Apache

ADMINISTRATOR'S HANDBOOK

Rich Bowen
Daniel López Ridruejo
Allan Liska

201 West 103rd St., Indianapolis, Indiana, 46290 USA

Apache Administrator's Handbook

Copyright © 2002 by Sams Publishing

International Standard Book Number: 0-672-32274-9

Library of Congress Catalog Card Number: 2001092348

Printed in the United States of America

First Printing: March 2002

05   04   03   02   4   3   2   1

Trademarks

Warning and Disclaimer

ACQUISITIONS EDITORS
Shelley Johnston
Jennifer Kost-Barker

DEVELOPMENT EDITOR
Heather Goodell

MANAGING EDITOR
Charlotte Clapp

PROJECT EDITOR
Elizabeth Finney

PRODUCTION EDITOR
Chip Gardner

INDEXER
Aamir Burki

PROOFREADER
Melissa Lynch

TECHNICAL EDITORS
Carlos Ramirez
Allan Liska
Patrick Grip-Jansson

TEAM COORDINATOR
Amy Patton

INTERIOR DESIGNER
Anne Jones

COVER DESIGNER
Aren Howell

PAGE LAYOUT
Brad Lenser

Overview

Contents

Part IV   Security and Auditing

About the Lead Author

Rich Bowen has been running Apache since the initial public release, and was running NCSA HTTPd before that. Rich has been contributing to the Apache documentation project for about two years, and has written a number of tutorials for the Apache docs. You can see the Apache documentation, which is the result of the efforts of a large group of documentation writers, at `http://httpd.apache.org/docs/`.

Rich is the CTO of Cooper McGregor, Inc, in Wilmore, Kentucky. Cooper McGregor specializes in Apache training and services, offering training courses on the Apache Server, Web application development in `mod_perl` and CGI, and a variety of consulting and support services for Apache and related technologies, including technical support for the Apache Server itself. Cooper McGregor can be found on the Web at `http://www.CooperMcGregor.com/`

Rich is a founding member, and Education Director, of the Lexington Professional Linux Users Group (`http://www.LPLUG.org/`), a professional organization dedicated to the promotion of Open Source technology, and Linux in particular, in the Lexington area.

Rich has spoken about Apache at a variety of conferences, including ApacheCon, Comdex, and the O'Reilly Open Source Software Convention.

You can reach Rich with questions, comments, errata, and kudos at `http://www.ApacheAdmin.com/`.

About the Contributing Authors

Allan Liska is a senior network engineer with WorldCom's hosting division. He has more than five years experience in the hosting industry, and is actively involved in the Apache Documentation Project. He likes spending his spare time with his wife, Roseanne, and collecting autographs from technology luminaries.

Daniel Lõpez Ridruejo is a senior developer with Covalent Technologies, Inc., which provides Apache software, support, and services for the enterprise. He is the author of several popular Apache and Linux guides and of Comanche, a GUI configuration tool for Apache. Daniel is a regular speaker at open source conferences such as LinuxWorld, ApacheCon, and O'Reilly OSCON. He holds an Ms. Sc. in communications engineering from the University of Seville and Denmark Technical University. Daniel is a member of the Apache Group.

Dedication

To the fine developers who make up the Apache Software Foundation. Thanks for developing and maintaining this great product. Thanks for recognizing that everyone is able to contribute something. Thanks for the wonderful opportunities that have come my way as a direct result of my association with you. Thanks for the chance to be a part of something of consequence.

Acknowledgments

Writing a book is an interesting experience. It is equal parts delight and drudgery. I love writing, most of the time, and get real joy out of explaining something in such a way that others can understand it, learn from it, and go on to solve real-world problems. However, since I don't know everything, there's a lot of grunt work that goes into getting the facts straight and explaining concepts that I only recently learned myself.

Additionally, there are all the mechanics of taking my various text files and conglomerating them into the stack of pages that you now hold. For that part of it, I cannot claim any credit. If anything, I have hindered the process as much as I possibly could by a variety of means, from insisting on using a document format that none of the editorial staff was familiar with, to consistently having too many things going on to meet any of my deadlines.

For assistance in this part of the process—for helping with the mechanics of putting together a book—I'd like to thank the following people.

Ken and Matt, thanks for twisting my arms until I consented to learn LaTeX, and then assisting me in making documents look like I actually wanted them to.

My coauthors, Daniel and Allan, came on board rather late in the game, after I started to realize exactly how far I was in over my head, and bailed me out. You are both great assets to the Apache project, and I deeply appreciate your help on this book.

Scott, thanks for always showing up at conferences and buying me dinner.

Heather and Jennifer and Shelley, thanks for dragging me through the process. Although I am writing this before the process is actually complete, you each have kept me motivated to keep moving, and I'm sure that you'll continue to do so. I'll try not to frustrate you too much. Thanks for trying to learn LaTeX, for putting up with the arcana involved in converting it to useful formats, and for going along with my insistence that it really is the best way for me to convert my ideas to something printable.

Carlos and Patrik, thanks for the helpful comments as we worked through the text. Elizabeth and Chip, thanks for your great job of helping me say what I meant in grammar that would not cause my high school English teacher to make disparaging remarks about Americans.

Joshua Slive, your involvement in the Apache documentation has really helped to make it a single cohesive document, rather than just a collection of documents that happen to be distributed together. It is a pleasure to work with you, and I hope that I'll be able to contribute more in the future.

To all the other folks on the `apache-docs` mailing list, especially Bill Rowe, thanks for handling my sporadic barrages of questions and always providing helpful and insightful answers.

I'd also like to thank some other folks, who, although they had nothing to do with the actual process of putting this book together, were nevertheless invaluable to me while that process was ongoing.

Chad, thanks for being so understanding as I traipsed around the country, and around the world, to a variety of conferences at which you believed I was learning more about Apache.

To the wonderful folks at Coffee Times, in Lexington, thanks for always remembering my daughter's name, even when you don't remember mine. Thanks for our table in the corner, where Sarah can play tea party with her Daddy. And even though you are not running Apache on your Web site (`http://www.coffeetimesinc.com/`) you are still some of my favorite people.

To the folks on `#perl`, thanks for offering just the right amount of support, and just the right amount of heckling, when I needed it. May each and every one of you finally get your pony.

srl, Skud, LotR, and the other folks on the Reefknot team (`http://www.reefknot.org/`), thanks for a refuge in other interesting projects when this one started to make me crazy (which was at least a few times a week). Hopefully, now that this book is on paper, I'll have a chance to fix some of the bugs that I introduced.

Ken Rietz, Wes Sheldahl, David Pitts, Dean Thomsic, Loren Lang, and a variety of other TM3 folks: Thanks for being my guinea pigs, reading the manuscript over my shoulder as I wrote it, and providing helpful feedback. The TM3 advisory board extends its blessing to you.

And, finally, to my wonderful little girl, Sarah. You are the most important part of my world. It's all for you.

Tell Us What You Think!

As the reader of this book, *you* are our most important critic and commentator. We value your opinion and want to know what we're doing right, what we could do better, what areas you'd like to see us publish in, and any other words of wisdom you're willing to pass our way.

You can e-mail or write me directly to let me know what you did or didn't like about this book—as well as what we can do to make our books stronger.

Please note that I cannot help you with technical problems related to the topic of this book, and that due to the high volume of mail I receive, I might not be able to reply to every message.

When you write, please be sure to include this book's title and authors as well as your name and phone or fax number. I will carefully review your comments and share them with the authors and editors who worked on the book.

E-mail: opensource@samspublishing.com

Mail: Mark Taber
            Associate Publisher
            Sams Publishing
            201 West 103rd Street
            Indianapolis, IN 46290 USA

What Is Apache?

Apache is a Web server. Unless you've been under a rock for the last 10 years, you've probably heard about the World Wide Web. And, chances are you would not be holding this book if you were not already familiar with the Apache Web Server. A Web server is a piece of software that is responsible for showing you the documents you ask for when you type Web addresses into your browser.

If you're looking for a book about the Apache Native American Indian tribe, and picked up this one by mistake, you should know that the Apache Server was named out of respect for the Apache system of social organization. Apache tribe leaders were selected based on the quality of their contribution to the community. This is the same way that the Apache Software Foundation manages itself.

Why Use Apache?

If you're reading this book in an attempt to determine whether you should use Apache, as opposed to one of the other Web server packages available, you should know that this book, for the most part, assumes that you've already made that decision. Although we'll briefly discuss the criteria that you should consider when choosing a server, no time is given to comparing Apache to IIS, Netscape, or any of the dozens of other Web servers out there.

Apache is a solid, dependable, reliable Web server, developed by talented, dedicated developers who are deeply concerned about the quality of the product, and the quality of the code that goes into the product. They are all amateurs, in the original sense of that word. That is, they are not doing this development because they are paid to do so (although some lucky guys are actually paid to do this). They do it because they love it and want to see something good come out of it, and see millions of people use the results of their work.

Who Else Is Using Apache?

According to Netcraft (`http://www.netcraft.com/`), more than 60% of all Web sites on the World Wide Web are running the Apache Web Server. That's nearly 18 million Web sites. The nearest competitor, Microsoft's Internet Information Server, has just more than 20% of the market.

Now, although the fact that everyone is doing something does not necessarily mean it's a good thing to do, numbers like this seem to suggest that Apache is doing something right.

Another good measure of the server's quality is to look at who is using Apache. Companies running Apache include Thawte (http://www.thawte.com/), the premier vendor of Web security technologies; The British Monarchy (http://www.royal.gov.uk/); Cisco (http://www.cisco.com/), which manufactures more than half of the hardware on which the Internet runs; and Slashdot (http://www.slashdot.org/), a popular technology news site, which gets thousands of visitors per minute.

Granted, similar impressive references could be provided for other Web servers. It is the responsibility of every Web site admin to consider all the options, and make the best decision for their particular situation. This subject will be addressed in Chapter 1, "Getting Started," because there are many more things to consider than just who else is using it.

Who Is This Book For?

This book is intended for the people that will be primarily responsible for an Apache Server—the Server Administrator. The Server Administrator is the person who installs the server, and gets called in the middle of the night when the server isn't working. He is also responsible for making daily changes to the server configuration, generating reports from the server logs, and giving people access to the portions of the Web site that they are supposed to update.

If any of those things describe what you do, or if you're just getting into this whole Web server thing and are not sure where to start, this book was written expressly with you in mind. We're taking our experiences running Web servers, both as server admins and as content providers, to give you the tools and information that you will need to avoid those calls at 3 a.m. and keep your Web site operating smoothly.

This book is not a comprehensive Apache manual, several of those are on the market. This book tries to be a little more focused than that.

Specifically, this book does not attempt to cover the aspects of the server that would be of interest to someone that wanted to work on the server code itself. For that, there is no substitute for downloading the source code and diving in.

Additionally, this book does not contain a complete listing of all the Apache directives, and their usage. If you want that, go to the Apache Web site (http://httpd.apache.org/) and start printing out the documentation. This book is intended to be a companion to the documentation, not a substitute for it. You should, however, check the Apache Web site for the most recent version of the documentation because it is being updated and improved almost every day.

What's with the Quotes?

I expect that some folks will wonder what significance the quotes throughout the book have. Do they have something to do with the chapter that they are attached to? Is there some overarching message conveyed by them? Or is there some secret code going on?

In college, I had a physics textbook that had strange quotes at the start of each chapter that had nothing at all to do with the chapter. Occasionally, there was a really bad pun in a quote that had to do—marginally, at least—with the content of the chapter.

I resolved then that if I ever wrote a book I would do something similar, putting in quotes that are significant to me in some way. For the most part, however, this means that you'll just have to endure my quotes without the benefit of knowing exactly *why* they are significant to me. If you happen to run into me at a conference, or if I'm doing training at your company, I'll try to explain a few of them to you, if you're really interested.

Conventions Used in This Book

Code lines, directives, variables, and any text you type or see onscreen, appears in a `monospaced` typeface.

Placeholders appear in an `italic monospace` typeface. Replace the placeholder with the actual filename, parameter, or whatever element it represents.

Errata, Updates, and More Information

The companion Web site to this book, which you can find at `http://www.apacheadmin.com/`, will contain a list of errata found in this book, as they are found, and other updates to the book's content. You will also find additional information about the topics covered in this book, one or two of the chapters, and a smattering of articles on Apache-related topics, as time permits.

There will also be a forum for discussion of Apache and related technologies, and, in particular, parts of the book on which you want clarification.

Installing and Configuring Your Apache Server

IN THIS PART

Getting Started

IN THIS CHAPTER

Quidquid latine dictum sit, altum viditur.

Before you start putting up your Web server and filling it with content there are a number of things to consider. However, if you're already running Apache you might want to skip this chapter and move on to the next one because this information might not apply to you.

Choosing a Web Server

The task of choosing a Web server is not always as simple as choosing the best one available.[1] Other things should be considered, but how important those things are depends entirely on your particular situation.

It is the responsibility of every Web site admin to weigh these considerations, and arrive at the decision that is in the best interests of their Web site, their company, and their customers.

Some of these considerations are discussed here, but there will certainly be others in some situations.

Compatibility Requirements

Frequently, you will have to make software choices based on the need to be compatible with existing installed software. For example, if there is a software package that you are required to run that only runs on IIS, then there is no further need to consider other servers.

Existing Knowledge

Although you should never be afraid to learn something new, there is certainly something to be said for sticking to your strengths. If you have people on staff that are already Lotus Domino server experts you might be better off sticking with Domino.

Executive Edict

Let's face it. In most companies, the software that you run is what your manager tells you to run. And what his manager tells him, and what her manager told her, and so on. The fact is that a lot of technical decisions are made for very non-technical reasons. Although it is your responsibility to present the pros and cons of various solutions, it's not always going to make a difference.

The Customer

If you're in a service provider role—either at an ISP or in the IS department of a company—you will frequently be faced with customer demands to run particular software to meet their particular needs. The customer is always right, even when the customer is not right.[2]

---

[1]*If it were, everyone would be running Apache!*

[2]*Note that the term "customer" is applied generically, and applies as much to people inside your organization as to those billed for your services.*

Hardware and Software Requirements

Apache has very minimal requirements. If you are running a machine as a server, then it probably already satisfies the minimum requirements for Apache. However, as with any software package, Apache runs better on faster systems with more memory.

Having run Apache on everything from a 486/33 to a Pentium-III 850, and several dual-processor machines along the way, the question of minimal hardware requirements seldom comes up. Apache will run on just about anything.

Apache also runs on just about any operating system that you've ever heard of, and several that you haven't. Anything vaguely Unix-like will almost certainly run Apache, and most Unixes ship with Apache installed in a default configuration.

Apache has been able to run on Microsoft Windows since version 1.3, which was released in 1997. It will run on Windows 9x[3] and Windows NT.[4]

Having said that, the INSTALL documentation that comes with Apache makes the following more specific statements:

- You will need at least 12MB of temporary free disk space for the build process. When the installation is completed, it will take up approximately 5MB of drive space. Of course, this number will vary based on which third-party modules that you add to the installation. Also, you will need to take into account the data that you will actually serve from the Web site, which is, of course, not included in that number.

- You will need an ANSI-C compiler, such as GCC, for the compilation of the source code. Unless you install one of the binary (precompiled) distributions, in which case you don't need a compiler at all.

- A Perl 5 interpreter is recommended, but not required. Several of the utilities that ship with Apache use Perl, but you can make do without these utilities.

- Dynamic Shared Object support is also useful to have, but not required. Most modern operating systems support this in some fashion or other, so this is not a very stringent requirement.

Connectivity

If you're going to run a Web server, you probably want a connection to the Internet so people can see your Web site. In order for this to work, you'll need the following:

---

[3]"Windows 9x" is a generic term which is used to refer to Microsoft Windows 95, Microsoft Windows 98, and Microsoft Windows ME, which share major architectural features, and behave much the same, as far as Apache is concerned.
[4]And "Windows NT" is the generic term used to refer to Windows NT 3.51, Windows NT 4.0, and Windows 2000, which, likewise, share major architectural similarities.

- **Internet connectivity:** A modem connection is a possible configuration, but if you expect to have more than a handful of people look at your Web site you would be well advised to get a higher-speed connection, such as DSL, cable modem, or some variety of leased-line solution. Your connection needs to be running 24 hours a day, all year long, so that your Web site is accessible whenever someone wants to use it.
- **Fixed IP address:** Although it's possible to play fancy games with DNS (domain name system) to make a dynamically allocated IP address appear to be in the same place all the time, the techniques for doing so are beyond the scope of this book. If you're actually going to run a real Web site you need to have a fixed IP address and a hostname (or more than one) in DNS that resolves to your address. You will need to check with your ISP to find out what your address is, and if you are not running your own DNS server, you will need to arrange to get your name(s) to resolve correctly with whoever is doing so.

Should I Host Somewhere Else, or Do It Myself?

An important question to consider is whether you want to host your Web site on your own server, in your own facility, or at someone else's facility, either on one of their servers, or at your own collocated server. This will depend on a number of factors, only a few of which are discussed here.

Connectivity

Can you afford the necessary connectivity? If you put up a Web site that suddenly becomes popular, will you have sufficient bandwidth to service the traffic? If you host it in your own facility, you will be entirely responsible for the cost of that connectivity, and scaling your connectivity to meet the demand can become costly. If you host at an ISP's facility they will likely have more connectivity than you will ever need, and you won't be shouldering the entire cost for all that bandwidth.

Reliable Connection

Is your connection reliable? If you have a small office, and are considering hosting your Web site on your own Internet connection, you should consider the possibility that your connection might go down occasionally. If this happens, and it stays down for a considerable period of time, you will need to consider alternative ways to provide service to your site's users. On the other hand, if your server is hosted at a remote facility, they will likely have redundant connections to the Internet, so when one goes down, the others will pick up, with no noticeable downtime to the users.

How Much Access Do You Need?

What level of access to your servers do you need? If you are running a fairly simple site, on a normal day you might only need to put content on the server. However, if you have a site that relies on a large amount of custom software, or even nonstandard hardware, you might need to have physical access to your server on a regular basis.

If you are running your server on a Windows operating system, or any other operating system for which remote management is problematic, you might not want to have that server very far off site in case you need to do something that requires direct access to the console. (You might also need to consider a remote control application, such as VNC or PC Anywhere, which enables you to export your desktop across the network and work on that machine from anywhere. There are, however, security considerations in doing this.)

If you are running a Unix-like operating system, then you need to make sure that you have as much access to your hosted server as required. If you need daily root access, you need to make sure that your ISP permits this. Some ISPs are reluctant to permit this, because they are then unable to guarantee that the system will stay up.

Questions To Ask Your ISP

If you choose to host your Web site at some other facility, rather than having it in house, you need to make sure that you understand your ISP's policies, and make sure that you're getting what you think that you should be.

The following are some of the things that you should ask your ISP, and things that you need to consider yourself, to make sure that there are no unpleasant surprises.

Shared Space, Dedicated Server, Colloc?

There are a number of different ways to lease space at an ISP. The two primary categories of service are leasing space on a server owned by the ISP, and putting your own server, completely managed by you, at the ISP facility. The latter is referred to as collocation, or a colloc.

If you are leasing space, you need to know to what extent you have control over that machine. Do you have your own server, or are you sharing it with someone else? This knowledge will affect the manner in which you will need to secure your files. If there are other users that will have login privileges on your server, you will need to be much more cautious about files with group and world permissions on them.

Do you have root access to the machine? Normally, if you are not collocating your own server, you will not have root access to the machine. This is necessary for the ISP to have sufficient control over the machine to guarantee its performance. If you do have root access to the machine, it is typical for the ISP to withdraw guarantees of any kind because they no longer have any control over the things they would be guaranteeing.

What Happens When Something Goes Wrong?

Is the server monitored by a package such as Watchers (`http://www.cre8tivegroup.com/web/watchers.html`), which will send notification in the event of system outages? If so, to whom do those notifications go? In the event of a catastrophic system failure (such as a kernel panic on Unix, or a blue screen on Windows, will someone at the ISP be willing to reboot the machine? If not, what is the procedure for getting your server back up?

Do you have an emergency contact number? Will a real person answer it? During what hours is there actually someone in the office that will be able to help you with problems?

Backups?

Are there any backups run, and if so, how often? Are the backup tapes stored on site, or off site in a safe box? What is the procedure for getting a file restored? How long are backups kept before the tapes are cycled?

Installing Software

If your server is not a dedicated server on which you have root access, then you need to know what the policy is on installing new software. Whether you need the latest Text::Template Perl module installed from CPAN, or you want Majordomo installed, or you want to have the installation of BIND upgraded to fix the latest security alert, you need to know what the procedures are for getting this done, what you can expect for turnaround on installation, and whether they are even willing to do such things. Although some ISPs are very willing to accommodate your whims, others have very strict requirements about what can and cannot be installed.

Small ISPs, such as cre8tivegroup.com, where I host my Web site for example, are often willing to install things for you, make small configuration changes, and keep up to date on the latest security alerts. However, much larger shops tend to be less flexible, insisting that every server have identical loads of software, so that they don't have to do any custom maintenance. Consequently, if there is anything fancy you want to do, such as mod_perl, mailing-list software, or custom Perl modules, you are probably better off going with a smaller ISP that is likely to be more flexible.

FTP, Telnet, SCP, SSH: Getting Content To Your Site

After you have your server set up and configured, you'll need a means of providing content to the server. This will ordinarily be done in one of two ways. Either you will log in to the server itself and create content there, or you will create the content somewhere else and copy it to the server machine after it is complete.

Most Web-development professionals agree that it's always a good idea to develop on a machine that is not your production machine, and then copy content to the live server after you have verified that it works. There will, however, frequently be situations where emergency fixes are required, and in those cases, you should work directly on the server.

Telnet and SSH—Connecting To the Server

If you have any Unix experience, you are probably at least somewhat familiar with telnet. You might be unfamiliar with SSH, however. If your experience is primarily on Microsoft operating systems, you might be unfamiliar with both of them. Although a telnet client is provided with most versions of Windows, neither a telnet server nor an ssh server are widely available for Windows.

Telnet is simply a means of logging in to a remote server (that is, not the machine you're sitting at) and getting a command line, just as you would if you were at that machine. The telnet client is part of most modern operating systems. On either a Windows or Unix machine, you'll find a telnet client. This can ordinarily be accessed directly from any command line by typing `telnet hostname`, where `hostname` is the network name of the machine to which you want to connect. After you have connected to the remote machine, you will get a login prompt, where you will need to provide a valid username and password for an account on that machine. After you have successfully logged in, a command prompt will appear.

Advantages of Using Telnet

There are a several reasons to use telnet.

Because you are working directly on the live server your changes will be immediately available on the Web site.

Also, you are working in exactly the environment where the Web site is running, so there will not be any strange system dependencies between one machine and another. That is, occasionally you'll find that, for some reason, something that works fine on your test server somehow inexplicably does not work on the live server.

Disadvantages of Using Telnet

The main disadvantage of editing content directly on the live Web site via a telnet session is the same as what I listed as the first advantage. Because you are working directly on the live server, your changes will be immediately available on the Web site. Consequently, when you mess something up, it will be immediately evident to your viewing public.

SSH—Exactly the Same, Only Different

SSH (the Secure Shell) is effectively the same thing as telnet, with one important difference. SSH provides you with a connection that is encrypted.

With telnet, your username, password, and all your data, is passed in plain text across the Internet. Anyone with a little bit of knowledge, and the right tools, can intercept this traffic, and either snoop on what you are doing (for example, steal your username and password) or alter the data as it goes past. And, there's very little you can do about this.

With SSH, on the other hand, everything is encrypted, so even if someone does intercept your data, it will be meaningless to them. SSH uses a public/private key system, so that the data can be viewed only by the two endpoints of the conversation. Decrypting this data is extremely difficult and time-consuming.

You can find out more about SSH, and download the free clients and servers for a variety of platforms at `www.openssh.org`.

FTP and SCP—Getting Content To Your Server

If you develop your content on a test server, and then copy it up to your live Web server—which is really what you ought to do—you will probably use FTP or SCP.

Like telnet and SSH, FTP and SCP, respectively, are the insecure and secure versions of file transfer.

Using FTP

FTP, which stands for File Transfer Protocol, is the most common way to copy files around the Internet. It requires an FTP server, which you will connect to with an FTP client, and transfers files from one machine to another. FTP is fairly easy to use, and there are an enormous number of available FTP clients, from standard console (command line) FTP clients to very sophisticated GUI (graphical user interface) FTP clients that make the remote server look like a part of your local file system.

To connect to a remote FTP server with a console FTP client, you will type

```
ftp remote.host.com
```

You will be prompted for a username and password, and then you will be logged in. You can navigate around on the remote server with the cd (change directory) command. `cd directory-name` changes into a particular directory, whereas `cd ..` moves back up one directory. To move around on your local filesystem while you are logged into the remote server, use the `lcd` (local change directory) in the same manner.

When you are in the place you want to be, use the put and get commands, respectively, to put and get files.

```
put index.html
```

```
get otherfile.html
```

Disadvantages of FTP

Two primary disadvantages of using FTP are the clients are insecure, and the servers are insecure.

Due to the nature of FTP, FTP connections are insecure. Like telnet, all data, including your username and password, are passed in the clear across the network, and could be captured as they go across the Internet.

A huge number of the available Unix-security exploits are performed by compromising an FTP server. There are a number of known FTP exploits, and it seems that more of them show up all the time. Although a vigilant system administrator should be able to stay abreast of the latest security exploit, many sysadmins will simply choose to avoid the problem all together.

The Solution—SCP

SCP, which stands for *Secure CoPy*, can be thought of as an encrypted FTP, although that's not quite accurate. Technically, SCP is file copy *tunneled* over SSH. Exactly what that means is probably not terribly important for our purposes here. The important thing is that it enables you to copy files across the Internet in a secure manner. Neither your authentication information, nor the data itself, is passed in the clear, and so it cannot be intercepted in a useful manner.

You can find out more about SCP at http://www.openssh.org/, and you'll likely get it when you install SSH.

There are SSH and SCP clients for Windows, the best of them being the ones that come with Cygwin.[5] Cygwin is available from http://cygwin.com/.

Summary

Although it is assumed that if you're reading this book, you're already sold on Apache, the decision of which Web server to use must still be carefully considered to make sure that you're making the right choice.

The decision of whether to host your Web site at your own facility or at an ISP, is also an important one, and there are a variety of considerations that you need to think about.

---

[5]*In my humble opinion, anyway*

Acquiring and Installing Your Apache Server

IN THIS CHAPTER

Everything that Mr. Smallweed's grandfather ever put away in his mind was a grub at first, and is a grub at last. In all his life he has never bred a single butterfly.

Bleak House—Charles Dickens

Apache is an Open Source product. This means that the source code is freely available for you to download and tinker with. This also means that most people will install Apache by downloading that source and compiling Apache their own particular way. This chapter walks you through that process. By the end of this chapter, you should have Apache installed and ready to start using.

Overview for the Impatient

For those of you who want to get something installed immediately, and don't care about all the details, this is for you. This is labeled "Overview for the Impatient" in the INSTALL file that comes with Apache. After you have unpacked the archive file, do the following:

```
./configure —prefix=PREFIX
make
make install
PREFIX/bin/apachectl start
```

There, you're done. Note that PREFIX should be replaced with the base directory under which you want everything else installed. For example, throughout this book we will be making the assumption most of the time that you have installed Apache in the directory /usr/local/apache, so in the above code example you would use the commands:

```
./configure —prefix=/usr/local/apache
make
make install
/usr/local/apache/bin apachectl start
```

OK, now some of the details.

Where Do I Get It?

The Apache Software Foundation (ASF) Web site is http://www.apache.org/. The part of the Web site specific to the Apache Web server is http://httpd.apache.org/. The Web site contains comprehensive documentation about the server software, information about the ASF, and, of course, the software itself.

Additionally, there are a number of mirrors around the world, so you can usually find a server that is near to you, particularly if you live outside of the United States. To find the mirror closest to you, go to http://www.apache.org/dyn/closer.cgi, which will dynamically figure out your closest mirror and send you there. After you click the Download link, you'll find yourself in the directory of downloadable files, `http://httpd.apache.org/dist/httpd/`, where you can select a file to download. Which file you choose depends on what format you're most comfortable with, and what version you want. Several versions are usually available for download—usually the most recent, and one or two versions back, in each of the various branches that are currently being supported. At the time of this writing, for example, 1.3.19, 1.3.20, and 1.3.22 are available for the 1.3 branch, whereas 2.0.16 and 2.0.18 are available for the 2.0 branch.

For each version there are usually six different files. The software is available in three different compression formats, and a .asc file accompanies each format, which is a PGP signature that verifies the authenticity of the file.

The three compression formats are `.tar.Z` (compressed tar archive), `.tar.gz` (gzipped tar archive), and `.zip` (pkzipped or Windows zip). The different compression formats are purely for the convenience of people that like the different formats, or might be more familiar with tools for extracting a particular format. All of the files contain the identical contents.

If you're not sure what you want, you should get the file labeled Current release in whatever compression format you're familiar with.

The `.asc` files enable you to verify that the files you are downloading are actually the same files that the Apache developers put on the site for you to download, and have not been tampered with by a third party. This is particularly important if you are downloading the files from a mirror of the Apache site, rather than the main download site.

You can check the validity of the signature files using PGP, which you can acquire at `http://web.mit.edu/network/pgp.html`. If the signature on the file matches, then you can be certain that the file has not been tampered with.

Unpacking the Source

The method used to extract the archive will, of course, depend on which compression format you download.

Move the archive to a convenient location for unpacking. `/usr/local/src` is a good place.[1]

To extract a `.tar.Z` file, type the following command:[2]

```
tar -vZxf httpd-2_0_xx.tar.Z
```

To extract a `.tar.gz` file, type the following command:

```
tar -vzxf httpd-2_0_xx.tar.gz
```

---

[1]*You don't have to move the archive if you don't want to. Just change to the directory where you want to unpack the file, and provide the full path to the file when you type the following commands.*

[2]*In each of these command lines, xx will be replaced with the particular version of the code you have downloaded.*

Or, if you are using a version of tar that does not accept the -z argument, try:

```
gunzip < httpd-2_0_xx.tar.gz | tar -zx
```

To extract a .zip file, type the following command:

```
unzip httpd-2_0_xx.zip
```

Or, if you are uncompressing this file on a platform other than Unix, there are a variety of decompression utilities available, such as WinZip, which simplify the process of extracting compressed files.

The Source Tree

After you have unpacked the source code, a directory listing will show you several files in the top-level directory—most of them documentation—and several subdirectories. Although it is not essential that you know everything about the source code to be a good system administrator, it's a good idea to understand something about the code that you're installing on your server.

There are six subdirectories created when you unpack the source archive.

cgi-bin

The cgi-bin directory contains two very simple CGI programs, one in shell, and the other in Perl. They both perform the same function—displaying the contents of your CGI environment. They are not particularly useful, but we'll refer to them again when we get to the chapter on CGI (15). A number of other CGI programs used to be distributed with Apache, but most were removed because of security concerns. If everyone on the planet knows what CGI programs are preinstalled on a default installation of Apache it gives them an upper hand when trying to compromise your server through Apache.

conf

The conf directory contains the default configuration files that will be installed on your server. During the configuration process variables in this file will be filled in with values that you provide to the configure script, or with default values if none are provided. These configuration files enable you to get a default Apache installation up and running in just a few minutes.

See Chapter 4 "Configuration Directives," for more information on these configuration files.

htdocs

htdocs contains a default index page for the server, with the Apache logo and some text explaining that this is a new installation of the server, and providing links to the ASF Web site for more information about the Apache server. This page is available in a number of languages and a variety of character sets. Apache's content negotiation ensures that (correctly configured) browsers will get the document in their own language.

The htdocs directory also contains the Apache users' manual in a subdirectory called manual, which contains exhaustive documentation on the server, as well as a number of "how to" style tutorials on a variety of topics. You need to be aware that although the documentation contained in this directory was the best thing available when that version of Apache was released, the Apache documentation gets updated almost on a daily basis, and the online docs (at http://httpd.apache.org/docs-project/) will be more up-to-date than what you have installed.

icons

icons contains a number of images that are used in directory listings and other automatically generated documents, as well as some you can use for your own documents.

logs

The logs directory is empty. This is where your log files will be put when you start up your server.

src

The most fun, of course, is in the src directory. src contains the source code for the server. This directory is subdivided into a number of subdirectories, but we won't talk about them all right now. If you are going to hack on the Apache server code, it is in this directory that you will be working. However, modifying the Apache server code is beyond the scope of this book.

Later in the book we'll talk more about modules (Chapter 26, "Modules Included with Apache") and at that time we'll refer to the modules directory inside src.

Installing Binary Distributions

Before we proceed with what happens next, we need to address binary distributions. If you are using some non-Unix operating system, such as Windows, Mac OS, or OS/2, it is very likely that you don't have a compiler installed, or even available to you. Outside of the Unix world, a compiler is typically a software package that you'll have to pay a good amount of money for, therefore, relatively few people are going to have them.

For these folks, the ASF provides binary distributions, which means that someone else has gone to the trouble of compiling the source code for you, and all you have to do is download the files and install them on your system.

Binaries are provided for an impressive list of platforms. Most of them are there either because compilers for those platforms are expensive or difficult to use. Some are just there for the convenience of people who don't want to spend the time building it themselves. In any case, the user will just need to download the package, and run the installation program, to have a fully functional installation of Apache server.

Installing on Windows

On Windows, the provided installation file is a familiar InstallShield file, which will ask you for some information such as where you want to install the server. It will then place the various files for you.

If you are installing on an NT operating system[3] you will further want to install Apache as a service, which can be done by selecting "Install as a service" from the Start menu.

See Chapter 12, "Apache on Microsoft Windows," for more detail on installing Apache on Windows.

Binary Versus Source Installation

Some folks will wonder why they would want to go to all the trouble to build their own installation when someone has already provided binary installations for their specific operating system. There are a number of reasons that you might want to build it yourself. Some of them are philosophical, but most of them are very pragmatic.

The spirit of the Open Source movement is that you have the source code, and can do whatever you want with it. This necessitates, in many cases, a large degree of understanding of what's going on behind the scenes, even to the point of hacking on the source code to get it to work. As more and more Open Source projects spring up, and as the quality of the source code improves, it becomes less and less necessary to work directly with the source code. This is definitely a good thing. But, for the present at least, it has left behind it a strong sentiment that to be a responsible system administrator, you should really understand the code that you are running on your system. Security reasons are hidden somewhere in there—someone could hide something malicious in code that you blindly install on your servers—but most of it is a philosophical belief that as a system admin, you should know as much as possible about what is on your servers.

Although I personally believe these sentiments, it might ring a little hollow to the sysadmin who has about 12 free minutes on a good day, and really doesn't have the time to mess with the source code of everything she installs. If it works, that's sufficient.

However, a number of more practical reasons exist to build Apache from source yourself.

---

[3] *"NT" is used here, and throughout the book, to refer to Microsoft's server operating systems, including NT and Windows 2000. The desktop operating systems are referred to generically as "Win9x", which includes Windows 95, Windows 98, and Windows ME.*

If you install binaries, you trust someone else to make the decisions about what the best configuration is for your server. Although this person has tried to make those decisions in the best interests of the majority of installations, he did not know the particulars of your server—what sort of load it will be under, what sort of content it will be serving, or what expectations your users have about performance. And, necessarily, when trying to make everyone happy, decisions are made that are not the best for everyone.

By building the source yourself, you can make decisions in the configure process that will accurately reflect how you want your servers to work. During the configure process, you can decide where files are put, what modules are installed and which ones are left off, and a variety of other things. This way, Apache is built in such a way that is most fitted to your system, the way that you work, and what you expect the server to do. It won't leave out modules that you will want, and perhaps as importantly, it will not be weighted down by a bunch of modules that you will never use.

configure

The next step in the installation process, if you have chosen to install from source, is to configure the build process. This is done with a script called `configure`, which is in the main directory where you unpacked the source archive file. `configure` enables you to specify a large number of options about how your server will be compiled and installed.[4]

To run the `configure` program, change into the directory where the archive has been unpacked, and type

```
./configure
```

Running `configure` without any arguments at all causes it to get ready for a default installation, taking all the default arguments to all options.

Upon typing this command, you'll see a large number of messages scroll by that will say "checking for," "checking if," and "checking whether" various things are available, installed, or working. You'll then see a lot of messages stating that it is creating various files for your particular configuration. This means that by the time you get around to compiling the code, it already knows all about your system, and it can do the right thing for your particular situation.

However, it will also make a lot of decisions for you that you might want to make for yourself.

By typing `./configure —help`, you can see a complete list of the things that you are able to configure. Most of them you'll just want to leave as the default, and in each case the default is specified in square brackets [].

---

[4]*Please note, going into this section, that there is another way to configure your installation, with the deceptively similar name of* `Configure` *(uppercase C, rather than lowercase c), which does much the same thing, in much the same way. This might seems a little silly, but there are some historical reasons that we'll touch on very briefly later.*

Rather than wasting two pages reproducing this here, I encourage you to run this command on your own system while you read along, so that you can see what we're talking about. Or, you can look in Appendix B, "configure Command-Line Options," for the complete listing.

Configuration options are divided into four main sections: configuration options, directory and filenames, host type, and features and packages.

Configuration Options

The Configuration options are those that affect the configuration itself, and apart from the −help option, it is probable that you will not want any of these options, at least the first few times you build Apache.

These options enable you to do things such as suppress the rather verbose output of the configuration process; run the configuration, but not create any of the resultant files after it is done; and cache the test results (where it is checking for various files and utilities) in a cache file for later use.

Directory and Filenames

The next set of options deals with directories and filenames. The bulk of this is specifying where particular files are put. In a default installation, all the files are put in /usr/local/apache, but you can change this, and you can change where particular parts of the installation are put.

Some people have very strongly held beliefs that certain files should go in certain places, regardless of their origin. For example, these people would hold that configuration files should go in /etc, log files in /var/log, and man files (documentation) in /usr/man or /var/man.

Other people feel that one application (such as Apache) should keep all its files in one place, so that they can be easily located.

This portion of the configuration process is there to keep everyone happy. Although the default is to keep everything together by specifying such arguments as −prefix (The directory which, by default, everything else will go under), −bindir (where the compiled binary executables will be placed), and −mandir (where the man pages will be placed), you can specify where each type of files in the installation will be placed.

Host Type

You are unlikely to have to change these options in a normal installation. They enable you to specify a few options about the host on which you are building Apache. If you do not specify these options, the configure process will automatically look up your hostname and type, and fill in these values for you.

Features and Packages

This is where things get really interesting. In this portion of the configuration you can specify which packages get installed, what features are enabled or disabled, and a variety of other options.

The most commonly used aspect of this section is turning various modules on or off, so they are built into the server, or not. Once again, see Appendix B for the complete list of modules that you can enable or disable in this step.

A Default Installation

Note again that if you don't specify any options, Apache will be built with a sensible default list of modules, or some definition of sensible, and with files in some sensible place, so you can run a normal Web site without too much difficulty. Consequently, the first few times you build Apache, at least until you think you have a good idea of what is happening, it is recommended that you accept the defaults to learn the ropes.

The technique for a default installation is covered at the beginning of the chapter in the "Overview for the Impatient."

make && make install

The final step of this process is very simple. You type the following command:

```
make && make install
```

And then you wait. This can take a while, but the time will vary depending on your processor, the amount of memory you have, and what you consider to be a long time.

During this time, the C source code that comprises the Apache server will be compiled into executable binary files, which it will then put in the locations that you specified during the configuration process.

These are actually two commands. `make` does the compilation, and `make install` puts the various files in their correct locations. The `&&` between the two commands means that upon the completion of the first command it should proceed immediately to the second. If there is a problem of some kind during the build process, execution will be aborted, and the installation process will not be run.

If you want to see where the installation will put all the various files, type the following:

```
./configure —show-layout
```

This will show you a full listing of the various directories that the installation will create and put things into:

```
root@rhiannon:/usr/src/apache_1.3.17# ./configure —show-layout
Configuring for Apache, Version 1.3.17
 + using installation path layout: Apache (config.layout)

Installation paths:
              prefix: /usr/local/apache
         exec_prefix: /usr/local/apache
              bindir: /usr/local/apache/bin
             sbindir: /usr/local/apache/bin
          libexecdir: /usr/local/apache/libexec
              mandir: /usr/local/apache/man
          sysconfdir: /usr/local/apache/conf
             datadir: /usr/local/apache
            iconsdir: /usr/local/apache/icons
           htdocsdir: /usr/local/apache/htdocs
              cgidir: /usr/local/apache/cgi-bin
          includedir: /usr/local/apache/include
        localstatedir: /usr/local/apache
           runtimedir: /usr/local/apache/logs
           logfiledir: /usr/local/apache/logs
         proxycachedir: /usr/local/apache/proxy

Compilation paths:
           HTTPD_ROOT: /usr/local/apache
      SHARED_CORE_DIR: /usr/local/apache/libexec
       DEFAULT_PIDLOG: logs/httpd.pid
    DEFAULT_SCOREBOARD: logs/httpd.scoreboard
     DEFAULT_LOCKFILE: logs/httpd.lock
      DEFAULT_XFERLOG: logs/access_log
     DEFAULT_ERRORLOG: logs/error_log
    TYPES_CONFIG_FILE: conf/mime.types
   SERVER_CONFIG_FILE: conf/httpd.conf
   ACCESS_CONFIG_FILE: conf/access.conf
 RESOURCE_CONFIG_FILE: conf/srm.conf
```

This option is not available in Apache 2.0 as of this writing.

Summary

By this point, you should have Apache successfully installed. It's OK if you have done a default installation the first time through. You can move on with that for a while, and then when you understand things better, you can come back to this chapter and customize your installation a little more.

Starting, Stopping, and Restarting

IN THIS CHAPTER

There are two kinds of fool. One says, "This is old, and therefore good." And one says "This is new, and therefore better."

The Shockwave Rider—John Brunner

Now that your server is installed, you need to get it running. Don't be concerned that we've devoted an entire chapter to this. It really is simple. But, there are some additional things that you'll want to know about starting, stopping, and restarting your server.

apachectl

Most of the time, you want to use apachectl to start and stop your server. apachectl is a handy little script designed to take the grunt work out of starting, stopping, and restarting Apache.

You'll find apachectl in the bin directory of wherever you installed Perl. You might want to copy, or symlink, it into /usr/local/bin, or somewhere else in your path, because you might need it frequently, at least while you're learning about Apache.

apachectl can be run with one of eight different options.

A complete listing of the options can be obtained by running apachectl with the help option:

```
% apachectl help

usage: /usr/local/bin/apachectl (start|stop|restart|
        fullstatus|status|graceful|configtest|help)

start      - start httpd
stop       - stop httpd
restart    - restart httpd if running by sending a SIGHUP or start if
             not running
fullstatus - dump a full status screen; requires lynx and mod_status enabled
status     - dump a short status screen; requires lynx and mod_status enabled
graceful   - do a graceful restart by sending a SIGUSR1 or start if not running
configtest - do a configuration syntax test
help       - this screen
```

These options are, for the most part, self-explanatory.

status and fullstatus will be covered in more detail in Chapter 14, "Handlers and Filters," when we discuss mod_status. configtest will be discussed in more detail when we discuss configuration directives in Chapter 4, "Configuration Directives."

The start, stop, restart, and graceful options are of particular interest to this section of the book. The first two do exactly what you would expect. restart does what you would expect also, but it's important to know that it also rereads the configuration files, so if any changes have been made, those changes go into effect on a restart. graceful is useful because any connections to the server that are currently active will be completed before the server is restarted. This is important because it means that nobody's connection will be unceremoniously dropped in the middle of receiving a file, therefore, the perceived downtime of the server will be lessened.

For both restart and graceful, if there is a syntax error in the configuration file(s), Apache will not successfully restart. However, Apache is smart enough to check the syntax of the configuration files before shutting down, rather than waiting until it is time to start back up. So, if there is a problem with the configuration files, Apache won't even shut down in the first place. This was not true with earlier versions, where a restart would occasionally leave you with your server down, if you did not check your configuration syntax before attempting the restart.

httpd

httpd is the server binary—that is, this is the actual executable file that is run when you start up your Apache server. You'll find this file in the bin directory of your Apache directory tree. The size of this file will vary depending on what you have built into your server, but it will be around 1MB in size, and will be the largest file in that directory.[1]

apachectl is just a wrapper that feeds arguments directly to the httpd binary for common options. There are a number of other things that you can do by passing arguments directly to httpd.

Starting and Stopping with httpd

To start the Web server, without any special options, simply invoke httpd directly:

```
/usr/local/apache/bin/httpd
```

To stop the Web server, you'll need to know the PID (process ID) of the Apache parent process. You can acquire this PID from the file httpd.pid, which is located in the directory with your log files—usually /usr/local/apache/logs.

```
cat /usr/local/apache/logs/httpd.pid | xargs kill
```

---

[1]*Note that if you installed Apache from a binary distribution, or built Apache with a file and directory layout different from the standard,* httpd *might be located elsewhere. See Chapter 2, "Acquiring and Installing Your Apache Server," for more information.*

Command-Line Flags

By passing additional arguments to httpd, you can have it behave in ways slightly different from what you have configured in the server configuration files.

For a complete listing of the available command-line options, invoke httpd with the -h option:

```
# /usr/local/apache/bin/httpd -h
Usage: /usr/local/apache/bin/httpd [-D name] [-d directory] [-f file]
                                   [-C "directive"] [-c "directive"]
                                   [-v] [-V] [-h] [-l] [-L] [-S] [-t] [-T]
Options:
  -D name            : define a name for use in <IfDefine name> directives
  -d directory       : specify an alternate initial ServerRoot
  -f file            : specify an alternate ServerConfigFile
  -C "directive"     : process directive before reading config files
  -c "directive"     : process directive after  reading config files
  -v                 : show version number
  -V                 : show compile settings
  -h                 : list available command line options (this page)
  -l                 : list compiled-in modules
  -L                 : list available configuration directives
  -t -D DUMP_VHOSTS: show parsed settings (currently only vhost settings)
  -t                 : run syntax check for config files (with docroot check)
  -T                 : run syntax check for config files (without docroot check)
```

We'll come back to a number of these options as we talk more about the surrounding information necessary to understand what they do, but of particular interest at this time are the following options:

- **httpd -v**: Shows you what version of the server you are running. This is a good way to convince yourself, after a new install, that you are in fact running the new version, and not some old version that happened to be laying around in your path somewhere.

- **httpd -V**: Tells you what compile settings were in effect when you built Apache.

- **httpd -l**: Lists the compiled-in modules. This will give you some assurance that what you did in the configuration phase actually paid off, and you got the modules that you wanted.

Starting on System Startup

If you are going to run Apache on a production system—that is, if you want people to be able to look at your Web site all the time—then you need to make sure that Apache starts up when you reboot your computer.

This is accomplished a variety of ways on different systems, but they are all typically just a small variation on the same theme.

In `/etc/rc.d` you will find a collection of scripts, typically with filenames starting with `rc.` (such as `rc.inet1`, `rc.firewall`, and `rc.local`) which run when your system starts up. The exact layout of this directory varies. Sometimes these scripts are located in subdirectories. Sometimes there are several subdirectories, corresponding to the various runlevels[2], containing the scripts, or symlinks to the scripts, and sometimes the scripts are all directly in `/etc/rc.d`.[3]

When you know how your system does things, you should create a startup script (called `rc.httpd`, for example) which contains a call to either `apachectl` or `httpd`, as you prefer, telling it to start your server. Alternately, many systems have a script called `rc.local`, which is specifically for you to put in your customizations to the startup process; this enables you to keep all your startup alterations in the same place.

So, for example, you can add the following line to either your `rc.local`, or to a separate file called `rc.httpd`:

```
/usr/local/httpd/bin/apachectl start
```

Or, if you want to start Apache with a configuration file other than the one in the default location, you could use the following line instead:

```
/usr/local/httpd/bin/httpd -f /etc/httpd/host2.conf
```

Microsoft Windows

As should be expected, Microsoft Windows does things a little differently. Apache on Windows offers a few other ways to manage things, more in line with the expected Windows way of doing things. For example, you can install Apache as an NT service, or start and stop it from the Start menu. However, there are also several ways to start and stop Apache from the command line as well.

---

[2]*A Unix machine can start up in one of several runlevels, or modes of operation, such as single-user mode or multiuser mode. The details of this are not particularly important for this discussion. Consult your OS documentation for further information.*

[3]*And, of course, other systems put it yet other places. Some systems, such as HP/UX, SuSE, Digital Unix, and others, like to put these startup scripts in* `/sbin/init.d` *or* `/sbin/rc[0-6].d`. *It can be a little hard to keep up with. Contact your local guru if you don't know how your system does things.*

Starting from the Command Line

The various command-line options previously listed for `httpd` also work on Windows, except that the executable on Windows is called `apache`, and is (by default) located in `c:\program files\apache group`

```
cd "\program files\apache group"
apache
```

After doing this, you might need to press `control-C` to regain control of your command prompt. Apache will continue running. Make sure that you can start Apache in this manner and that it is serving pages correctly before you proceed to the next step, to ensure that things are mostly set up OK.

Installing as a Service

As previously described, if you are running a production server, you'll want to install Apache as a service. This is done with the following commands.

To install Apache as a service with no special options, do the following:

```
apache -k install -n "service name"
```

If the `"service name"` option is omitted, the service name `"Apache"` is used as the default name of the service.

If you want to install the service to use a particular configuration file, different from the default location for configuration files that you specified during the installation process, you can specify a different configuration file when you install the service. This way, you can have multiple Apache services, with different configurations.

```
apache -k install -n "service name" -f "\path\to\alternate\conf"
```

To remove the Apache service after it is installed, you can use the following command:

```
apache -k uninstall -n "service name"
```

Starting and Stopping Your Apache Service

After you have Apache installed as an NT service, you can start and stop it a number of different ways.

apache -n "service name"

You can call the Apache binary directly from the command line if you like, passing it arguments as we discussed previously with `httpd`. To start, restart, or stop the Apache service, you would use the following three commands, respectively:

```
apache -n "service name" start
apache -n "service name" restart
apache -n "service name" shutdown
```

Where, in each case, `"service name"` is whatever you called the service when you installed it.

NT NET Command

Alternatively, you can use the NT NET command, which can start and stop any NT service:

```
NET START "service name"
NET STOP "service name"
```

Services Control Panel

Finally, there's the NT GUI (graphical user interface) way to do things. NT provides you with a Services dialog, which lists all of the NT services, and enables you to start and stop each one. Additionally, it enables you to set properties on each service, such as whether they start automatically on server boot.

The Services applet is located in the Control Panel.

Console Application

Under Windows 9x (Windows 95, Windows 98, and Windows ME), Apache does not, by default, run as a service. Windows 9x, not being server operating systems, do not have the concept of a service.[4]

Consequently, under Windows 9x, Apache runs as a console application. Which means, as it sounds, that Apache runs in a console (DOS window), and that console stays open for the entirety of the time that Apache is running. This is a little less than convenient, but then you really should not be using Windows 9x as a server platform, so hopefully this will only inconvenience you during testing.

If you are running Apache as a console application, you will launch it from the Start menu, in the Apache submenu. This will open up a console in which you will see an indication that Apache is running. To shutdown Apache, or restart it, the recommended method is to open another console, and type the commands

```
apache -k shutdown
```

to shutdown the process, and

```
apache -k restart
```

to restart it.

---

[4]*Yes, there are third-party applications that enable you run things as services. They are, however, not part of the base operating system.*

Doing this with the -k option, rather than just pressing control-C in the console window, or just closing the console window, is preferable, because it enables Apache to shutdown cleanly, rather than abruptly disconnecting from any open connections. However, because you are hopefully not running this in a server environment, it probably does not matter much.

Summary

Apache provides a variety of ways to start, stop, and restart your server. This makes it easy to automate these processes, and ensure that your server is always running when it needs to be.

Configuration Directives

IN THIS CHAPTER

Oh I have slipped the surly bonds of earth
And danced the sky on laughter-silvered wings

High Flight—John Gillespie Magee

Apache's behavior is configured via one or more text configuration files. These files are read on server startup, and contain directives that control everything about the server. In this chapter, we'll talk about how these configuration files work, and what you need to do to get your server acting exactly the way that you want it to.

Please note that this is not a comprehensive blow-by-blow, talking about every configuration directive that Apache supports. There are two main reasons for this.

One is that the Apache documentation itself, which is available free online, contains just such a comprehensive listing. There is a copy of this documentation on the CD that accompanies this book, but the version online is guaranteed to be the absolute latest information, including changes and corrections that are made on almost a daily basis by the Apache documentation team. This documentation can always be found at `http://httpd.apache.org/`.

The other reason is that it seems to make more sense to divide configuration directives into the various topics that they address. CGI directives, therefore, appear with Chapter 15, "CGI Programs," virtual host directives appear with Chapter 7, "Virtual Hosts," and so on.

This chapter discusses the configuration files themselves—their formats, their syntax, and techniques that can be used to simplify their maintenance.

Configuration Files

Apache has one main configuration file in which all the parameters controlling the operation of the server are specified. This file, called `httpd.conf`, is located in the `conf/` subdirectory of wherever you installed Apache. Ordinarily, this is `/usr/local/apache/conf`.

When you first install Apache, you'll find a number of different files living in that directory. Most of these files, however, are example files, put there as a sort of tutorial by demonstration.

The first files you will see in `conf` are `highperformance-std.conf` and `highperformance.conf`. These files are identical—the idea is that the `-std` version, you'll keep around as a backup in case you do things to the other one, and want to get it back the way that it was originally. This configuration file is intended to give you a head start in configuring a Web server that is tuned to peak performance in your particular setting. See Chapter 13, "Performance Tuning," for more information on tuning your server for maximum performance.

The next set of files, `httpd-std.conf` and `httpd.conf`, are the main server configuration file. We'll come back to this in a moment.

`magic` is the configuration file for `mod_mime_magic`, which is a module dealing with mime types.

`mime.types` is a configuration file relating file extensions with MIME types. See Chapter 8, "MIME and File Types," for more details about this file.

`httpd.conf` is the main server configuration file, and the file that you will most often be working with. `httpd-std.conf` is there so that you can make changes to the configuration file with impunity, and not be concerned that you won't be able to remember how to get it back to its original state.

It is a very good idea to make backup copies of known-good configuration files, particularly when you are going to try some modifications. In particular, you should keep around the configuration file that is distributed with Apache, as a good example of a well-formed configuration file. This file is usually called `httpd.conf-dist`.

Configuration File Syntax

`httpd.conf` consists of just a few types of lines.

Directives actually make configuration changes to the server, so these are what you will become the most familiar with. Sections, although technically a form of directive, divide your server into different pieces on which different sets of directives are to act. Comments provide documentation so that you remember why you made particular configuration changes.

Directives

The basic currency of the Apache configuration file is the directive. A directive is a keyword that is followed by a value, or values, which dictates one particular aspect of the server's behavior.

Here are some examples of directives:

```
KeepAlive On

MaxThreadsPerChild 20

ServerAdmin rbowen@rcbowen.com

Alias /icons/ "/usr/local/apache/icons"

IndexOptions FancyIndexing VersionSort
```

4

The directives that are available for you to set is determined by what modules you have installed. A number of directives directly affect the Apache core, whereas others are for configuring the behavior of individual modules.

To show a complete listing of all directives that are available to you on your particular server, you can use the -L flag with httpd, as shown here:

```
/usr/local/apache/bin/httpd -L
```

This will list every module that you are able to set, listing the name of the module that provides the directive, the expected argument or arguments, the contexts[1] that the directive can be used, and what override conditions, if any, must exist in order for the file to be permitted in a .htaccess file. (See Chapter 6, ".htaccess Files—Per-Directory Configuration," for more information on .htaccess files.)

Sections

A section[2] is a method for limiting the scope of one or more directives to a particular directory, a set of files, or a set of URLs. Sections look similar to HTML tags, and enclose one or more directives.

```
<Directory /usr/local/apache/htdocs/private>
    Deny from all
    Allow from 192.168.1.105
</Directory>
```

The directives enclosed in the section apply only to the limited subset of your server's space, which is specified by the section. In the previous example, the Deny and Allow directives will apply only to files located in the /usr/local/apache/htdocs/private directory, and any subdirectories thereof, unless overridden by a directive applied to a specific subdirectory.

There are a number of different types of sections, specifying a number of different ways to divide up the content served by your Web server.

Directory and DirectoryMatch

A <Directory> section, as you would expect, specifies that the enclosed directives apply to the particular directory listed, and all subdirectories thereof, unless overridden by another directive applied to a deeper directory. The directory path specified is the full path.

---

[1]*This concept will be covered in more detail in the next section on containers, and in the upcoming chapter on .htaccess files.*

[2]*Note that the documentation alternately refers to them as directives, sections, and containers, depending on the context, and the author of that particular part of the documentation.*

If a <Directory> section is used on Microsoft Windows, and if the directory being specified is on the same drive letter as the ServerRoot directory, then the drive letter doesn't need to be specified.

In the following example, the ServerRoot is on the D: drive, and so the <Directory> section is also assumed to be referring to the D: drive.

```
ServerRoot d:\apache\

<Directory \apache\docs\private>
    AllowOverride None
</Directory>
```

Directory sections are easier to use when your site has been well planned out, and the content in a particular directory is of a particular type.

A Directory section is used to indicate that a particular part of your site contains resources that are to be treated somewhat differently from files in the rest of the site. These files are treated differently because they are either a different file type (such as being image files, or CGI programs), or because there are different restrictions on their use (such as a requirement of a certain authorization to get in).

A <DirectoryMatch> section behaves much the same way as a Directory section, except that instead of taking an exact directory path as its argument, the argument is a regular expression. The enclosed directives are then applied to any directory that matches the regular expression.

Stated simply, a regular expression is a way of describing a particular pattern of characters. The regular expression engine will compare the pattern to a given directory, and determine whether or not it matches. This allows you to specify more than one directory in a single section, if there are multiple directories that share common traits.

For more information on regular expressions as they are implemented in Apache, please see Appendix C, "Regular Expressions."

In the example that follows, the <DirectoryMatch> section specifies that the enclosed directive (the AllowOverride directive) is to be applied to all directories that look like /users/, followed by a string beginning with either A or B (uppercase or lowercase):

```
<DirectoryMatch /users/[aAbB].* >
    AllowOverride All
</DirectoryMatch>
```

So, for example, the directory /users/Bowen would have the directive AllowOverride All applied to it, by virtue of matching the specified pattern.

4

CONFIGURATION
DIRECTIVES

This gives you a lot more control over which directories directives are applied to, and allows you to do in one directive what otherwise could potentially take a large number of individual directives.

Files and FilesMatch

<Files> sections indicate that the enclosed directives should be applied only to the specified files. Wildcard characters can be used. A ? will match a single character, and * will match any sequence of characters.

```
<Files *.gif>
    DefaultType image/gif
</Files>
```

As with <Directory>, <Files> has a sibling <FilesMatch>, which accepts extended regular expressions as arguments.

These directives are particularly useful for restricting access to some files in a particular directory, but not others, as shown in the following examples.

If you have several CGI programs, one of which is intended solely for site admins, you could use a Files directive to restrict access to just that one file:

```
<Files admin.cgi>
    AuthName Admin
    AuthType Basic
    AuthUserFile /usr/local/apache/passwords/admin.passwd
    AuthGroupFile /usr/local/apache/passwords/admin.groups
    Require group siteadmins
</Files>
```

(See Chapter 21, "Authentication, Authorization, and Access Control," for more details on authentication and authorization.)

Alternatively, if you have been a little less consistent in your naming scheme, but your admin files have somewhat similar names, you can still restrict access to them all with one directive.

```
<FilesMatch "admin.(cgi|pl|exe)">
    AuthName Admin
    AuthType Basic
    AuthUserFile /usr/local/apache/passwords/admin.passwd
    AuthGroupFile /usr/local/apache/passwords/admin.groups
    Require group siteadmins
</Files>
```

Because the Files directive accepts wildcard characters, creative use of that directive is often simpler and more intuitive than resorting to the FilesMatch directive.

IfDefine

The `<IfDefine>` section will be applied only if a particular parameter is defined. A parameter can be defined when the server is started up, with the `-D` command-line option.

Thus, if your `httpd.conf` were to contain directives as follows:

```
<IfDefine ReferLog>
    LogFormat "%{Referer}i -> %U" referer
    CustomLog logs/referer referer
</IfDefine>
```

And, if you were then to start your Apache server with the command line:

```
/usr/local/apache/bin/httpd -D ReferLog
```

Then the directives enclosed in the `<IfDefine>` section will be applied. In this case, starting your server with the `-D ReferLog` flag would cause the server to maintain a log file listing of the URLs from which people followed links to your site.

An `<IfDefine>` section can also be defined to apply directives when a particular parameter is not set. This is done by prepending a `!` to the specified parameter:

```
<IfDefine !ReferLog>
...
```

The directives enclosed in the previous section would be applied to the server if the `ReferLog` variable were *not* defined. That is, if you start your server *without* the `-D ReferLog` flag, these directives would be applied.

IfModule

Placing directives for a particular module inside of a `<IfModule>` section ensures that they are only applied if that particular module is loaded. This is a convenient way to have a standard configuration file, and not have to make per-system configuration changes just because a particular module is not installed. This is also the way that the default Apache configuration file is distributed, so no matter which modules you choose to build into your server, the configuration file will still work.

In the following example, the directives are applied only if the `threaded` module is loaded.

```
<IfModule threaded.c>
    StartServers        3
    MaxClients          8
    MinSpareThreads     5
    MaxSpareThreads     10
    ThreadsPerChild     25
    MaxRequestsPerChild 0
</IfModule>
```

4

CONFIGURATION DIRECTIVES

Limit and LimitExcept

<Limit> and <LimitExcept> sections refer to request methods. The enclosed directives are applied only if the HTTP request was made with one of the specified methods.

A request method is the manner in which the document, or resource, was requested from the Web server. This will usually be GET, POST, or HEAD, but will occasionally be something else. Without going into too much detail GET is usually used to get a document or resource. POST is usually used to send in the contents of a Web form. HEAD is a way to check the status of a document, typically to see if it has changed since the last time you looked at it, or if you can just reuse the copy you already have cached.

The <Limit> directive, then, allows you to restrict access to a particular document based on how that document (or resource) is being accessed.

<LimitExcept> is the opposite of <Limit>, limiting access for methods not listed.

Location and LocationMatch

When Apache receives a request for a resource, there is a phase during which Apache maps the URL to either an actual file on the server, or to some resource. A <Location> section defines a mapping from a URL to some non-file resource. And, as with the other Match directives, <LocationMatch> maps from a URL pattern to a resource.

The resource can be just about anything, but generally it will be a handler of some variety. A handler is an action that is to be taken when particular files, types of file, or particular URLs, are called. Some handlers are part of the core server, and others are included in modules.

Handlers will be discussed in detail in Chapter 14, "Handlers and Filters."

VirtualHost

When multiple Web sites, with different hostnames, are served from one Web server machine, they are referred to as virtual hosts. Chapter 7 is dedicated entirely to virtual hosts, so we'll just say that directives enclosed in a <VirtualHost> section apply only to documents served from that virtual host.

Comments

Lines beginning with the hash character (#) are comments, and are completely ignored by Apache when it reads through the configuration file on server restart.

Note that the line must begin with the hash. You can't start a comment mid line.

The default configuration file that comes with Apache is very heavily commented. Many beginning Apache users find that they can configure their server just by looking at the comments in that file and making changes based on the recommendations outlined there. All the basic directives are discussed, with examples and default settings, right in the comments.

As a result of this, the default configuration file is rather large, and nearly half of it is comments. That can be a little frustrating for an experienced user who already knows what he's looking for but has to scroll through dozens of lines of comments.

When you make configuration changes, it's a good idea to add comments explaining what the configuration is for, when it was made, and who made it. This will help you to remember, when you look back at the file several months later, why you were doing it.

It is also a very good idea to put your configuration file into some sort of revision management system, such as CVS, so that you can track changes, and undo them if they have undesirable effects.

Specifying a Different Configuration File

There are a variety of different circumstances in which you would want to load your configuration from somewhere other than your main server configuration file. If, for example, you are testing a different configuration, but don't want to overwrite your existing configuration file, you might want to maintain multiple config files, and switch among them.

You can do this with the -f flag when you start Apache:

```
/usr/local/apache/bin/httpd -f /path/to/alternate/apache.conf
```

Note that the specified configuration file is loaded in place of your regular configuration file, and therefore must specify a complete configuration.

apachectl is not aware of what configuration file you have loaded, nor does it allow you to pick an alternate configuration file. So if you apachectl restart when you are running with an alternate configuration file, Apache will be restarted with the default configuration file, rather than the one that was specified by -f.

Testing Your Configuration

Apache reads your configuration files only on server startup. This means that when you make changes to your configuration file, they do not take affect right away, but only when you restart the server. This gives you a chance to test your changes before putting them into production.

You can test your new configuration file using the configtest argument to the apachectl command. This is done simply by typing

```
apachectl configtest
```

apachectl will read through your configuration file and ensure that you have used correct syntax in the file. It is important to note that it does not verify that your configuration will work, but merely that it is correct syntax. If, for example, you refer to a `DocumentRoot` that does not exist, this error will not be caught at this stage, but only when you restart the server with the new file.

If the configuration file has bad syntax, `apachectl` will report this condition to you, and tell you which line the bad syntax appears on, as shown in the following example:

```
% apachectl configtest
Syntax error on line 26 of /usr/local/apache/conf/httpd.conf
Illegal option FollowSumLinks
```

In this example, I had misspelled the option `FollowSymLinks` as `FollowSumLinks`, and this was identified as an invalid configuration directive.

Having corrected this error, and running the command again, I get an indication that the problem has been resolved:

```
% apachectl configtest
Syntax OK
```

Note that if you have bad syntax in your configuration file when you try to start your server, it will not start. If you try to restart your server with a bad configuration file, it will ignore the restart and continue running so that it does not get stuck in a state of not running, and be unable to start up.

We highly recommended you run `apachectl configtest` each time you make any modifications to your configuration file. Apache gives you the option of including a file into your `httpd.conf` configuration file at the time that the server is restarted and the configuration files are loaded. This is accomplished with the `Include` directive, as shown here:

```
Include conf/modperl.conf
Include /etc/apache.otherconf
```

If the file path does not start with a leading slash (or, on Windows, with a drive designation) then the path is assumed to be relative to the `ServerRoot`. Why would you want to do this?

As your server configuration becomes more and more complex (Which it will, unless you have a very simple site, and are content to leave it that way forever), it becomes increasingly desirable to split it up into smaller, more manageable parts. Although this might, in some way, harken back to the day when there were three configuration files,[3] if handled carefully, this can greatly simplify your server administration. I'll give three examples where this might be a good thing to do, but I expect that your own situation will suggest other possibilities.

---

[3]*srm.conf, httpd.conf, and access.conf, presumably split the directives into sensible categories, but the distinctions were always rather nebulous.*

First, there's the situation when you have a very large, very complex module, which you have built into your server for some added functionality. `mod_perl`, `mod_ssl`, and `mod_rewrite` come to mind. These are very useful, very powerful modules, which can double the size of your configuration file.

In Apache 2.0, the default SSL configuration is in a separate file, which is loaded with an `Include` directive.

By separating the directives for that particular module out into a separate configuration file, you can make both parts of the configuration easier to read.

There is, of course, a slight performance hit on server start, because there is additional file I/O, but this only happens once, and is a very minor consideration.

Second, and perhaps most commonly, included configuration files are very useful when managing a large number of virtual hosts. By putting the configuration for each virtual host into its own file you can very swiftly locate the configuration for a particular host, and modify it without having to paw through dozens of other lines of configuration files looking for a particular host.

However, before you rush out and implement this plan, make sure you read the next section on including directories.

Note also that the performance hit on server start is going to go up as you add additional files. If you have hundreds of virtual hosts, and each one is in a separate file, not only will you have hundreds of include lines, but you'll have to open and read in those hundreds of configuration files. You might want to consider using `mod_vhost_alias`, which is discussed in Chapter 7. `mod_vhost_alias` allows you to configure large numbers of virtual hosts with just a few directives, rather than needing directives for each virtual host.

And third, there's the question of multiple people managing different parts of the Web site. By putting these different parts of the configuration into different files, and giving the necessary file permissions so the right people can edit them, you can delegate responsibility for the configuration file without letting everyone in the company have write access to the main server configuration file. This is particularly useful in the case of virtual hosts, where you are very likely to have a different person managing each virtual host.

Note, of course, that you will still have to have someone with root privileges restart the server in order for the configuration changes to take effect.

4

CONFIGURATION
DIRECTIVES

Including Directories

Of course, if you really buy into this notion of splitting configuration off into other files, you might end up with an inordinate number of Include directives in your configuration file. This is particularly the case if you are using this scheme for virtual hosts.

Fortunately, there's a really good solution for this. The Include directive also takes a directory, instead of a file, as the value of the argument. When given a directory, the Include directive reads every file in the specified directory and includes it into the configuration.

So, if you have dozens of virtual hosts, you can put all those configuration files in a single directory, and include them all with one directive:

```
Include conf/vhosts
```

When you start (or restart) your Apache server, you'll see something like the following in your error_log:

```
[Sat Jun 30 21:52:58 2001] [notice] SIGHUP received.  Attempting to restart
Processing config directory: /usr/local/apache/conf/vhosts
 Processing config file: /usr/local/apache/conf/vhosts/apache
 Processing config file: /usr/local/apache/conf/vhosts/boxofclue.com
 Processing config file: /usr/local/apache/conf/vhosts/buglet
 Processing config file: /usr/local/apache/conf/vhosts/cpan
 Processing config file: /usr/local/apache/conf/vhosts/cvs
 Processing config file: /usr/local/apache/conf/vhosts/dates
 Processing config file: /usr/local/apache/conf/vhosts/drbacchus.com
 Processing config file: /usr/local/apache/conf/vhosts/gaddisphoto.com
 Processing config file: /usr/local/apache/conf/vhosts/photos.tm3.org
 Processing config file: /usr/local/apache/conf/vhosts/reefknot.org
 Processing config file: /usr/local/apache/conf/vhosts/rt
 Processing config file: /usr/local/apache/conf/vhosts/tm3
 Processing config file: /usr/local/apache/conf/vhosts/zzz_last
[Sat Jun 30 21:52:59 2001] [notice] Apache/1.3.19 (Unix) mod_perl/1.25
     ➥configured — resuming normal operations
```

Notice that the files are included in alphabetic order. More specifically, they are included in the order that they appear in a directory listing. In the previous example, you'll notice a zzz_last file on the end. This is the one containing the virtual host settings for the _default_ virtual host, and perhaps some other global server configuration directives.

It is also very important to note that every file in the directive will be included, therefore, you should make sure that no stray files end up in the directory, which can cause Apache to fail on startup. Temporary files generated by your editor are a frequent source of problems, for example.

Options: Turning on Features

The Options directive is one of the main tools for turning features on and off in various parts of the site. Judicious use of this directive will allow you to control very tightly what is allowed, and not allowed, in each content directory. It can be set in your main server configuration, in a VirtualHost section, in a Directory section, or in a .htaccess file. For the scope of the section in which you set it the specified options will be turned on.

Options takes one or more of seven possible values, All of them, or None of them. Most of these possible values will also be discussed in other chapters because they turn on (or off) major functionality of the server.

General Syntax

The syntax of the Options directive is as follows:

Options [+|-] *option* [+|-] *option*Prepending a [ps] to a particular option adds that option to those that are turned on, whereas prepending a ñ turns off that particular option.

```
Options +ExecCGI +Includes -FollowSymLinks
```

In this example, the ExecCGI and Includes options are turned on, and the FollowSymLinks option is turned off.

Although the [ps] and ñ are optional, omitting them means that you are turning off all other options that might have been set, and turning on only those that you have specified. The following directive, for example, turns on Indexes, but also turns off any other options that might have been turned on. It helps to remember that directives set in a particular directory also apply to any subdirectories of that directory.

```
Options Indexes
```

ExecCGI

```
Options +ExecCGI
```

The ExecCGI option turns on the capability to execute CGI programs inside the specified scope. This option will be discussed in greater detail in Chapter 15, "CGI Programs."

CAUTION

Although this directive allows you to execute CGI programs in a directory which is not marked with a `ScriptAlias` directive—that is, to execute CGI programs in a document directory—this is generally not a good idea for two reasons. First of all, it makes it very difficult to track down all the CGI programs on your site if and when you are having problems. Secondly, it is a potential security problem. Any CGI program is a potential security hole, and permitting them in directories where the file permissions are typically a little more lenient is asking for trouble.

FollowSymLinks

```
Options +FollowSymLinks
```

By default, symbolic links are ignored when they appear in a directory served by Apache, which makes it impossible to escape from the document directory. If, for example, you had a link to /home in your document root, following that symbolic link would permit Web users to download arbitrary files from anyone's home directory, which would clearly be a security problem.

However, if you have `Options +FollowSymLinks` turned on, then Apache *will* follow these links.

CAUTION

Make very sure you are aware of the security implications in turning on this option. Make sure that you do not have any symbolic links to directories that might contain files that should not be available to the general public. Never permit this option for directories that are managed by potentially untrustworthy people. If you absolutely must have symbolic links from your content directories, see the `SymLinksIfOwnerMatch` option as a possible alternative.

Because Microsoft Windows does not permit symbolic links, this option does not apply to Apache on Windows.[4]

---

[4]*No, shortcuts are not the same as symbolic links, and Apache will not follow shortcuts.*

SymLinksIfOwnerMatch

```
Options +SymLinksIfOwnerMatch
```

This is the same as the previous option, with one important difference. Apache will follow symbolic links only if the target of the directory is owned by the same user as the link itself. That means a user cannot link to a directory that they do not own, and thus get access to the contents of that directory.

As with `FollowSymLinks`, this option is not available on the Windows version of Apache.

Includes

```
Options +Includes
```

`Options Includes` turns on the capability to have Server-Side Includes (SSI) in files. SSI gives you the ability to embed a variety of commands in HTML documents, and have them evaluated when the page is served to a client.

SSI is discussed in detail in Chapter 16, "Server-Side Includes."

CAUTION

SSI has many of the same security concerns as CGI programs, in that it allows the execution of arbitrary commands on the server. To defang this beast, consider using `IncludesNOEXEC` instead.

IncludesNOEXEC

```
Options +IncludesNOEXEC
```

This directive turns on permission to use SSI, but forbids the use of the `#exec` command, or using `#include` to load a CGI program. This removes most of the security risk associated with permitting Server-Side Includes.

Indexes

```
Options +Indexes
```

This option enables the generation of automatic indexes in directories that do not have an `index.html` file (or whatever file you have indicated with the `DirectoryIndex` directive.

You can find out more information about automatic generation of indexes in Chapter 11, "Directory Indexing."

> **CAUTION**
>
> Turning on this option means that files in directories—even if you don't have links to them from anywhere on your site—will be visible to anyone looking at your Web site. However, if you are planning the security of your Web site around the principle of "hoping nobody notices," then you will have larger problems than this. That is to say, if you would not want random strangers to be in possession of certain files, you should never have them available on an unauthenticated Web site.

MultiViews

```
Options +MultiViews
```

The `MultiViews` option turns on a very powerful aspect of content negotiation. `MultiViews` is a feature whereby Apache figures out which document is most likely to be acceptable to the client, and gives them that one. `MultiViews` and content negotiation in general, will be discussed in Chapter 10, "Content Negotiation."

All

```
Options All
```

As you would expect, `Options All` turns on all the various `Options`. Well, almost all of them. `MultiViews` is not turned on with `All`, and must be explicitly asked for.

None

```
Options None
```

And, of course, `None` turns off all the available options.

Configuration Security Considerations

Please remember that there are serious security concerns when you start splitting up your configuration file and putting it all over the place; particularly if you start giving out permissions to edit those files.

Being able to edit those subfiles is no different from being able to edit your main server configuration file. Any directive can be put in those included files, and will have every bit as much weight as though it had appeared in the main server configuration file.

Make very sure of two things. First, ensure the files themselves are in secure directories. If the file is world-writeable, so are all the files in it, and even if they can't edit the file itself someone could delete or rename them. For example, if `/usr/local/apache` is world-writeable[5] someone can remove the directory `apache`, and replace it with his own directory, with anything he wants in it. So it's not enough that the individual files in that directory have the correct permissions on them.

Secondly, make sure that you trust the folks that you're giving file write permission to.[6] If they can edit these files, they can do whatever they want to your server configuration.

Summary

Apache configuration files contain three types of things. Sections, specified with HTML-like tags, delineate the scope, or range, of a particular set of directives. Directives, specified as a directive name, followed by a value, configure all the individual settings on the server. And comments, specified with a leading pound sign (#), are ignored by the server, and serve only to annotate the configuration file.

Apache ships with heavily commented default configuration files to get you started quickly.

4

CONFIGURATION
DIRECTIVES

---

[5]*Yes, I know, that's a horrible thought, but I've seen it happen.*

[6]*And, of course, the first law of security is "Don't trust anybody." See Chapter 19, "Apache Security," on Security Considerations.*

Configuration Utilities

IN THIS CHAPTER

"Software suppliers are trying to make their software packages more user-friendly...Their best approach, so far, has been to take all the old brochures, and stamp the words, 'user-friendly' on the cover."

Bill Gates

GUIs and Configuration Files

Apache, in the Unix-server tradition, is configured via text-based files. This has several advantages, including:

- You only need a simple text editor such as vi or emacs to modify the configuration of an Apache server.
- It is possible to access the machine through a remote shell (using telnet or ssh, a secure version of the Unix remote shell command).
- The bandwidth requirements are small and you can administer servers over slow links. You can connect a modem to a serial port and be able to dial-in and administer the machine remotely, even if it is unreachable from the Internet.
- You can put the configuration files under a source control system such as CVS, and keep track of who changed what and when. You can easily maintain different configuration versions and revisions, and you can safely return to the last set of configuration files known to work.
- The Apache configuration file format enables insertion of comments alongside directives. This provides valuable information about the configuration and provides administrators the opportunity to document, in detail, specific settings. This is useful in environments where more than one administrator modifies the same set of Apache server configuration files.
- You can automate the generation and modification of the configuration files using shell commands of scripting languages such as Perl or Tcl. This is useful if the same task has to be repeated over time, for example for different ISP customers. The configuration files are usually generated via template files from customer information stored in relational databases or LDAP directories.

Text-based configuration systems have several disadvantages. The following reasons are why GUI or Web-based installation and configuration tools are useful, especially for new or inexperienced administrators.

- The configuration file formats vary significantly from one program to another. Even if you are familiar with the Apache configuration syntax, other popular server packages such as Sendmail or Samba use different configuration formats. A well-designed GUI will provide you with a centralized, consistant interface to a variety of server programs, thus lowering the learning curve.

- The number of available directives is overwhelming. Setting up a server such as Apache usually involves reading a long set of documentation and manual pages. This is necessary even if you only need a handful of options to configure a typical installation. A well-designed GUI will organize the options in a sensible, task-oriented interface that will guide the user, collect the information needed, and produce the appropriate configuration.

Other advantages of well-designed, GUI-based administration tools are context-sensitive help, delegated administration, and the capability to abstract the specific configuration syntax details.

Poorly designed GUIs have disadvantages. A GUI can be unstructured, offering configuration screens with a myriad of options that confuse the user. Some GUIs can only configure a limited set of functionality, thus being useful only for initial configurations. When users need the advanced functionality, they must access the configuration files directly, defeating the purpose of the GUI. In some cases the GUI does not interact nicely with the underlying configuration files, keeping its own metadata and overwriting the configuration files when needed. Thus, any configuration changes done by editing the file directly will be lost because the GUI will not recognize those changes.

This chapter introduces you to two popular GUI configuration tools for Apache. You will learn how to install and use them to configure your server.

Webmin

Webmin is a Web-based administration system for Unix-like operating systems. It is Open Source under the GPL license and James Cameron is the main author. It is written in Perl and is extensible, meaning that developers can write modules to configure different programs, including one to configure Apache.

In this section you will learn how to install and configure Webmin and use it to perform basic Apache-administration tasks. These tasks include starting and stoping the server, changing server parameters, creating new virtual servers, protecting directories, and so on.

Before using Webmin or any other configuration utility make sure you backup your Apache configuration files. In particular you need to backup `httpd.conf` and any other files referenced in it via the `<Include>` directive.

Existing Webmin Installation

You might have Webmin already installed if you are using a recent Linux distribution. You can use package management utility of your distribution to check if Webmin is already installed.

> **TIP**
>
> If your system is rpm-based (such as the ones from Red Hat, Suse, or Mandrake) you can check if Webmin is already installed by issuing the `rpm -q webmin` at a shell prompt.

If you do not have Webmin installed, please proceed to the next section where you can learn the steps necessary to get Webmin up and running.

Webmin is accessed via a Web browser. Before you can do so, you need to start the Webmin Web server. The Webmin application is protected by a password.

To change the Webmin default password issue the following command:

```
/usr/share/webmin/changepass.pl /etc/webmin/ admin newpassword
```

Substitute *newpassword* with the new password to protect access to Webmin. The command needs to be executed as root.

> **TIP**
>
> Each distribution places files in a slightly different location. You can check where the files are installed in your system by issuing the following command:
>
> ```
> # rpm -q -l webmin | more
> ```
>
> If you want to know where `changepass.pl` was installed in your system, you can issue the following command:
>
> ```
> # rpm -q -l webmin | grep changepass.pl
> ```

Installation

If you don't have Webmin installed in your system, you can download it from `http://www.webmin.com/webmin/`

Users of any of the BSD-Unix variants such as FreeBSD or OpenBSD have Webmin available via the ports collection.

You can download an rpm package from the Webmin site. If you are using an rpm-based Linux distribution you might want to check if your distribution already includes a Webmin rpm and install that one instead. You can check your vendor's Web site or an rpm repository like `http://rpmfind.net`. In any case, make sure to check the Webmin Web site for the latest version, to make sure your rpm is up to date.

Issue the following command as root to install a new rpm in your system:

```
# rpm -q -i webmin*.rpm
```

Installing Webmin from Source

Webmin is written in Perl, so you need to have a version of Perl installed in your system. You can verify that you have Perl installed in your system by typing `perl` in the command-line prompt. Executing the command `which perl` will give you the exact path of the program being executed.

If you do not have Perl installed in your system, you can install the package that came with your Unix distribution or visit `http://www.perl.com`. The Webmin Web site also provides precompiled packages for Solaris and HP-UX.

The installation of Webmin is straightforward. The steps need to be performed as root. After you have downloaded the Webmin compressed sources package (tarball) from the Webmin Web site, you need to uncompress it and execute the installation script:

```
# gunzip < webmin-xxx.tar.gz | tar xvf -
# cd webmin-xxx
# ./setup.sh
```

xxx needs to be replaced by the version of Webmin you are installing.

You will be prompted for the information Webmin needs:

- You need to specify where Webmin will install its configuration and log files: `/etc/webmin`, `/var/webmin`
- You need to enter the path to the Perl interpreter, which you already learned about earlier in this section.
- You need to provide the specific vendor name and version for your operating system. This is necessary because each operating system distribution places configuration files in a different place.
- Finally, you provide the required values for the Webmin server such as the listening ports and the username and password, to protect the pages.

Webmin usually listens on port 10000 and the Web server might or might not allow for secure access depending on whether the appropriate libraries were installed in the system. You might want to change this port number if you are concerned about people scanning your computer for services at specific ports.

You can access the specific configuration of your Webmin server via the `miniserv.conf` file, located in `/etc/webmin`.

Starting Webmin

To access Webmin, assuming it is configured with the defaults outlined in the previous sections, you need to type the following URL in your Web browser:

```
http://127.0.0.1:10000/
```

If your Webmin server has SSL support, the URL changes from `http://` to `https://`.

This will take you to the Webmin login page if Webmin is already running. Webmin can be configured to run at startup time. You can start and stop Webmin manually with the following commands:

```
/etc/webmin/start
/etc/webmin/stop
```

Using Webmin

You need to enter the appropriate username and password to access Webmin (see Figure 5.1). After a successful login you can access the main Webmin page. Here you can configure different aspects of Webmin itself. It even includes support for themes.

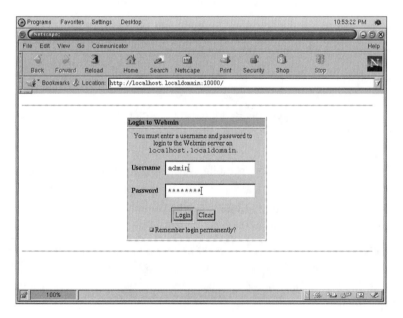

FIGURE 5.1

Webmin login screen

You can navigate the different sections by clicking on the different tabs (see Figure 5.2). The System tab enables you to configure the underlying operating system, including users, file systems, and packages. The Hardware section enables for configuration of bootloaders, disk partitions, networking, and printers.

In the Others section you can access Webmin modules that permit the execution of remote commands, a Web-based file manager, and so on.

You can find Apache under the Servers section, together with the configuration options for mail, DNS, and FTP servers.

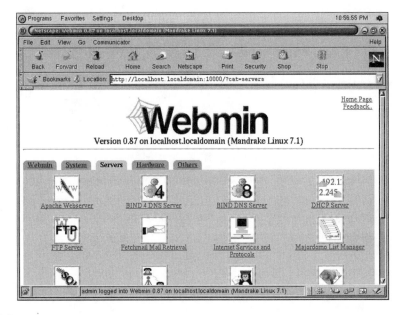

FIGURE 5.2

Webmin server screen

You can click in the Apache icon to enter the main Apache configuration page.

The first time you enter Apache configuration you might be asked to provide information about available third-party Apache modules. If you are not sure about what modules are installed click OK because Webmin tends to guess right and you can always change that selection afterwards.

5

- Top area, where you can find links to configure the Apache instances being managed and links to start the server.
- Global Configuration, with links to configuration options.
- Virtual Servers, which is a list of all the available servers to be configured.

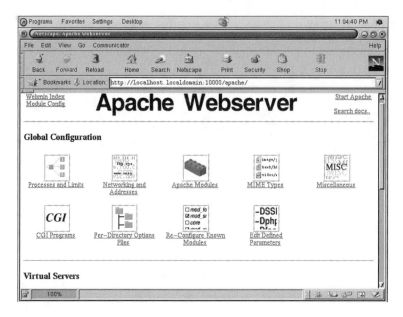

FIGURE 5.3

Webmin Apache main configuration screen

Top Area

If the Apache Web server came installed with your operating system distribution then Webmin knows how to find it and you can configure it right away. If you are using a custom installed Apache you can specify the location of the relevant files by clicking on the module configuration link (see Figure 5.4). You need to provide the commands for starting and stopping the server, the location of the httpd executable, and the root directory of Apache. Other options enable you to specify how virtual hosts will be displayed in the Web interface.

You can start the Apache Web server by clicking the link on the top-right corner (see Figure 5.3). After Apache has been started, a new link will appear that enables you to stop the running server.

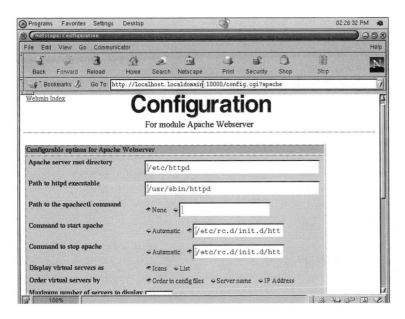

FIGURE 5.4
Apache Web server configuration options

Global Configuration

You can configure parameters that affect the server as a whole via the links in this area. Most of the options here are usually required only for advanced configuration scenarios. The default settings are usually appropriate for most situations. Under the Processes and Limits section you can configure the number of Apache processes and the number of requests these servers will process. You can define which modules will be loaded by the Web server at the Apache modules section.

Apache enables you to specify certain configuration options on a per-directory basis, via special files called `.htaccess`. You can configure them in the per-directory options files section.

Virtual Servers

Here you have access to a list of virtual hosts available for your Apache installation. You can configure the default Web server. Other virtual hosts will also inherit the properties specified here.

Configuring a Virtual Host

You can add a new virtual host (see Figure 5.5) by providing the address and port the new server will listen to, the document root where documents will be served, and the server name for the host.

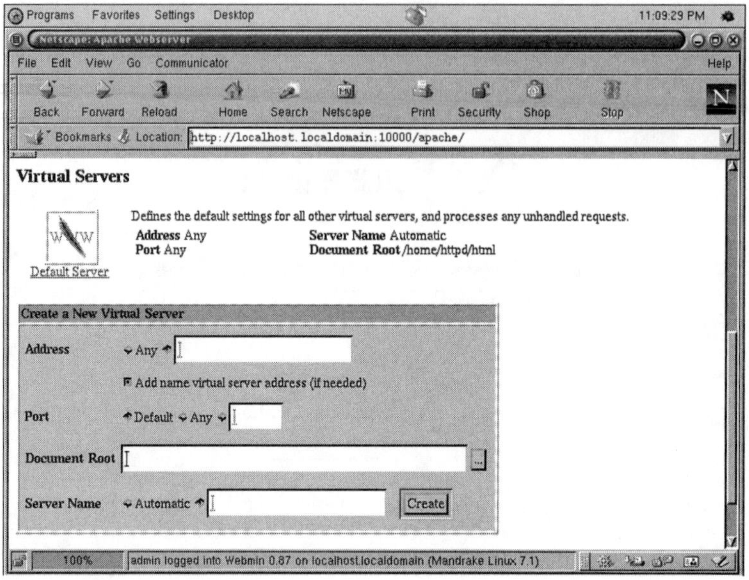

FIGURE 5.5

Adding a new virtual server

You can delete a virtual server by clicking the virtual server link, server configuration, and then selecting to delete the server.

You can configure the properties of the virtual server via the configuration links. Some of the practical configuration parameters include:

- **Error Handling:** You can customize the pages to be displayed in your Web site when an error occurs. For example, when a document is not found you can present the user with a page that explains the error and allows them to search the Web site for similar documents.

- **Log files:** You can define the location of the files where Apache will log the Web server accesses, the possible errors encountered, and the format of the information recorded.

- **Aliases and redirects:** You can associate directories in the hard disk with specific URLs that are easier to remember and type. You can also specify the permanent or temporary redirection of certain URLs in your Web site. This is useful if the Web site has gone through layout changes. Your users will not encounter "Document not found" errors, they will be redirected to the appropriate page instead.

- **Show directives and Edit directives:** These allow you to have a direct look at the underlying configuration directives. You can edit specific directives or even add new directives for custom or not supported modules.

- **CGI:** You can mark certain directories as containing and allowing the execution of CGI scripts.

You can configure directory, location, and file sections in each of the virtual servers. As well as define specific portions of the URL space that you can configure separately.

You can configure these sections by clicking them and then selecting one of the links. The Access Control (See Figure 5.6) section enables you to restrict access based on the IP address the user is coming from, its username and password, or the browser he is using.

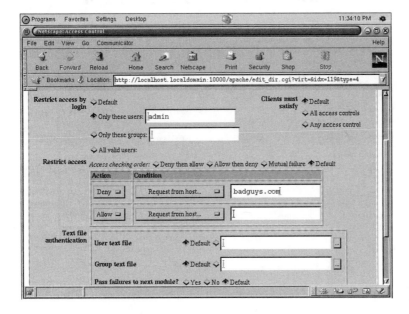

FIGURE 5.6
Restrict access screen

Delegated Administration

More than one user can administer the Apache installation with Webmin. You can restrict access and configuration rights on a per-user or per-group basis

You can accomplish this by following these steps:

- **Create a new Webmin user:** Click the Webmin tab, select Webmin users, and then select Create a new Webmin user. Select Apache module as part of the creation process.
- **Restrict configuration:** You can now select the created user link and configure the level of configuration access. You can restrict the ability of the user to start or stop the server, change addresses, pipe logs to programs, or manage only a certain virtual Web server (See Figure 5.7).

You can also create Webmin groups and set policies based on them.

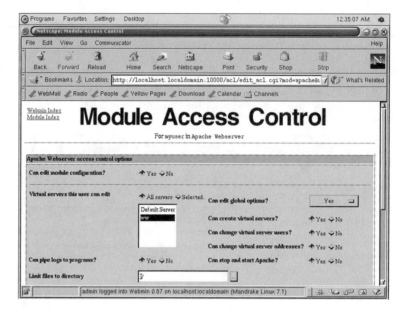

FIGURE 5.7

Restricting configuration on a per-user basis.

Related Links

You can learn more about Webmin by visiting the following Web sites:

- Official Webmin site: `http://www.webmin.com/webmin`
- Joe Cooper's Webmin guide:
  `http://www.swelltech.com/support/webminguide/index.html`

Comanche

Comanche stands for Configuration Manager for Apache. It is a standalone GUI (not Web-based) distributed under an Apache-style license, and its primary author is Daniel Lopez. It is written in the Tcl/Tk scripting language and works on Unix and Windows platforms. Although it can be extended to easily configure other servers, its primary focus is Apache.

Before using Comanche or any other configuration utility make sure you backup your Apache configuration files.

Installation

You can download Comanche from the Comanche Web site at http://www.comanche.org.

You can download binaries for a variety of Unix and Windows platforms.

If you want to download the source, you need to make sure you have a recent version of Tcl/Tk installed in your system, together with the [incr Tcl] object-oriented extension to the Tcl language. You can get this software at the Tcl developer exchange http://tcl.activestate.com/.

Unix

After you have downloaded the tarball, you need to uncompress it, change your working directory to the newly created directory, and start Comanche:

```
# gunzip < comanche-xxx.tar.gz | tar xvf -
# cd comanche-xxx
# ./comanche-xxx
```

Where *xxx* is the Comanche version.

If you downloaded the source distribution itkwish main.tcl is the command you need to start Comanche.

The first time you start Comanche no Apache installations will be available. You can press the New Installation link to provide Comanche with the location of the Apache Web server. You can select one of three options—you compiled Apache manually, you are using the Apache bundled with your installation, or you are using a custom Apache installation. After you have provided the data, you are ready to proceed with the configuration of the server.

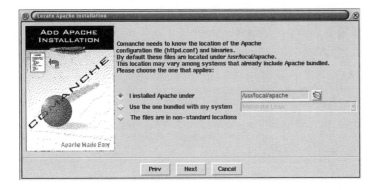

FIGURE 5.8

Initial Comanche setup

Windows

You need to have Apache installed in your system prior to installing Comanche in Windows. Comanche supports Windows 95/98/NT/ME/2000, but you should only run production Apache versions on server versions of Windows, such as Windows 2000.

The Windows binary is contained in a zip file. You can use Winzip or any other Windows compression utility to extract the contents of the archive.

You can start Comanche by double-clicking the Comanche.exe icon. Comanche will read the location of Apache installations directly from the registry, so you do not need to perform any extra configuration steps.

Using Comanche

The Comanche configuration screen is divided in two main areas (see Figure 5.9). The left area is a tree-like structure that enables you to navigate Comanche nodes. The right pane displays information about the selected nodes. You can create, delete or perform actions on nodes by right-clicking them.

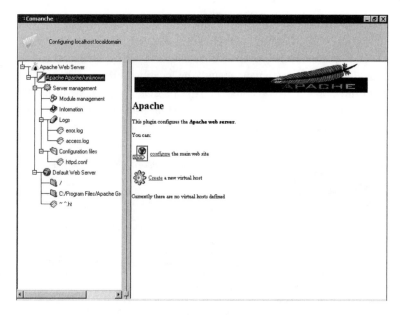

FIGURE 5.9

Main Comanche screen

Node Structure

The Apache Web server node enables you to add or remove Apache installations.

Each one of the Apache installations contains a node called Server management. Under Server management you can start or stop Apache (only in Unix), as well as create and restore backups of the configuration files.

Under Server management you can find several nodes:

- **Module management:** Enables you to select which Apache modules Comanche will configure (See Figure 5.10). Selecting a module here means that the associated options will appear later when configuring Apache. Deselecting a module means that those options will be preserved in the configuration file, but you will not see them when configuring Apache.

- **Information:** Displays information about the Apache instance being configured (only in Unix).

- **Logs:** Provides access to the log files being configured.

- **Configuration files:** Provides access to the contents of the configuration files.

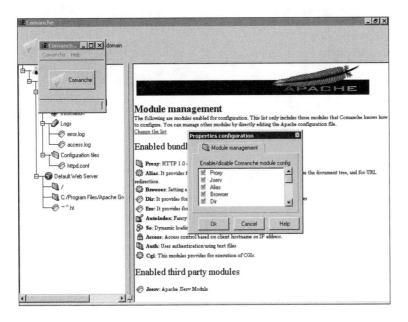

FIGURE 5.10
Module management screen

Each Apache installation contains a Default server node. You can configure the properties of the default Web server in this node. The other virtual hosts will inherit most properties, but some properties, such as number of processes, apply to the server as a whole and you can only configure them here.

You can configure the default server by clicking on the properties link in the right pane or by right-clicking on the node and selecting the properties entry in the pop-up menu. A window containing different property pages will appear. When you are done configuring properties you can press Ok and the changes will be applied to the configuration file. You need to restart the server before the changes affect a running server.

Under basic properties (see Figure 5.11) you can configure the document root for the default server. This is where Apache looks for requested documents. If the document root is /usr/local/apache/htdocs then a request for http://localhost.localdomain/index.html will return /usr/local/apache/htdocs/index.html.

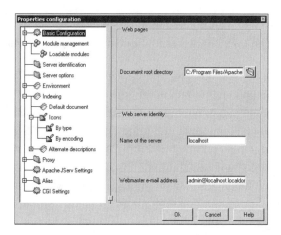

FIGURE 5.11
Configuring basic properties.

You can also define the server hostname and the administrator e-mail address. Under the basic properties node, in the listening properties node, you can configure the addresses and ports you want Apache to listen to.

Virtual Hosts

You can create virtual hosts by right-clicking the Default Server and selecting New virtual host.

You can configure the virtual host properties by right-clicking the virtual host node and selecting properties.

You can define basic and advanced parameters. The changes will be incorporated when you press OK.

Some of the advanced parameters include options for redirecting links, associating files with MIME types and directory listen formatting.

Containers

You can create location, directory, and file nodes. They relate to the corresponding `<direc-tory>`, `<location>` and `<file>` sections in the Apache configuration file. This enables you to apply specific configuration directives to certain portions of the filesystem or URL space. For example, by clicking on the security node on the directory or location property pages window, you can restrict access based on where the client is coming from (IP-based access is shown in Figure 5.12), or who he claims to be (User auth).

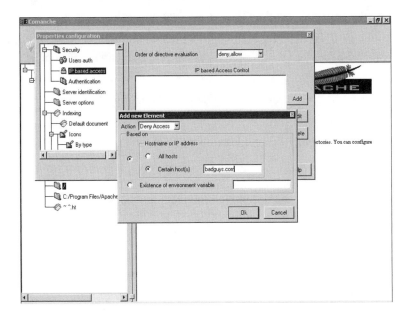

FIGURE 5.12
Restricting access

Containers can be created by right-clicking Virtual hosts or other containers and selecting the add option in the pop-up menu.

Comanche provides context-sensitive help. In any of the property pages you can press Help to have access to the Apache directives related to the information present on the screen. In the basic properties screen you will get information about the `ServerRoot`, `ServerAdmin` and `ServerName` directives.

Summary

In this chapter we have described two of the most popular GUI tools for configuring Apache. You can find other tools at Open Source sites such as http://freshmeat.net and http://sourceforge.net. We have analyzed the drawbacks and advantages of GUI tools. Whether or not you use them depends a lot on your personal level of comfort with Apache, Unix, and command-line tools. As the tools mature, they become more and more attractive, even for experienced system administrators.

Webmin is a powerful tool for configuring Apache. Its main strength is the capability to remotely configure the server.

Webmin respects the original Apache configuration file structures and contents. It is possible to alternate between the configuration of Apache via Webmin and editing the configuration files directly. Indeed, it is possible to edit those files via Webmin itself.

Webmin only runs on Unix, but it includes support for a wide variety of platforms, providing a consistent, easy-to-use interface for a variety of system configurations and popular Internet servers.

Comanche provides a powerful cross-platform tool for configuring Apache. Its main strengths are structured, user-friendly interface, and context-sensitive help.

You can still edit Apache configuration files with a file editor. Comanche will detect and incorporate those changes.

Comanche can be easily extended via XML files to support additional directives.

.htaccess files—Per-Directory Configuration

IN THIS CHAPTER

*And everyone said, "If we only live, We too will go to sea in a Sieve—To the hills of the
Chankly Bore!"*

The Jumblies—Edward Lear

When you have multiple people managing different parts of your Apache server, it is often
very useful to be able to give each person the ability to configure the particular directories for
which they are responsible. This can, of course, be done with directives contained in `<Directory>`
sections. However, it is often desirable to restrict the number of people that have direct access
to the main server configuration file.

`.htaccess` files, described in this chapter, give you the ability to allow this sort of per-directory
configuration without giving access to the main server configuration file, and without having to
add directives for everyone, each time they want something changed.

A `.htaccess` file can be placed in any directory on the server, and may contain almost any
configuration directive. The directives in each file apply to resources served out of that directory,
and any subdirectories thereof, unless they are further overridden by directives appearing in other
`.htaccess` files within deeper subdirectories.

Finally, directives in `.htaccess` files take effect immediately, as opposed to restarting your
server for them to take effect, as is necessary for changes to the main server configuration file(s).

However, there are tradeoffs associated with using `.htaccess` files, and you should make sure
that they are actually needed on your site before you put a lot of your configuration into them.

AccessFileName

Although the filename `.htaccess` will be used throughout this chapter, and in the rest of this
book, to indicate the file in which you put per-directory configuration directives, this filename
is configurable, using the `AccessFileName` directive. This directive appears in the main server
configuration file, and tells Apache what files to look in for per-directory configuration directives.

The default value for this directive is `.htaccess`. However, on Microsoft Windows, where filenames starting with a dot are problematic, the directive should be given the value of `htaccess`,
or some other file without a leading dot.

You can set this to whatever value you like, if there is some name that you find to be more
intuitive. For example, if you would prefer to call your per-directory configuration files
`directory.conf`, the following directive would let you do this:

```
AccessFileName directory.conf
```

You will notice, if you look at the documentation for this directive, that it is possible to set more than one filename to be used for per-directory configuration. Just because it's possible doesn't mean it's a good idea. Setting multiple values for this directive should be avoided for two reasons.

First and most importantly, it's confusing. If there are two (or more) possible files in any given directory where directives can be lurking, it will take longer for you to find that rogue directive that is causing undesired or unexpected results on your server. Likewise, if you are working in one file, but there are conflicting directives in the other file, then you might spend unnecessary time trying to figure out why your configuration is producing unexpected results.

Secondly, as is explained in more detail in the "Performance" section, looking for, and parsing the contents of .htaccess files takes time. And doubling the number of possible locations of .htaccess files by giving it two names to look for, rather than just one, will cause Apache to spend twice as much time looking for these files than it would with just one, *even* if you are not using any per-directory configuration files.

AllowOverride

Because this feature allows anyone with write access to any directory served by your Web server to make configuration changes, you will be glad to know that you can limit what you permit these files to override.

The AllowOverride directive can have one or more of five possible values, specifying what category of directives will be permitted in the files. In addition to these limitations, the documentation for each directive indicates the contexts it is permitted in, and this will specifically indicate whether that particular directive is permitted in .htaccess files.

The syntax for this directive is as follows:

```
AllowOverride All|None|directive-type1 [directive-type2] [directive-type3] etc
```

The possible directive types are detailed in the following sections.

AuthConfig (Authentication)

```
AllowOverride AuthConfig
```

The presence of the previous directive will allow use of the authorization directives (AuthDBMGroupFile, AuthDBMUserFile, AuthGroupFile, AuthName, AuthType, AuthUserFile, Require, and so on) in .htaccess files. These directives are covered in more detail in Chapter 21, "Authentication, Authorization, and Access Control," but an example follows.

To require password authentication in a particular directory, you might add the following to a .htaccess file in that directory:

```
AuthType Basic
AuthName admins
AuthUserFile /usr/local/apache/secure/passwords
AuthGroupFile /usr/local/apache/secure/groups
Require group admin
```

If AuthConfig is not one of the directive types permitted by your AllowOverride directive, directives that fall into this category will be ignored.

FileInfo

```
AllowOverride FileInfo
```

The presence of the previous directive will allow use of the directives controlling document types (AddEncoding, AddLanguage, AddType, DefaultType, ErrorDocument, LanguagePriority, and so on) in .htaccess files.

You can learn more about the directives that fall into this category in Chapter 8, "MIME and File Types." An example of how this might be used is shown here.

To specify the error document for a particular directory, you might add the following to a .htaccess in that directory:

```
ErrorDocument error.html
```

(See Chapter 9 for more information on the ErrorDocument directive.)

Indexes

```
AllowOverride Indexes
```

The presence of the previous directive in your server configuration file will allow the use of the directives controlling directory indexing (AddDescription, AddIcon, AddIconByEncoding, AddIconByType, DefaultIcon, DirectoryIndex, FancyIndexing, HeaderName, IndexIgnore, IndexOptions, ReadmeName, and so on) in .htaccess files.

Chapter 11, "Directory Indexing," covers the use of these directives in more detail. These directives are primarily used when there is no index file in the directory, and Apache automatically generates a directory listing. The DirectoryIndex directive, on the other hand, tells Apache which file to use as the default for a particular directory, when there is no filename specified.

The following example sets the default file for a particular directory to something other than what is configured for the rest of the server.

```
DirectoryIndex menu.shtml
```

Placing the previous directive in a .htaccess file in a particular directory will cause that file to be displayed when no other file has been specified.

Limit

```
AllowOverride Limit
```

The presence of the previous directive in your server configuration file will allow use of the directives controlling host access (Allow, Deny, and Order) to be used in .htaccess files.

For example, in a directory containing documents internal to your company, you might want to restrict access to hosts within your own network. This could be accomplished with the following directives, placed in a .htaccess file in that directory.

```
Deny from all
Allow from yourcompany.com
Order Deny,Allow
```

See Chapter 21 for more detail about using these types of directives.

Options

```
AllowOverride Options
```

The presence of the previous directive in your main server configuration file allows use of the directives controlling specific directory features (Options and XBitHack).

XBitHack turns on (or off) the capability for Apache to determine what files to parse for SSI (Server Side Include) directives. This functionality will be discussed in detail in Chapter 16, "Server-Side Includes."

The Options directive is rather powerful, turning on or off a variety of different behaviors such as CGI execution, SSI, directory indexing, and following symbolic links. The directive itself is discussed in Chapter 4, but is mentioned in many other places because of its widespread effects. Consider carefully before permitting this functionality in .htaccess files.

All

```
AllowOverride All
```

The previous directive will enable all the previously listed categories of directives in .htaccess files.

None

```
AllowOverride None
```

The previous directive will cause Apache not to honor any directives placed in `.htaccess` files. In fact, it will cause Apache to not even look for these files. This has performance implications. See the section on Performance for more details.

Caveats and Limitations

Use of `.htaccess` files has two primary consequences, which you should carefully consider before allowing their use: performance and security.

Performance

To understand the performance impact of `.htaccess` files, you need to know a little about how they work.

When a client requests a resource from your server, that resource request is mapped to a directory path, or perhaps to some nonfile resource. If the target of the request is a file living in a directory, Apache then has to determine what additional configuration directives, if any, apply to that directory, and perhaps also to that particular file. The main server configuration file has already been parsed, and that configuration information is stored in memory. Therefore, this can be very quickly checked for references to the affected directory and/or file.

However, if the use of `.htaccess` files is enabled, there's another step that must be taken. For each directory along the path to the file, Apache has to check for a `.htaccess` file. Remember that `.htaccess` files apply not only to the directory they are in, but also to all subdirectories thereof. Therefore, to know what has to be applied to a particular directory, you have to check all parent directories, all the way to the root.

For example, if you are serving a file out of `/usr/local/apache/htdocs/products/watchers`, Apache has to check for following files:

```
/.htaccess
/usr/.htaccess
/usr/local/.htaccess
/usr/local/apache/.htaccess
/usr/local/apache/htdocs/.htaccess
/usr/local/apache/htdocs/products/.htaccess
/usr/local/apache/htdocs/products/watchers/.htaccess
```

Apache checks for the existence of each of these files, in that order. If it finds one of these files, it opens it and parses it for directives. If not, it moves on. It does this every time a file is requested out of any directory in which `.htaccess` files are permitted. Note that it does this whether or not there are any `.htaccess` files in any of those directories, so you pay this penalty even if you don't have *any* `.htaccess` files. As you can imagine, this slows things down.

It is therefore preferable, if it's at all possible, to set AllowOverride none and put any per-directory configurations inside of the <Directory> sections in your main server configuration file.

Security

When you allow per-directory configuration, you're allowing whoever has write access to directories on your server to affect the behavior of your Apache server. A few security considerations go along with this.

For the most part, the people that have access to make these configuration changes can only make changes that affect things in their own directory. In a sense, they can only screw up their own stuff. However, this is not true for several reasons.

Insufficient Directory Security

First, it is likely that you have directories on your server that are insufficiently secured. This is particularly going to be the case if you have multiple people providing content for your server. File and directory permissions might be a little relaxed so that more than one person can modify the content. Yes, you should use user groups for this, rather than making the files world-writable, but perhaps you were a little sloppy with a directory or two. You've now made a situation where someone can come in and add a .htaccess file to change the behavior of files served out of that directory. Whether this is done in malice, as a practical joke, or for some other reason, it can result in a denial of service by making files load with incorrect MIME types, redirecting content to other locations, or other configuration changes.

The solution to this problem, of course, is to be vigilant about security. You need to read Chapter 19, "Apache Security," and you need to make sure that any new directories that are created have reasonable file permissions on them. This can best be accomplished by a nightly cron job that sets the permissions to what they should be.

CGI and SSI

If you allow AllowOverride Options, your users have the ability to add Options ExecCGI and Options Includes. These two abilities—to execute CGI programs and to have Server Side Includes (SSI) in their files, are potentially pretty big security problems. So, be very cautious about allowing Options in your AllowOverride policy.

CGI programs can contain any code whatsoever, and can potentially do malicious things. You are somewhat saved by the fact that CGI programs are run (usually) as the "nobody" users, or some other unprivileged user, but even that user can do a lot of damage doing a rm -rf / [1] because there are always a number of files with world-writable permissions.

---

[1]*Windows users, think* format c: -y -y

Likewise, SSI can execute arbitrary code, with the added benefit that with the #exec cmd syntax you can embed arbitrary system commands in the HTML and have them executed.

See Chapter 15, "CGI Programs," and Chapter 16, for more information about the capabilities of these two options, and how to be more careful about security issues.

More importantly, if your users don't really need to be able to do these things, don't enable AllowOverride Options. If users really need this functionality, still don't enable it. In your server configuration file, simply enable Options ExecCGI for perhaps one directory that only trusted users have access to. You can also enable a tamer version of Includes by enabling Options IncludesNOEXEC in your configuration file. As the name implies, this enables SSI, but does not enable the use of the #exec directive.

Symlinks

For Windows users, this is not an issue. For most other operating systems, symbolic links are not, by default, followed by Apache. That is, if you have a symbolic link to a directory, within a directory you're serving content out of, Apache will not allow retrieval of content out of that directory. This is for security reasons.

If, for example, you were to create a symbolic link to /etc, within your document directory, then anyone could happily download /etc/passwd or /etc/shadow, and crack your passwords at their leisure. That would not be desirable.

However, with Options FollowSymlinks turned on, Apache will follow symlinks quite happily. Although there are cases where this is useful, you don't generally want nonadmin users to add Options FollowSymlinks to their .htaccess file and be able to then serve your entire hard drive on their Web site.

As with CGI and SSI, the solution to this is to not allow Options to be overridden. If there is some reason that users really do need to follow symlinks in their file space, you can add, in your main server configuration, an Options SymlinksIfOwnerMatch directive. This allows Apache to follow symlinks, if and only if the directory or file it is linked to is owned by the same user as the link itself.

Summary

.htaccess files allow users to set per-directory configurations without modifying the main server configuration file. This is handy on sites where users are running content out of their home directory, or any other situation where you have more than one person providing content on a Web site. They should, however, be avoided if they are not actually necessary, because there are performance and security concerns with using them.

Virtual Hosts

IN THIS CHAPTER

"Pilgrim, how you journey on the road you chose
To find out where the winds die and where the stories go"

*Pilgrim—A Day Without Rain—*Enya

Fortunately, you don't need a separate Apache server for each Web site that you want to run. Virtual hosting is the term given to the capability to run multiple Web sites on the same computer and on the same Apache server process[1].

There are a number of different techniques for setting up virtual hosts. This chapter covers these various techniques and offers some examples for setting up common configurations.

In all the various methods for doing virtual hosting, the concept is basically the same. The user goes to a URL specifying a particular hostname and gets different content for each hostname. Generally, the user is not aware that they are loading content from the same physical computer system. Somehow, Apache determines which Web site you are requesting content from, and gives that to you, even though all the different sites are running on the same Apache daemon.

The two most common ways of accomplishing this are IP-based and name-based virtual hosting.

IP-Based Virtual Hosts

With IP-based virtual hosting, each hostname on the server is given its own IP address.

Setting Up Multiple IP Addresses

All modern operating systems allow you to have more than one IP address on one physical network card. Earlier operating systems actually required you to add an additional network card for each new IP address. That is no longer the case, however, in any operating system you are likely to encounter.

The specific details of how this is accomplished—the exact procedure for putting multiple IP addresses on your network interface—will vary from OS to OS and you need to consult your documentation.

On the other hand, if you do have multiple network cards in your machine, IP-based virtual hosting will work for that also.

---

[1]*Webster's dictionary defines the word "virtual" as follows: "being such in essence or effect though not formally recognized or admitted." I'm not sure what is "virtual" about a virtual host. It's just as real as the main host is, but in the mid-90s everything* was *"virtual."*

In addition to setting up the IP addresses on your machine, you will also need to set up the DNS records that will direct the hostnames to the IP addresses you have assigned to your server. That, also, is beyond the scope of this book. Contact your DNS administrator to add the hostnames to your DNS zone, or to register a new DNS domain. You can't just make up hostnames and have them magically work.

If you are not able to add records to DNS, or if you just want to test, you can access the IP-based virtual hosts by simply using the IP address in the URL. For example:

```
http://192.168.5.10/
```

Configuring the Virtual Host

After you have your IP addresses set up and have the DNS records pointing the correct names to the correct IP addresses, you can proceed with configuring your Apache server to answer to these names.

This is done in a `<VirtualHost>` section, as was mentioned in Chapter 4, "Configuration Directives." All the configuration directives for a virtual host are contained in the `<VirtualHost>` section, with one section per virtual host. A `<VirtualHost>` section looks like the following:

```
<VirtualHost 192.168.1.2>
  ServerName vhost1.apacheadmin.com
  ServerAlias www.vhost1.apacheadmin.com
  DocumentRoot /usr/local/apache/vhosts/vhost1
  ErrorLog logs/vhost1.error
  AccessLog logs/vhost1.access
</VirtualHost>
```

The address in the `<VirtualHost>` directive can be specified as a hostname, rather than as an IP address, but it is highly recommended that you use the IP address instead. The reason for this is simple. If, when the server is rebooting, it cannot immediately contact a DNS server to determine the IP address of the `VirtualHost`, it will simply start up without that particular `VirtualHost` being loaded. Apache needs the IP address, not the name, to answer requests, so if it cannot determine the IP address from the name it is simply unable to load the configuration. Using the IP address avoids this lookup and ensures that the server will start correctly, with all host configurations loaded, even if the network is unavailable at the time the server is coming up.

The server uses the name of the virtual hosts, specified by the `ServerName` directive, when it constructs self-referential URLs, such as for a redirect.

It's a good idea to have a separate log file for each of your virtual hosts, although it is not required. By logging each host separately, you can much more easily determine problems on a per-host basis. If all your hosts log to the same log files it becomes very difficult to isolate problems when they occur because they become buried in with entries from all the other hosts. See Chapter 24, "Logging," for more information.

You only need to put directives in a VirtualHost section when the values are different from those set in the main server configuration. All other values are inherited from the main server.

Name-Based Virtual Hosts

Name-based virtual hosts are the same as IP-based virtual hosts in almost every way, except you don't need more than one IP address. By having more than one name pointing to the same IP address, you can arbitrarily host many virtual hosts on the same IP address.

> **NOTE**
>
> Multiple host names pointing to the same IP address are referred to in DNS lingo as "cnames."

The configuration is almost identical to that of IP-based virtual hosts, except that you need to tell Apache, with the NameVirtualHost directive, which IP addresses on your server will be used for name-based virtual hosts.

```
NameVirtualHost 192.168.1.3

<VirtualHost 192.168.1.3>
    ServerName vhost1.apacheadmin.com
    ServerAlias vhost1
    DocumentRoot /usr/local/apache/vhosts/rhiannon/htdocs
</VirtualHost>

<VirtualHost 192.168.1.3>
    ServerName vhost2.apacheadmin.com
    ServerAlias vhost2 www.vhost2.apacheadmin.com
    DocumentRoot /usr/local/apache/vhosts/demo/htdocs
</VirtualHost>
```

The name of the server, specified by the ServerName directive, is used to determine which virtual host is displayed. The browser supplies the name of the host that it is trying to connect to in the request headers, and Apache uses this information to map the request to the correct files or other resources.

Older browsers[2] were unable to use name-based virtual hosts because they did not supply this request header.

More specifically, clients or proxies that support only the HTTP 1.0 protocol might fail to get the right virtual host because the Host header is not part of the HTTP 1.0 protocol, and is required for name-based virtual hosting.

However, all currently available browsers support the HTTP 1.1 protocol, which contains name-based virtual host support as one of its requirements. And almost all HTTP 1.0 clients and proxies support the Host header as an extension to the 1.0 protocol.

The Apache documentation contains instructions for working around this limitation in older browsers, if you think that it is worth the effort. However, the solution is inelegant and might not be necessary for your site. You should watch your server logs to see if you are getting visits from browsers old enough to warrant this sort of work-around. You might want to consider using IP-based vhosts if you feel older browsers are a large enough portion of your visitors.

Note the use of the ServerAlias directive in the previous examples. This directive is useful when a particular site can be accessed by more than one name. Two specific examples, illustrated previously, come to mind. In the first example, I have a host that can be accessed from the inside, or from the outside, of my network. Inside the network, or from the machine itself, I don't need to type the entire name of the machine because it will check the local domain first, so the ServerAlias allows me to do this. In the second example, I have added a ServerAlias of www followed by the original hostname. It has been my experience in recent years that people are so trained to expect Web addresses to start with www that they are incapable of typing a URL without it. Simply adding that to the hostname saves a lot of time on the phone explaining to people that the www is not necessary.

Port-Based Virtual Hosts

It's not a very common practice, but it is also possible to set up virtual hosts by varying the port number that the server is running on, rather than the host name or IP address. The configuration for such a setup would look like this:

```
<VirtualHost 192.168.1.103:75>
ServerName vhost.apacheadmin.com
ServerAlias vhost
DocumentRoot /usr/local/apache/vhosts/strange
</VirtualHost>
```

---

[2]*Really older versions you are unlikely to see in any real-world setting.*

You must also add a `Port` directive for each additional port on which you want your server to listen. The `Port` directive would look like this:

```
Port 75
```

If you choose a port below, or equal to, 1024, you will need to be root to start the server. Stated differently, you can run a Web server as an unprivileged user by choosing a port higher than 1024.

This host can be accessed via the URL `http://vhost.apacheadmin.com:75`

Note that SSL, which runs on a different port from unencrypted HTTP, is generally set up in the configuration file as a port-based virtual host. However, browsers know that when a URL is prepended with `https://` rather than `http://`, the connection is to be made on port 443 rather than 80.

In Chapter 22, "SSL," you'll learn about SSL, which is a technology that provides for secure encrypted connections on the Web. For reasons that will be made more apparent there, you cannot use name-based virtual hosting in conjunction with an SSL site.

The short form is that the negotiation of the connection encryption takes place before the client has a chance to tell the server which named host it wanted to connect to. Consequently, by the time it gets to that stage, it might have already negotiated a secure connection to the wrong site.

So, if you want to put up a secure Web site using SSL, you have to have a unique IP address for each SSL-enabled virtual host.

Bulk Virtual Hosting

Frequently, when you're running virtual hosts, you'll find that the number of hosts grows faster than your ability to sensibly manage them. A few techniques you might use to simplify the task of managing these hosts' configurations follow.

Per-vhost Configuration Files

As recommended in Chapter 4, when you are configuring your virtual hosts, you might consider putting each virtual host's configuration into its own individual file. Then you could place these files into a subdirectory of your `conf` directory, perhaps called `vhosts`. Then add the following directive to your main configuration file, `httpd.conf`:

```
Include conf/vhosts/
```

Note that the directory path given in the example is relative to the `ServerRoot`, and not an absolute path.

Apache will read all files in the specified directory and parse directives found in those files. Therefore, you cannot have any files in this directory that are not configuration files, such as temporary files, Readme files, and so on.

The more virtual hosts you have the longer it is going to take to parse all the vhost configurations[3], and, therefore, the longer it is going to take for your server to start up.

mod_vhost_alias

When you are running more than just a few virtual hosts—when you start getting into the tens, or even hundreds, of virtual hosts, you will notice a substantial time taken to start your Apache server. During this time, your server is not responding to HTTP requests. That is, while your server is starting, or restarting, it is effectively unavailable to the end-users. When you are a service provider—which, as a server admin, you really are—this sort of downtime needs to be avoided whenever possible.

mod_vhost_alias is one of the modules available for making bulk virtual hosting more efficient. If each of your virtual hosts has essentially the same configuration, you can configure them all with one set of directives.

mod_vhost_alias provides just four directives—two for use with name-based virtual hosts, and two for use with IP-based virtual hosts.

If you are using name-based virtual hosts, the directives that you will be using are VirtualDocumentRoot and VirtualScriptAlias. These directives mean exactly what their names imply, but the syntax is a little unusual. The value given to the directives will contain one or more variables into which will be substituted all or part of the hostname being requested by the client. If you are familiar with C, or similar programming languages, these variables will remind you of arguments to the sprintf function. The following things can appear in the directive value.

Template	Meaning
%%	A literal % character.
%p	The port number of the virtual host being requested.
%N.M	All or part of the host name, depending on the values of N and M.

The values N and M are, respectively, the portion of the dot-separated hostname to be inserted, and the number of characters from that portion to be used.

---

[3]This will be the case whether the configurations are in external (Include'ed files) or in your main configuration file.

7

VIRTUAL HOSTS

The interpretation of the value of N is as follows:

0	The whole name
1	The first part
2	The second part
-1	The last part
-2	The next-to-last part
2+	The second and all following parts
-2+	The next-to-last part, and all preceding parts

1+ and -1+ would mean exactly the same thing as 0.

If the value given results in selecting more of the name than there actually is available to select, then a single underscore is interpolated in place of the given variable.

This will all be made much clearer by several examples.

The trivial example is to use the full hostname in the directive, as follows. In your configuration file, put a directive that looks this:

```
VirtualDocumentRoot /usr/local/apache/vhosts/%0/htdocs
```

Then, any incoming request for a valid virtual host—that is, any hostname that DNS points to your server—will have files served out of a directory named by the hostname. For example, a request for the URL http://www.boxofclue.com/vhosts.html will get the file located at /usr/local/apache/vhosts/www.boxofclue.com/htdocs/vhosts.html.

This technique has one large problem: Most virtual hosts can be accessed by more than one hostname. For example, if the previous URL was requested instead as http://boxofclue.com/vhosts.html, which should give the same resource, Apache will attempt to serve the file /usr/local/apache/vhosts/boxofclue.com/htdocs/vhosts.html, which is not the same file path it tried in the other case. It might either be a different file or not exist at all.

This dilemma can be solved in a few different ways. The simplest way around this is to simply create symbolic links from all alternate possible file paths to the "correct" file path, and allow Apache to locate the files in that way. However, one of the major reasons for using this module in the first place is to reduce the amount of administrative tasks required to create a new virtual host, so this is hardly ideal.

The better way to solve this is to use a different combination of variables provided by mod_vhost_alias to construct unique filepaths per virtual host.

The following example proposes one such configuration option. Put this directive in your configuration file:

```
VirtualDocumentRoot /usr/local/apache/vhosts/%-1/%-2/htdocs
```

The variable `%-1` will evaluate as the last part of the hostname—usually `com`, `net`, `org`, or some other top level domain (TLD). So, your virtual hosts will be divided into subdirectories by their TLD.

The second variable, `%-2`, evaluates as the next-to-last (or, as the documentation refers to it, the penultimate part) of the hostname. For example, for the hostnames `www.boxofclue.com` and `boxofclue.com`, `%-2` will evaluate to the string `boxofclue`, and files will be served out of the directory `/usr/local/apache/vhosts/com/boxofclue/htdocs`, giving you a more manageable subdivision of your virtual host directories.

In the event that you have many hundreds of virtual hosts, as is the case for some large ISPs, you might want to subdivide your directories even further. For example, you might split hosts into subdirectories alphabetically, as follows:

```
VirtualDocumentRoot /usr/local/apache/vhosts/%-1/%-2.1/%-2/htdocs
```

In this configuration, files for the host `www.boxofclue.com` will be served out of the directory `/usr/local/apache/vhosts/com/b/boxofclue/htdocs`.

This subdivision can continue to any depth you like, as required by the number of virtual hosts you are serving, you could, for example, further subdivide with the following directive:

```
VirtualDocumentRoot /usr/local/apache/vhosts/%-1/%-2.1/%-2.1%-2.2/%-2/htdocs
```

In this case, files for the host `www.boxofclue.com` will be served out of the directory `/usr/local/apache/vhosts/com/b/bo/boxofclue.com`. The variable combination `%-2.1%-2.2` gets evaluated is the first, followed by the second, letters of the next-to-last part of the hostname; this is what gives the subdirectory `bo`.

Continue this subdivision until you have sufficiently few hosts per-directory to keep track of them.

Note that you can use this same technique to have each virtual host served out of the home directory of the particular user, if you choose usernames appropriately to map directly to the hostnames of their respective sites.

Running Multiple Daemons

In very rare cases, you might want to run more than one Apache server process on the same machine to handle different virtual hosts. This might be done, for example, when you need a very different set of modules for different Web sites. You could run one Apache process to serve static HTML pages and images, and a separate Apache process running `mod_perl` to serve your dynamic content.

In these cases, all that is required is that you maintain separate configuration files, and start the Apache server with the `-f` flag to specify a configuration file located somewhere other than the location specified when the server was built.

```
/usr/local/apache/bin/httpd -f /usr/local/apache/conf/host_two.conf
```

Summary

Virtual hosts provide the best way to serve multiple Web sites off of the same physical server machine, and, therefore, make the best use of your available resources.

Advanced Configuration Techniques

IN THIS PART

MIME and File Types

IN THIS CHAPTER

"Whoever we are, we will become what is said about us."

David Williamson

MIME, which stands for Multipart Internet Mail Extensions, is defined in RFC's 2045–2049, and was initially developed to allow e-mail messages to contain non-ASCII information.

In this chapter, we'll talk about the use of MIME in HTTP, and the available configuration directives that Apache provides to use MIME.

MIME and HTTP

HTTP is heavily dependent on MIME. Each file that is sent to a client browser is prefaced by a MIME header, which tells the browser what sort of document it is receiving. In the absence of a MIME header, the browser would know only that it was receiving a series of bits, and would not know what to make of them. Introduced by a MIME header, that stream of bits becomes a useful piece of data, and the browser can display it appropriately.

HTTP includes a great deal of information in headers, which are in the form: `Variable: value` and come before the body, or main content portion, of the HTTP transaction. The particular header that specifies the content type of the data that is being sent, is the `Content-Type` header, and has a very specific format.

`Content-Type: major/minor`

`major` indicates the major category of content to which this content stream belongs. This is a general term that describes the content type, such as `text`, `image`, `video`, `audio`, and `application`.

`minor` indicates the specific type of file that this content should be treated as. Typically, this is a specific file format, such as `html`, `gif`, `quicktime`, `mp3`, or `msword`.

Armed with these two pieces of information, we have a very specific idea of how to deal with the file. The browser will know how to render the file into a readable (or viewable, or audible, or whatever) format, or what external application to launch to deal with the data. Or, for a MIME type of `application/unknown`, or anything else that the browser does not recognize, the typical behavior is to ask you to download the file and save it somewhere, or specify some particular application with which to open the file.

MIME Types Configuration Directives

`mod_mime` provides several directives for manipulating MIME information, both for setting particular MIME types, and for telling Apache how to react in the presence of particular MIME types.

MIME Types Configuration

The following directives affect the usage of MIME type on files. All these directives, except where specified, can appear anywhere—in the main server configuration file, `VirtualHost` sections, `Directory` sections, or in `.htaccess` files.

TypesConfig

The `TypesConfig` directive specifies the location of the MIME types configuration file. This is the primary location where MIME types are mapped to filename extensions. The filename specified is assumed to be relative to the `ServerRoot` directory, unless it starts with a slash, in which case, it is assumed to be a complete absolute path.

The default location of this file is `conf/mime.types`.

The format of this file is very simple, listing a MIME type, followed by one or more file extensions that are to be mapped to that type. The following is an excerpt from the `mime.types` file that comes with Apache:

```
application/mac-binhex40     hqx
application/octet-stream     bin dms lha lzh exe class so dll
application/x-tex        tex
audio/x-realaudio        ra
image/gif           gif
image/ief           ief
image/jpeg          jpeg jpg jpe
text/html htm html
text/sgml           sgml sgm
text/tab-separated-values    tsv
video/mpeg          mpeg mpg mpe
```

If you want to add additional MIME types to the server mapping it is recommended that you use the `AddType` directive, rather than adding them to the `TypesConfig` file. The reason for this is very simple—it gives you a more reliable way to keep track of which MIME types ship in the default configuration and which were added later. Knowing what you changed is an important part of figuring out what went wrong when something is not working as expected.

Note that the file extension is case insensitive, and can be specified with or without the period.

AddType

The AddType directive has the same syntax as a line in the `TypesConfig` file, and serves the same purpose. It can be placed in the main server configuration file, in any restricting section (such as a `<Directory>` section, or a `<Files>` section), or in a `.htaccess` file.

```
AddType image/png .png
```

8

MIME AND FILE
TYPES

Note that the extension is case insensitive[1], and can be expressed with or without the leading dot.

RemoveType

To go with the AddType directive, there is a RemoveType directive. This is particularly useful if you use AddType for a particular directory, but don't want its subdirectories to inherit the configuration.

```
<Directory /www/docs/products>
Options +Includes +ExecCGI
AddType application/x-httpd-cgi cgi
</Directory>

<Directory /www/docs/products>
Options -ExecCGI
RemoveType cgi
</Directory>
```

You only need to mention the name of the extension, and any and all MIME types that are associated with that extension will be removed. It will then revert back to the default type, specified by the DefaultType directive.

DefaultType

The DefaultType directive is not part of mod_mime, but is instead part of the core Apache API. The value of this directive determines how files are sent to the client if Apache is unable to determine what MIME type should be associated with it from the file extension.

The default value of this directive[2] is text/html so files of unknown type are served to the client as HTML. This is more important than it might initially appear. What this means is that if you start serving files of a new variety off of your site, such as gzipped tar files with a tgz file extension, Apache will quite cheerfully tell the browser that they are HTML files, and you will get garbage in your browser window. This can be especially confusing if you do your testing with Microsoft Internet Explorer, which usually tries to be helpful and figure out the file type, even if there is not a valid MIME type associated with the HTTP transaction. Thus, if you were to test such a file with Internet Explorer, you would mistakenly think that things were correctly configured. This emphasizes the importance of setting up MIME types correctly, and also of testing with more than one browser.

---

[1] *That is, it can be upper or lowercase.*

[2] *The default default type, if you will.*

The `DefaultType` directive, in addition to being set for the main server, can be set in `<Directory>` sections as well, to specify that files of unknown types in that directory should have a particular type.

ForceType

Similar to the `DefaultType` directive, `ForceType` indicates a MIME type for a set of files. However, rather than setting the type on files of unknown type, it forces all matching files (all files in the `<Directory>`, or files matched by a `<Files>` directive, for example) to a particular MIME type, regardless of file extension. Note that it can be used only in one of these sections, or in a `.htaccess` file.

Encoding

A file of a particular MIME type can additionally be encoded a particular way to simplify transmission over the Internet. Although this usually will refer to compression, it can also refer to encryption, or to an encoding such as UUencoding, which is designed for transmitting a binary file in an ASCII (text) format.

By using more than one file extension (see the section in this chapter titled "Files with Multiple Extensions") you can indicate that a file is of a particular type, and also has a particular *encoding*.

For example, you might have a Microsoft Word document file, which is pkzipped to reduce its size. If the `.doc` extension is associated with the Microsoft Word file type, and the `.zip` extension is associated with the pkzip file encoding, then the file `Resume.doc.zip` would be known to be a pkzipped Word document.

The Encoding directives (`AddEncoding` and `RemoveEncoding`) are provided by `mod_mime` to specify these encodings.

The default, if no Encoding directives are specified, is that there is no encoding—that is, the file is simply sent as is. For this reason there is no `DefaultEncoding` directive.

AddEncoding

The `AddEncoding` directive associates a particular content encoding with a particular file extension. This directive can be used in any context, for example:

```
AddEncoding pkzip .zip
```

This directive will ensure that any file with a file extension of `.zip` will be delivered with a `Content-encoding: pkzip` header.

RemoveEncoding

It is often also desirable to *not* send the Content-encoding header in certain situations. For example, you might have a directory of .gz files—gzipped distributions of software packages, perhaps. These .gz files are sent with a Content-encoding of gzip. In a subdirectory, you have files containing descriptions of each of the gzip files. For convenience, you give these files the same name as the file they describe. These description files are to be downloaded as plain text. The following configuration, which could be placed in the main server configuration file, or in a .htaccess file, would accomplish this:

```
<Directory /path/to/downloads>
  AddEncoding gzip .gz
</Directory>

<Directory /path/to/downloads/descriptions>
  RemoveEncoding gz
  ForceType text/plain
</Directory>
```

The ForceType directive is used here to ensure that the files are displayed as plain text in the browser window.

Character Sets and Languages

Finally, in addition to file type and the file encoding, another important piece of information is what language a particular document is in, and what character set the file should be displayed in. For example the document might be written in the Vietnamese alphabet, or Cyrillic, and should be displayed as such. This information is also transmitted in MIME headers. Although the character set is useful for the browser to determine how to display the document, the language and the character set are also used in the process of content negotiation (See Chapter 10, "Content Negotiation"). It determines which document to give to the client when there are alternative documents in more than one language or more than one character set.

To convey this further information, Apache optionally sends a Content-Language header, to specify the language that the document is in, and can append additional information onto the Content-Type header to indicate the particular character set that should be used to render the information correctly.

```
Content-Language: en, fr
Content-Type: text/plain; charset=ISO-8859-2
```

The language specification is the two-letter abbreviation for the language. The charset is the name of the particular character set that should be used. For a full listing of the two-letter abbreviations that may be used, see the documents ISO 639 and ISO 639-2.

Mirroring the directives for MIME types, languages, and character sets have directives provided my mod_mime for adding, and removing, associations with particular file extensions.

These directives are AddCharset, RemoveCharset, AddLanguage, RemoveLanguage, and DefaultLanguage.

There is not a DefaultCharset directive, because the default character set is defined by the HTTP 1.1 specification as ISO-8859-1, and so it is unnecessary to have a directive to set this.

AddCharset

The AddCharset directive associates a character set with a file extension, and causes Apache to send the character set information with the Content-type header when files with that extension are served. This directive can be set in any context, for example:

```
AddCharset ISO-2022-JP .jis
```

RemoveCharset

The RemoveCharset directive removes any association attached to the given file extension, for example:

```
RemoveCharset .jis
```

AddLanguage

The AddLanguage directive creates an association between a file extension and a particular language. Apache will send a Content-language HTTP header, indicating the language of the document, when files with this extension are served. This directive can be set in any context, for example:

```
AddLanguage en .en
AddLanguage fr .fr
```

Note that there can be only one language associated with any given file extension.

RemoveLanguage

The RemoveLanguage removes any language associations currently in effect for the specified file extension, for example:

```
RemoveLanguage .fr
```

DefaultLanguage

The DefaultLanguage directive determines the Content-language header that should be sent with files for which no explicit language association has been set. If your site is primarily an English-language site, for example, you should set this to en as shown in this example:

DefaultLanguage en

Files with Multiple Extensions

With the capability to set attributes on a file by virtue of the file's extensions, the obvious question is: What if I want to set the language *and* the character set? Or the encoding and the language? Or all three?

This is accomplished very simply by giving the file several extensions. You can stack as many file extensions as you like onto a file, and the file attributes are accumulated, with the following rules:

- If you give two (or more) file extensions that map the same attribute (such as two extensions that specify the file language, for example) then the one seen last (reading from left to right) is the one that is used.
- index.html.en.fr will be served with a Content-language header specifying that it is French, not English, and will be served with a Content-type of text/html.
- If you use an extension that is not recognized at all, it will cause Apache to forget the extensions it had figured out so far, and start all over again.
- example.fr.pop.gif will be served with a Content-type of image/gif, but with no Content-language, because the pop extension does not map to anything, and thus causes the mappings up to that point to be forgotten.

Handlers

mod_mime also defines directives for specifying handlers. A handler is a process that is defined for dealing with files of a particular type. For example, if we associate the handler cgi-script with files with an extension of .cgi, then those files will be executed, and the output sent to the client, rather than sending the file itself.

The directives AddHandler, RemoveHandler, and SetHandler are all provided by mod_mime.

Handlers actually have a chapter of their own, Chapter 14, "Handlers and Filters," where these will be discussed in detail.

Summary

HTTP relies heavily on MIME headers for the delivery of content, both to tell the browser what to expect and to have it display the content correctly. mod_mime provides most of the directives that deal with setting the MIME types on particular files.

8

MIME AND FILE TYPES

URL Mapping

IN THIS CHAPTER

"When you've only got two ducks, they're always in a row."

Me

When Apache receives a request for a URL it has to figure out how that URL maps to actual content that it needs to send back to the client. Usually, the URL gets mapped directly to a file that is read off of the disk and sent as-is out to the client. Occasionally, the URL maps to a program of some variety that generates content, which then gets sent out.

This phase of figuring out what to send in response to a request is called the URL mapping phase. There are a number of directives that assist Apache in figuring out how to perform this mapping.

Location

The `Location` directive defines how a particular URL is to be treated, and does not necessarily indicate a file path, or refer to the file system at all. A `Location` directive will usually map a URL to a handler. A handler is a process that generates the content that will be displayed in response to the request. Handlers are described in additional detail in Chapter 14, "Handlers and Filters."

The `Location` directive creates a section, like the `Directory` or `Files` directive. This section contains directives that will apply to requests matching the specified pattern.

For example:

```
<Location /server-status>
    SetHandler server-status
    Order deny,allow
    Deny from all
    Allow from .your_domain.com
</Location>
```

In the previous example, requests starting with `/server-status` will be answered by the handler `server-status`. Additional directives might be placed in the section. In this case, access restrictions have been placed on who can get to the content served by this handler.

Alias

The `Alias` directive, and its close relative the `AliasMatch` directive, tell Apache to map URLs beginning with a certain thing to a particular part of the file system. Typically, this is used to map a URL to somewhere outside of the `DocumentRoot`, the place where documents are supposed to be served. (See the `DocumentRoot` section later in the chapter for more information).

The syntax of the `Alias` directive is as follows:

```
Alias /icons/ /usr/local/apache/icons/
```

If a server called www.apacheadmin.com had a directive such as this one, then a request for http://www.apacheadmin.com/icons/unknown.gif would result in Apache attempting to serve a file called unknown.gif out of the directory /usr/local/apache/icons rather than out of the main document root.

ScriptAlias

The `ScriptAlias` directive is a special case of the `Alias` directive. It indicates that, for the specified alias, files should be served out of the specified directory, and that it should be assumed that they are all CGI programs and, therefore, should be executed. (See Chapter 15, "CGI Programs," for more details.)

The syntax of the `ScriptAlias` is as follows:

```
ScriptAlias /cgi-bin/ /usr/local/apache/cgi-bin/
```

The previous example is the equivalent of the following set of directives:

```
Alias /cgi-bin/ /usr/local/apache/cgi-bin/
<Directory /usr/local/apache/cgi-bin/>
Options +ExecCGI
AddHandler cgi-script *
</Directory>
```

You can refer to Chapter 4, "Configuration Directives" section `Options +ExecCGI`, and Chapter 14, "Handlers and Filters," for more detail on these other directives.

Usually, the `ScriptAlias` directory will be where you will put all your CGI programs, although this is not required. Also, you might have more than one `ScriptAlias` directory.

AliasMatch and ScriptAliasMatch

In addition to the regular form of the `Alias` and `ScriptAlias` directives, there are also versions that use regular expressions to match a class of things, rather than just one particular string. For example, if you find that a large number of your users are misspelling a URL, you can compensate for that.

```
AliasMatch ^/[dD]rbacc?h?[ui]s(.*) /usr/local/apache/vhosts/drbacchus\$1
```

This regular expression will match URLs that start with /drbacchus (with an upper or lowercase D) with one or two c's, perhaps missing the h, and with a, u, or an i before the s. This one directive fills the place of the 16 `Alias` directives that would be needed to check for these four possible variations.

See Appendix C, "Regular Expressions," for a more complete treatment of the regular expression syntax available in Apache directives.

Redirect

The various `Redirect` directives (`Redirect`, `RedirectMatch`, `RedirectPermanent`, and `RedirectTemp`) serve a rather different purpose than the `Alias` directives. The `Alias` directives define an accepted URL and tell Apache where to serve the content from for that URL. The `Redirect` directives say that a particular resource is no longer at a given location, or never was, and tell the client to go elsewhere to get it.

```
Redirect /apache http://www.apacheadmin.com/
```

This directive actually sends a `Redirect` back to the browser, telling it to go to the new location. Because the redirect is actually handled by the browser, and not by the server, the browser will (usually) have the new URL displayed in the Location box, and the user will be able to see that they have been taken to a different site. Likewise, if they attempt to bookmark the site that they have arrived at, they will get the new URL, rather than the one they typed.

`Redirect` directives are very useful, and important, if and when you redesign your Web site. Your old URLs should continue to work, so that you don't confuse your loyal users. So, you should provide redirects from all the old URLs to the new places where that information is kept.

The `Redirect` directive takes an optional additional argument, which can set the status of the redirect. The status argument can be one of permanent, `temp` (the default), `seeother`, or `gone`. These arguments cause mod_alias to send different HTTP status codes, as shown in Table 9.1.

TABLE 9.1   HTTP Status Codes

Argument	Status code	Description
permanent	301	The resource has moved permanently.
temp	302	The resource has moved temporarily.
seeother	303	The resource has been replaced by another resource.
gone	410	The resource has been permanently removed. In this case, the URL argument should be omitted.

For example:

```
Redirect seeother /apache http://www.apacheadmin.com/
```

This informs the browser that the resource that was at the URL /apache on your server has been replaced with the new resource which is at http://www.apacheadmin.com/. Whether the browser chooses to do anything about this or not is a separate issue. For example, an intelligent browser would use this as a hint to update your bookmarks with the new location.

RedirectMatch

RedirectMatch, much like the AliasMatch directive described previously, accepts a regular expression, rather than the literal path, as its first argument. Otherwise, the syntax is the same as for Redirect.

For example:

```
RedirectMatch permanent ^/[dD]r[Bb]acc?h?us http://www.drbacchus.com/
```

The previous example will redirect any URL that looks like /drbacchus, but with the d and the b optionally uppercase, and the c and the h optionally missing, to the new URL http://www.drbacchus.com, and tell the client that the redirection is a permanent one.

RedirectTemp and RedirectPermanent

The RedirectTemp and RedirectPermanent directives are exactly equivalent to Redirect temp and Redirect permanent, respectively. That is, using the RedirectTemp directive is no different from using Redirect with the optional temp argument. These directives are for convenience only.

DocumentRoot

When Apache has finished running through the various Alias and Redirect directives as well as the Location directives, the assumption will be reached that the resource requested is simply a file resource, and should be loaded off of the file system and sent out to the client.

The DocumentRoot directive tells Apache where in the file system it should start looking for this file. The syntax of the directive is as follows:

```
DocumentRoot /usr/local/apache/htdocs
```

Apache will take the path of the requested document, prepend the value of DocumentRoot, and attempt to serve that file.

For example, if the requested URL is http://www.apacheadmin.com/services/apache/index.html, and the DocumentRoot is set to /usr/local/apache/vhosts/apacheadmin/htdocs, the Apache will attempt to serve the file /usr/local/apache/vhosts/apacheadmin/htdocs/services/apache/index.html.

9

URL MAPPING

If that file is there one of two things will happen. If there is no handler associated with the file it will simply be sent to the client with the appropriate MIME headers. Or, if there *is* a handler associated with the file, then the handler will be called, with the path to the file as an argument. A handler, simply stated, is a process defined for preprocessing a resource before it is sent to the client. Handlers will be treated in more detail in Chapter 14.

If the file is *not* there, then the client will receive an error message of some description, telling them that the document was not found. This is a 404 (document not found) error. If there is no ErrorDocument defined for this type of error, they will receive a simple, dynamically generated error message, which will tell them that the document could not be found. See the following section for how to deal with this more elegantly.

Error Documents

When something goes wrong, the end users typically get an unhelpful message. It is not helpful to them because it does not tell them any information that they can actually use, and it is not helpful to you as the server admin because you don't get any useful report about what went wrong.

If they request a resource that does not exist, they will typically get a message that says something like:

```
Not Found

The requested URL /foo was not found on this server.

Apache/1.3.20 Server at www.apacheadmin.com Port 80
```

This does not help them. Sure, they know that what they were looking for is not there, but they don't know what to do about it. They don't know where the document has moved to, or if the information is just not available, and they don't know how to ask you, the site admin, where to go look for it. And, worse yet, they think that it is their fault.

And, as the admin, it does not tell you anything useful. In your logs, you'll see an entry like this:

```
[Sat Aug 11 22:32:25 2001] [error] [client 192.168.1.3] File does not
exist: /usr/local/apache/vhosts/apache/htdocs/foo
```

This tells you that someone was requesting a document you did not have, but you don't really know what he was looking for. You don't know if he made up the URL, followed a link from somewhere, or read it in the newspaper. And you don't have any way to contact him for this information.

The way around this is to provide a more useful error document. This is done with the ErrorDocument directive:

```
ErrorDocument 404 /errors/notfound.html
```

In the previous example, any "not found" error will receive the document located at the URL /errors/notfound.html, rather than the auto-generated "not found" error page.

This enables you to have a error document page that does not make the user feel like he broke something, but gives him useful information about how to find stuff on your site. Perhaps it could also provide a handy way to contact you about how he got to that page and what he was expecting to see when he got there.

If you make it a CGI program, or other dynamically generated page, you can capture their referrer—that is, where they came from, making it very easy for you to figure out who has bad links to your site.

Error documents can be more specific than this. For 404 pages (resource not found), for example, you might want different error documents per directory. In one directory, you might want to display a default document for all invalid requests. In another directory you might want to redirect the request to a CGI program that outputs a custom error message that helps the user find what they want—perhaps guessing an alternative URL based on the URL the entered—or helps him notify someone about what he was looking for.

You can provide custom error documents for any error condition. For a 403 (authorization require) you could display a page where the user can apply for a user account. For a 500 (server error) you can display a page that masks the fact that your CGI programs are not working, and sends the bug report to you in a useful form, rather than to the user in a useless one.

URL Rewriting

Occasionally, you'll want to take an incoming request, and, based on certain criteria, send it somewhere else. Perhaps you want to send people to different URLs based on what browser they are using, what time of day it is, or what IP address they are coming from. Fortunately, there is a way to do this.

mod_rewrite is a delightful module that enables you to take a request as it comes in, and modify the requested URL before it is passed on to the URL mapping process described previously.

For the full scoop on mod_rewrite, you need to read the URL rewriting guide, which you can find at http://httpd.apache.org/docs-2.0/misc/rewriteguide.html.

Summary

When the user requests a URL, Apache goes through a rather lengthy process to figure out exactly what it is that gets sent to the client. This is called the URL mapping phase. At the end of the process, if the document was still not located, or if there was some other error encountered, the user receives either an auto-generated error page, or a document specified by an ErrorDocument directive.

Content Negotiation

10

IN THIS CHAPTER

> *"In a defeat there would be a roundabout vindication of himself. He thought it would prove, in a manner, that he had fled earlier because of his superior powers of perception. A serious prophet upon predicting a flood should be the first man to climb a tree. This would demonstrate that he was indeed a seer."*
>
> *The Red Badge of Courage*—Stephen Crane

Content negotiation is another phase of URL mapping (see Chapter 9, "URL Mapping"), but sufficiently important to warrant its own chapter. When the client requests a document from the server, if there is any ambiguity as to what document to give to the client, there is negotiation between the parties regarding which document is the best suited to the needs of the client.

Which means that the end-user decides what representation of the document she most wants to see.

With the increasing diversity of your Web site's potential audience it is increasingly important to cater to their needs and provide them with content in a usable format. Content negotiation provides a way to do this seamlessly and invisibly. Two users might visit exactly the same URL on your Web site and get completely different content—perhaps in a different language, for example—based on the preferences they have set in their browsers.

The basic idea behind content negotiation is that the Web site should be available in a variety of different representations, and that clients should be able to select the one that best meets their preferences and needs.

For example, one user might need to view your Web site in English and likes to have documents as HTML, whereas another might prefer French and a plain text document so that it can be read to them by a screen reader.

Many Web sites provide links from their home page to the French or English versions, but content negotiation enables Apache to automatically figure out what version of the site the user needs, and just give it to them.

Content negotiation might better be called content selection, because no actual negotiation takes place. The term negotiation implies a conversation between the server and the client in which some sort of compromise is reached. What really happens is much simpler than that.

Client Preference

The first, and most important, part of the content negotiation is for the client to communicate the document types that she prefers to receive. This is done with one or more `Accept*`[1] header, each of which might have associated quality factors.

---

[1] `Accept*` *is used here to indicate that there are multiple headers starting with* `Accept`.

Accept Headers

When the client makes a request she sends with it a list of document types that she is willing to accept, and the relative preferences that she places on those document types. This is done with four `Accept` HTTP headers, which the client might send. These four headers—Accept, `Accept-Language`, `Accept-Encoding`, and `Accept-Charset`—list the document types that the client is willing to accept, as well as those that she prefers to accept.

For example, to indicate that a media type of HTML is acceptable to the client, the following `Accept` header would be sent:

```
Accept: Text/html
```

The server, on the other side of the equation, maps filenames to media types, language, character sets, and/or encoding method, with file extensions or other techniques discussed in Chapter 8, "MIME and File Types." These factors are compared to the various `Accept*` headers that the client has sent, and the most appropriate representation of the document is selected.

Quality Factor

The quality factor is an important consideration in the decision of which representation of the document will be the best for the client. The client has an opportunity to send a quality factor along with each of the document types that she has indicated she will `Accept`. The quality factor is a number between 0 and 1, which indicates the relative preference of receiving that document type in relation to the other specified document types.

The following example shows a client indicating that it most prefers to receive documents as HTML, but will accept any text document as a fall back if no HTML representation is available.

```
Accept: text/html; q=1.0, text/*; q=0.5
```

The quality factors indicate that resources of type `text/html` are most preferred, at a quality factor of 1.0. That means, if a representation of the resource is available in that media type, it should be given a preference (or probability) higher than any other media type. The second media type listed, `text/*`, indicates that any document with a major-media type of `text` should be considered, at a much lower preference. The `*` is a wildcard, matching any secondary media type. Thus, documents of type `text/plain` or `text/csv` would match that wildcard.

Because the quality factor is an optional argument, most browsers actually omit this part of the header. For example, the browser that I am currently using (Netscape 4.72) passes the following `Accept` header:

```
Accept: image/gif, image/jpeg, image/pjpeg, image/png, */*
```

Presumably, this is intended to indicate an order of preference of the given image formats. However, the specification indicates that types with no quality factor are all considered at the same level of preference, as you will see in the following description of the negotiation process.

The other `Accept` headers, also, can attach a quality type to the various accepted representations. For example, to indicate that the client prefers documents in the French language, but will also accept German documents, at a reduced preference, the following header might be sent

```
Accept-Language: fr; 1.0, de; 0.8
```

Similarly, preferences can be expressed regarding the content encoding, and the character set used.

Negotiation Methods

After the client has sent the preferences and the associated weighting factors for each preference to the server, the server then uses this information to determine which of the available representations of a given resource most closely matches the preferences of the user.

This is done in one of two ways: `MultiViews`, or by using a type-map file created on the server listing the various representations and the associated qualities of those documents.

Type Map File

A type map file, as the name indicates, is a file containing a map of the files in a particular directory, and the various MIME types that should be associated with each. For a given URL, all representations of that URL should be listed by filename, and their respective properties listed with it.

The name of the type map file is specified by using an `AddHandler` directive, with the `type-map` handler:

```
AddHandler type-map .var
```

With the proceeding example, files with an extension of `.var` will be used as type map files.

An example of a type map file follows:

```
URI: about

URI: about.html.en
Content-type: text/html
Content-language: en

URI: about.html.fr.de
Content-type: text/html;charset=iso-8859-2
Content-language: fr, de
```

The map above describes one resource, which can be retrieved with the URL (relative to whatever directory we are currently in) of `about.html`, or just `about`. The first entry in the map lists only the base reference of `about`. The next two entries list two alternate representations of the same document, the first one in English, the second in French and German, with a character set of `iso-8859-2`.

When a client sends an `Accept` header indicating that French or German is the preferred language, the second listed variant of the document is returned.

If you want to indicate that one particular representation of the document is a better quality than another , you can do so with the `qs` parameter. The following example, from the `mod_negotiation` documentation, shows a resource that is available as a `jpeg` image, a `gif` image, and as `ASCII` art, in decreasing order of image quality.

```
URI: foo

URI: foo.jpeg
Content-type: image/jpeg; qs=0.8

URI: foo.gif
Content-type: image/gif; qs=0.5

URI: foo.txt
Content-type: text/plain; qs=0.01
```

The `Content-type` attribute can also specify a level, which specifies the specification version for particular file types. For example, HTML 2 would be specified as

```
Content-type: text/html; level=2
```

In addition to the examples shown above, other attributes of the file can be specified from the list below:

- **URI:** The URI of the file containing the particular variant. These are interpreted as URLs relative to the current directory. They might not be a fully qualified URL pointing at a different server.
- **Content-Type:** The media type (or MIME type) of the resource. A quality factor (the `qs` parameter) may be given, and a character set may be specified.
- **Content-Language:** The language of the media type.
- **Content-Encoding:** The manner in which the content is encoded, if any.
- **Content-Length:** The size of the file in bytes.
- **Description:** A description of the file. If no variant of the file matches the client's requirements, a list of available variants is provided, with these descriptions.

10

CONTENT
NEGOTIATION

Given all of this information, Apache selects the variant that it is going to send to the client in the following way.

For each the various factors to be considered, the quality factor provided by the client (if any) is multiplied by the quality of service factor from the type-map file, if any, to arrive at the overall quality factor of the document. The document (or documents) with the highest value are selected. If, at any point, there is only one document remaining for consideration, this file is sent to the client.

The various factors are considered in the following order:

- Media type
- Language
- Media-type level
- Character set
- Content encoding
- Smallest content length

If, by the end of this procedure, a single document has not been selected, the user is presented with a list of the available documents, with their descriptions, and is able to choose one.

MultiViews

Content negotiation by MultiViews is simpler to configure, and does what you want most of the time. It does not allow you the fine level of control that actually writing a type-map file does, and it gives up most of your control over what resource the client gets, deferring entirely to the preferences specified by the client.

MultiViews is turned on via the Options directive:

```
Options +MultiViews
```

This can be set for a directory (in a directory section, or in a .htaccess file) or in the main server configuration. Note that setting Options All does *not* turn on MultiViews. It must be set explicitly.

When MultiViews is turned on, Apache will search the directory for files that match the requested resource, and create a type map for that resource on the fly. For example, if a URL http://www.example.com/testing/index were requested, Apache would look through the testing directory for files with names starting with index. For each one it would create an in-memory type map, using any associations that have been added to the file with one of the various directives used for this purpose.

These associations can be added to files in the following ways:

Media type (MIME type)	`AddType`, `ForceType`, entries in the `mime.types` file
Content encoding	`AddEncoding`
Character set	`AddCharset`
Language	`AddLanguage`, `DefaultLanguage`

For more details on this process see Chapter 8, "MIME and File Types," in which these directives, and various related ones, are discussed.

Mostly what you are missing when you use `MultiViews` rather than a type-map file, is the capability to indicate the relative quality of various representations of a file, therefore, control of the selection process is given entirely to the client, by way of the `Accept` headers.

In the event that a "best" language cannot be determined from the client configuration, the server is able to set a preferred order in which the languages should be considered. This is done with the `LanguagePriority` directive, which lists in order, the preferred languages on the server side. Presumably, this will express the order of quality of the document. Perhaps, for example, the site is a French site, which has been translated into German. The German documents, being translations, and not the originals, might have a lower quality of information. This would be indicated with the `LanguagePriority` directive below:

```
LanguagePriority fr de en
```

In this scenario, the English version of any given document will be served only if the client explicitly requests it, or if there are no French or German variants of the resource.

Noncompliant Browsers

As mentioned above, most browsers do not correctly[2] set the quality factor on `Accept` headers. By passing multiple media types in an `Accept` header, for example, in the order of preference, they make the assumption that the order has something to do with which media type will in fact be preferred. So you will often see Accept headers like the following.

```
Accept: text/html, text/plain, text/*, */*
```

Because of the ambiguity involved in this list, Apache applies the following rules to figure out what is meant:

Fully qualified media types for which no quality factor is specified (such as `text/html` or `image/png`) are interpreted as having a quality factor of 1.0.

Media types of the format `type/*` are interpreted as having a quality factor of 0.02.

The wildcard media type `*/*` is interpreted as having a quality factor of 0.01.

---

[2]*Or at all!*

With this scheme, types with the format `type/*` are preferred over a wildcard of the form `*/*`, and explicit media types are preferred over those. However, there is still no ordering of preference between various fully qualified media types.

These adjustments are made only if there were no quality factors specified anywhere in the `Accept` header. If any quality factors are specified in the `Accept` header, then the above scheme is not used, and it is presumed that the specified media types are the ones that should be used. The exception to this is that fully qualified media types (those with both a type and a subtype) are given a quality factor of 1.0 if none was specified.

Caching

Ordinarily, negotiated documents are not cached. This is so that multiple clients behind the same proxy all get the document that is best for them. If the `CacheNegotiatedDocs` directive is turned on, then negotiated documents might be cached. Although this reduces network traffic, it means that some clients behind a proxy might get the document that is best for someone else in their office, and not necessarily for them.

This configuration is set by adding the following directive:

```
CacheNegotiatedDocs on
```

The default value is off.

Summary

Content negotiation provides a transparent way to give clients documents that are best suited to their needs without them having to explicitly select it from a list of options. Using this technique eliminates the need to explicitly list the various languages in which your site is available, for example, because your clients will automatically get the version they need based on the language preference configured in their browser.

Directory Indexing

IN THIS CHAPTER

"And memories, he knew, were not glass treasures to be kept locked within a box. They were bright ribbons to be hung in the wind."

The Talismans of Shannara—Terry Brooks

When a user requests a directory without specifying a particular filename in that directory, there are a few different things that Apache can do to serve that request. For example, if a user types in a URL that looks like `http://www.example.com/directory/`, Apache will have to somehow figure out *which file* from the `directory` directory is to be sent to the user.

Apache can respond by sending the default document, defined by the `DirectoryIndex` directive. If certain options are enabled, and if there is no default document, it can generate a directory index. Or it can just return an error message, and not give the user anything at all.

DirectoryIndex

The `DirectoryIndex` directive tells Apache what file to serve when a directory is requested but no particular file in that directory is specified. The default value of this directive is `index.html`, so when you request a URL ending in a slash (`/`), or one that happens to specify a directory and not a file, Apache will attempt to give you the file `index.html` out of that directory.

For example, we'll consider a site configured with a `DocumentRoot` of `/usr/local/apache/htdocs`, with a hostname of `boxofclue.com`. If a client requests the URL `http://www.boxofclue.com/`, Apache will attempt to serve the file `index.html` out of the directory `/usr/local/apache/htdocs`.

If there is no such file in that directory (assuming that there have been no additional configuration changes), Apache will return a `404` error—file not found.

You can, however, set `DirectoryIndex` to any filename at all if you want to call your index file something else, or if you want to have somewhat different behavior for a particular directory. And you can set `DirectoryIndex` to several things at once, in order to give Apache several choices about what files it serves.

Example:

```
DirectoryIndex index.html index.htm default.html default.htm index.cgi
```

This example kills a variety of birds with one stone. If you have customers who are used to providing content for Microsoft IIS servers, they may be used to calling their default document `default.htm`, since that is the default document on an IIS server. By providing `.htm` and `.html` alternatives for each of the most common default filenames, you will catch most of your users and enable the server to do what they expect.

The last entry in the list, `index.cgi`, demonstrates that the default document does not necessarily need to be an HTML document, but can be a CGI program. If you have CGI execution turned on for the given directory, Apache will execute the CGI program and provide the output as the default document.

Finally, it is not even necessary that the default document be in the specified directory. By providing an absolute (but local) URL, rather than a relative one, you can specify any content on your server as the default content.

```
DirectoryIndex index.html /errors/notfound.html
```

Note that this same behavior could also be supplied with an `ErrorDocument` directive.

```
ErrorDocument 404 /errors/notfound.html
```

Options +Indexes

Things become somewhat more interesting if you allow Apache to generate content for you. This can be done at a variety of levels of complexity, from a simple bulleted list of filenames to a highly customized directory listing.

The automatic index generation is handled by a module called `mod_autoindex`. Most of the rest of this chapter discusses directives that are provided by that module. `mod_autoindex` is part of the core set of Apache modules, and is compiled into Apache by default.

> **NOTE**
>
> In order to use any of the directives and options discussed here, you must enable **Options +Indexes**.

The simplest level of auto-indexing is achieved by turning on the `Indexes` option:

```
Options +Indexes
```

For any directory where this option is turned on, if the default file is not found in that directory, Apache will generate a file listing. By default, this is a very simple bulleted list of filenames, with each filename linked to the appropriate file so that clicking it downloads the file. Any additional frills are provided using the `IndexOptions` directive.

IndexOptions—"Fancy" Indexing

For anything more than a simple bulleted list of filenames, you need to use the `IndexOptions` directive, which customizes the way that the directory listing is generated.

IndexOptions Syntax

The `IndexOptions` directive, like the `Options` directive, enables you to turn several options on or off by preceding them with a + or - sign.

```
IndexOptions +option -option
```

Specifying a list of options without the + and - signs turns on only the specified options.

FancyIndexing

```
IndexOptions +FancyIndexing
```

The very first option that you will want to turn on is `FancyIndexing`. In fact, you will almost certainly discover that it is turned on already in the default configuration file that came with Apache when you installed it. So when you tried out the previous example, adding an `Options` `+Indexes` to your server configuration,[1] you probably saw not a bulleted list of filenames, but something that looked much more like a directory listing in a GUI file manager or on an FTP site viewed in a browser (see Figure 11.1).

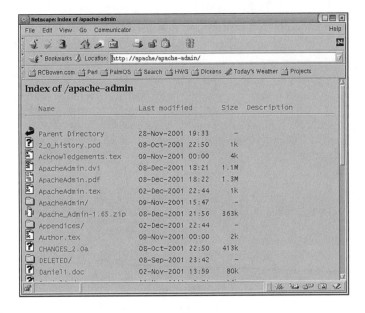

FIGURE 11.1

Fancy indexing

---

[1]You are *trying out all the examples as you come across them, right?*

This is the view that you are probably most accustomed to seeing on Web sites when there are file listings.

For each common file type, the filename will have a small (20×22 pixels) icon next to it, which will indicate that file type. The particular icon that is displayed is configured by the various `AddIcon` directives, and can be replaced by any icon or other image of your choosing.

There are three `AddIcon` directives—`AddIcon`, `AddIconByEncoding`, and `AddIconByType`—that you can use to associate a particular icon either with specific files or with types of files. Additionally, the `DefaultIcon` directive determines what icon will be displayed if none of the `AddIcon` directives matches the file.

DescriptionWidth

```
IndexOptions DescriptionWidth=30
```

or

```
IndexOptions DescriptionWidth=*
```

The description column is, by default, 23 characters wide. If your description is longer than that, it will be truncated. You can, with this option, make that column larger or smaller by specifying a column width in characters. Using an argument value of * will cause the column to be the width of the longest description that it needs to contain.

See the "`AddDescription`" section for more information on file descriptions.

AddIcon

`AddIcon` is the first, and most specific, of the three directives. You will see several examples of the `AddIcon` directive in your default Apache configuration file, where the mapping of files to icons is set up. There are no default values for these mappings, and they must be set up in the configuration files in order for any images to be displayed in the directory listing.

The syntax of the `AddIcon` directive is as follows:

```
AddIcon icon_url name [name]
```

The `icon_url` is the local URL for an image file. The `name` is a particular filename, some portion of a filename (such as the file extension), or a wildcard that could match a filename.

Files that match something in the argument list will be displayed in directory listings with that icon next to them.

Apache comes with about 70 icons, which are located in the `icons` directory, which is usually located in your `ServerRoot` directory at the same level as the `htdocs` directory. These icons, or any that you supply yourself, can be used for the icon URL.

Example:

```
AddIcon /icons/movie.gif .mov .avi .mpg
```

`AddIcon` optionally takes a somewhat different argument syntax if you want to provide alternate text for the image, in the event that the client has image loading turned off or is using a text-only browser. Figure 11.2 shows a directory listing customized by the addition of on icon associated with `.tex` files, which is accomplished with the following directive:

```
AddIcon (LaTeX,/icons/tex.gif) .tex
```

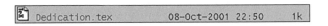

FIGURE 11.2
A customized directory listing using icons.

You can also use the `AddAlt` directive to add alternate text.

AddIconByType

`AddIconByType` is slightly less specific concerning the files you are adding icons for, and so should be used to pick up the files for which you don't have specific `AddType` directives.

As the name suggests, this directive specifies the icon to be displayed for files of a particular MIME type. Like `AddIcon`, this directive is only effectual when the `FancyIndexing` option is turned on in `IndexOptions`.

Example:

```
AddIconByType /icons/image3.gif image/*
```

As you can see in this example, wildcards can be used in the type argument, in order to match larger classes of content type.

AddIconByEncoding

This final `AddIcon` directive associates a particular icon with an encoding type. For example, you can display the "compressed" icon for all files that have an encoding type of `x-com-pressed`:

```
AddIconByEncoding (Compressed,/icons/compressed.gif) x-compress
```

In this example, I am again using the (*ALT,/image/url*) form of the arguments to provide alternate text for the image in the event that the client does not load this image. This is an important part of keeping your Web site accessible to people using alternate technology. Blind people using screen readers, people reading the site on a handheld computer, and people who for whatever reason prefer to use a text-based browser will thank you for using this argument style and making their lives easier.

DefaultIcon

When all else fails, auto-indexed directories will show the `DefaultIcon` next to images that don't match any of the `AddIcon` directives. In the default Apache configuration file, this is `/icons/unknown.gif`, which is a question mark. If you intend to use auto-generated directory listings as a major interface on your site, you should attempt to provide icons for as many of your common file types as you can so that people can very quickly ascertain what file types they are looking at.

FoldersFirst

```
IndexOptions +FoldersFirst
```

If you are used to using a graphical interface to your file system, such as the Windows file explorer, you may initially find the layout of the default directory indexing a little confusing, as the directories are mixed in with the files, in alphabetical order. In most graphical directory and file management tools, the directories appear at the top, and are followed by the actual files below.

The `FoldersFirst` option reorders the auto-index in this manner, as shown in Figure 11.3.

HTMLTable

```
IndexOptions +HTMLTable
```

This option formats the index listing as an HTML table, rather than as a preformatted list.

Icon Dimensions

```
IndexOptions +IconHeight=20 +IconWidth=22
```

The `IconHeight` and `IconWidth` directives determine the size of the icons displayed in the directory listing. They are, by default, 20×22 pixels, as this is the size of the images that are shipped with Apache. However, it will use whatever images you ask it to use, and they will be displayed at whatever their actual size is. By setting these directives, you can force all the icons to be displayed at the same size, for more uniformity in the listing. Additionally, using these directives causes the page to *appear* to load faster, since each image tag will include the `height` and `width` attributes, which permits the browser to precalculate the page layout and display the text items on the page while the images are still loading.

`IconHeight` and `IconWidth` should be used together—that is, you should not use one without the other.

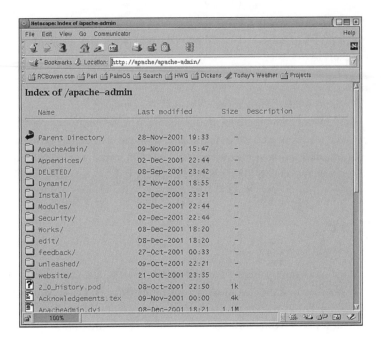

FIGURE 11.3
Directory listing with FoldersFirst

IconsAreLinks

IndexOptions +IconsAreLinks

By default, while the text name of the file is a link to download that file, the icon is not. Because people seem to intuitively click the icon rather than the name, this option makes the icon a link also.

IgnoreClient

IndexOptions +IgnoreClient

This option causes mod_autoindex to ignore all query variables from the client. This disables the ability to re-sort the file listing by columns, and so implies SuppressColumnSorting.

NameWidth

IndexOptions +NameWidth=*

Filenames will be truncated, as shown in Figure 11.4, if they exceed 20 characters in total file-name length.

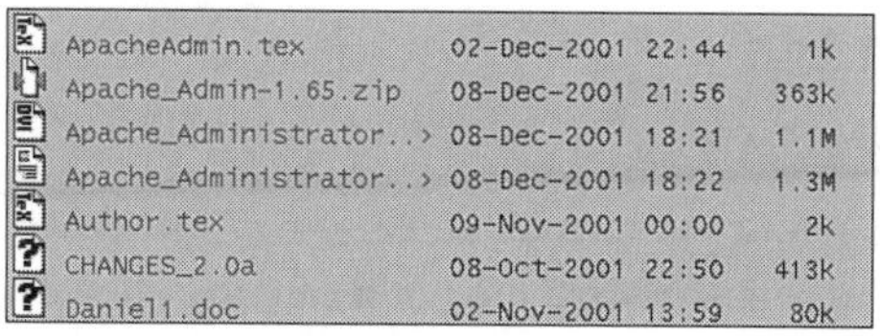

FIGURE 11.4
Directory listing with truncated filenames

The NameWidth option lets you set the maximum length, or, by using an asterisk (*) rather than a number as the argument, you can have Apache automatically use the length of the longest filename in the directory as the maximum.

ScanHTMLTitles

IndexOptions +ScanHTMLTitles

This option is not a particularly nice thing to do to your server, since it is extremely CPU- and disk-intensive. When a directory listing is generated, each HTML file will be opened, and whatever appears in the <TITLE> tag will be used as the file description. This is handy for a number of reasons during Web site development. It gives you a quick way to figure out what the various filenames mean, and to see whether you have put sensible <TITLE> tags in your files. However, once your site is live, leaving this option on will cause a significant performance hit, resulting in slow load times for this directory, and will also do unfriendly things to your server's hard drives. Remember that the HTML files are opened and read *each time* the directory is requested, as there is no caching mechanism built into this process.

SuppressColumnSorting

IndexOptions +SuppressColumnSorting

The names of the columns in the directory listing (Name, Last Modified, Size, and Description) are all links. Clicking a link re-sorts the view by that attribute.

The SuppressColumnSorting option turns off this behavior, and you are stuck with the default ordering. This is a good thing to do for performance reasons. Users like to tinker. Once they discover that they can reorder the directory listing, some people will sit for several minutes reordering the listing by the various options. This causes a drain on the server, because, as you might recall, it is not caching results, and so has to read and sort the directory listing each time, causing a large amount of disk I/O for no particularly good reason.

SuppressDescription

IndexOptions +SuppressDescription

This is a great option to set in order to recover some screen space. Most of the time, the file descriptions are blank, because most people are not aware that they can add a description for a file.[2] So you have a blank column taking up space over on the right side of the screen. By setting the SuppressDescription option, the description column is dropped, and the rest of the columns expand into the available space.

See the section "AddDescription" for information about adding descriptions to files.

SuppressHTMLPreamble

IndexOptions +SuppressHTMLPreamble

This option tells mod_autoindex not to generate the standard HTML header when displaying the file listing. You should use this directive if you are also using the HeaderName directive (See the "Headers and Footers" section) to place a customized HTML header on the index.

SuppressIcon

IndexOptions +SuppressIcon

SuppressIcon entirely turns off the displaying of icons in the directory listing. This results in a more lightweight, faster-loading directory index.

SuppressLastModified

IndexOptions SuppressLastModified

By default, the Last Modified column takes up 19 characters horizontally. The SuppressLastModified option prevents this column from being displayed at all, and these 19 characters are given to the Description column. Consider whether the date and time each file was last modified is a useful piece of information to your audience. If you are distributing software, this may be crucial information. If, on the other hand, you have a directory of MP3 files for download, this information is probably fairly unimportant.

SuppressRules

IndexOptions +SuppressRules

At the top and bottom of the auto-generated listing are horizontal rules, created with the HTML <hr> tag. Use of this option removes those rules. Technically, the HTML 3.2 specification does not permit either images or horizontal rules to appear in a preformatted block created

---

[2]*Of course, now that you are aware of this capability, you might want to use it and ignore this advice!*

with the HTML `<pre>` tag, which this directory listing is. Therefore, use of this option, and the `SuppressIcon` option, make this generated document HTML 3.2 compliant.

SuppressSize

`IndexOptions +SuppressSize`

As with the other `Suppress` options, this option causes one of the columns to be dropped from the index listing. The column containing the file size is not displayed when this option is in effect. However, the size of a file is usually a very important piece of information when you are providing files for download.

TrackModified

`IndexOptions +TrackModified`

I've mentioned more than once in this chapter that the directory index is generated each time a user requests the directory, and that this information is not cached for the next client. The `TrackModified` option goes partway to solving this problem.

If your operating system provides accurate information about the status of files (the `stat` command), `mod_autoindex` will include a `Last-Modified` HTTP header with the response so that a `HEAD` request can determine whether it actually needs to retrieve the document. This will also tell caching proxy servers that they can just return the copy of the document they already have, rather than forcing the server to regenerate the listing if none of the files in the directory have been modified since the last time the index was requested, or if no files have been added or removed.

Note that many operating systems don't return the necessary status information, and on some platforms, the `Last-Modified` header will not be changed if files change size or time stamp.

VersionSort

`IndexOptions +VersionSort`

Although filenames are usually sorted alphabetically,[3] this sorting scheme will not give the desired results when you have file version numbers as part of the filenames. For example, a file called `Date-ISO-1.14.tar.gz` will be listed before a file called `Date-ISO-1.3.tar.gz`, even though it was an earlier version of the file.

---

[3] *Or, more accurately, what is sometimes called "ASCII-betically," since names are sorted by the ASCII value of the characters. This is why all the filenames that start with capital letters appear before all the files that start with lowercase letters.*

The VersionSort option does the right thing with regard to versioned files, listing the files in version order rather than alphabetical order.

AddDescription

By default, the Description column will be empty, since there are no default file descriptions. This is not to say that the description feature is somehow turned off, just that there are no file descriptions set.

The AddDescription directive allows you to set the description for a particular file, or for a set of files that match a wildcard pattern.

```
AddDescription "Sarah at the lake" sarah_lake.jpg

AddDescription "gzipped tar file" *.tar.gz
```

This directive can be used in any context, but only has an effect if FancyIndexing is turned on. If you are not using this in a directory-specific context (that is, a <Directory> section or a .htaccess file), make sure you provide a full path to the file that you're talking about.

```
AddDescription "Mayan calendar" /home/www/images/maya.gif
```

A fairly small amount of space is available for your file description string. The documentation says the following:

> The typical, default description field is 23 bytes wide. 6 more bytes are added by the IndexOptions SuppressIcon option, 7 bytes are added by the IndexOptions SuppressSize option, and 19 bytes are added by the IndexOptions SuppressLastModified option. Therefore, the widest default the description column is ever assigned is 55 bytes.

Judicious use, therefore, of the various Suppress commands will gain you a decent amount of space for your file descriptions. However, you may not want to sacrifice these other fields just so that you can say more about your files.

The DescriptionWidth option of IndexOptions (discussed earlier in the chapter) enables you to further influence the size of this column.

It is also important to know that the file description can contain HTML markup. If you've permitted AllowOverride Indexes so that users can add their own file descriptions in generated index listings (among other index-related things), you may find that they are using this feature and getting strange results. If a description string containing HTML markup is truncated (because it is longer than the allotted space in the column) before an HTML tag is closed, this tag can influence the rest of the generated document.

Say, for example, you have the following:

```
AddDescription "<b>Long, bolded description goes here</b>" file.name
```

If the description were truncated after `description`, before the HTML `bold` tag was closed, the rest of the HTML document from that point on would be rendered in a bold font.

Headers and Footers

```
HeaderName /header.html
```

```
ReadmeName /footer.html
```

The `HeaderName` and `ReadmeName` directives give you the ability to add something to the top and bottom (respectively) of the auto-generated HTML page. Since these files can be HTML, you can make your auto-generated page fit in with the rest of your site look by simply inserting the list of files into your regular site template. And if you have `Options Includes` on for this directory, these files can even contain SSI directives (see Chapter 16, " Server-Side Includes").

If the file referenced by your `HeaderName` directive does in fact contain the start of an HTML page (`<HTML>`, `<HEAD>`, and so on) you will probably also want to enable `IndexOptions SuppressHTMLPreamble` so that these tags are not repeated in the generated HTML document. Also, you should make sure that there is a complementary `ReadmeName` file to close those HTML tags that you opened in the header.

Note also that the values for the `HeaderName` and `ReadmeName` directives are not necessarily just filenames in the current directory, but can be URLs, so you can use a single header and footer file for your entire site and merely load them into the various places where you need them.

This URL can even refer to a CGI program, which can produce the header and/or footer dynamically. However, these directives require that the file have a major content type of `text/*` (something like `text/html` or `text/plain`, for example). So to meet this requirement, one only has to add a content type of `text/html` to the CGI program in question:

```
AddType text/html .cgi
```

See Chapter 8, " MIME and File Types," for more information on this directive.

Ignoring Files

There are certain files that you never want showing up in directory listings. Things that come to mind are `.htaccess` files, `.tmp` files (or whatever you use to designate a temporary file), `.swp` files (something `vi` leaves lying around when you edit files), and a variety of other files that the end user never needs to know about.

The `IndexIgnore` directive lets you list those files that you don't want showing up. By default, the list contains the current directory (`.`), but you will need to add everything else yourself.

```
IndexIgnore README HEADER *.swp .htaccess
```

Searching and Sorting

Unless you have used the `SuppressColumnSorting` option, there is a link at the top of each column in your directory index that, when clicked, will redisplay the index sorted by that column rather than by name (the default).

`mod_autoindex` accomplishes this with very simple parsing of URL arguments, which are appended to the URL with these links.

NOTE

These arguments completely changed in version 2.0, so you need to make sure that you are reading the portion of this section that refers to the version you are running.

Sorting in Version 1.3

In version 1.3, there are four columns by which you can sort, and each column can be sorted in either ascending or descending order. This is accomplished by appending a query string to the URL.[4]

The query string can have one key, which is `N`, `M`, `S`, or `D`, and this key can have one of two values—either `A` or `D`. The key represents the column by which you want to sort, with the `A` meaning *ascending*, and the `D` meaning *descending*.

key	value
N	Name
M	Last Modified
S	File Size
D	Description

---

[4]*A query string is a series of one or more key/value pairs, appended after a question mark on the end of the URL. For example, `?name=Rich&occupation=author` is a query string with two variables. See Chapter 15, "CGI Programs," for more treatment of query strings and how to deal with them.*

When any key other than the name is selected, the secondary sort key is always the filename, sorted in ascending order (with the A's at the top, and the Z's at the bottom). When the page is sorted strictly by the filenames, there is no ambiguity, because filenames are guaranteed to be unique, so there is no need for a secondary sort key.

For example, if the URL `http://apache.rcbowen.com/apache-admin/` generates a directory listing, the URL `http://apache.rcbowen.com/apache-admin?S=D` will generate the same directory listing, but in descending order by the size of the files, with the largest files at the top.

> **NOTE**
>
> When sorting by file size, the actual file size in bytes is used, which is not necessarily what is displayed in the listing, since file sizes are rounded to the nearest number of kilobytes. Hence, two files that are displayed with file size 1K are actually sorted by the number of bytes, which may be, say, 1,203 bytes and 978 bytes.

The links at the top of each column are automatically generated by `mod_autoindex` to reorder the listing by that column. When the view is already ordered in one direction (say, ascending) by a particular column, the link will then be generated to re-sort the list in the opposite order (now descending).

Sorting in Version 2.0

In version 2.0.23, directory sorting was overhauled. The list of possible arguments and values has been expanded, and may be combined to produce a larger matrix of results. The following tables show the various options:

Argument C	Column by Which to Order
C=N	Order by the filename
C=M	Order by last modified date
C=S	Order by file size
C=D	Order by description

Argument O	Order in Which the Column Is to Be Sorted
O=A	Sort in ascending order
O=D	Sort in descending order

Argument F	Format in Which the Directory Should Be Displayed
F=0	A simple list. No fancy indexing used
F=1	FancyIndexing list
F=2	Displayed as an HTML table

Argument V	Ordered by Version Information
V=0	Version ordering disabled
V=1	Version ordering enabled

Argument p	Pattern for Which to Search
p=pattern	Only files that match the specified pattern will be shown.

Note that the pattern search supplied by the p argument is applied *after* the list of files to be displayed has already been filtered through anything you have put in IndexIgnore, and so cannot be used to get at files that you have explicitly excluded from directory listings.

If mod_autoindex encounters an argument with which it is not familiar, it will immediately stop processing the arguments.

The Apache documentation supplies the following HTML snippet, which you can paste directly into a file referred to by HeaderName, in order to provide an easy-to-use way for users to select how they want the directory to be ordered.

```
<FORM METHOD="GET">
    Show me a <SELECT NAME="F">
      <OPTION VALUE="0"> Plain list
      <OPTION VALUE="1" SELECTED> Fancy list
      <OPTION VALUE="2"> Table list
    </SELECT>
    Sorted by <SELECT NAME="C">
      <OPTION VALUE="N" SELECTED> Name
      <OPTION VALUE="M"> Date Modified
      <OPTION VALUE="S"> Size
      <OPTION VALUE="D"> Description
    </SELECT>
    <SELECT NAME="O">
      <OPTION VALUE="A" SELECTED> Ascending
      <OPTION VALUE="D"> Descending
    </SELECT>
    <SELECT NAME="V">
      <OPTION VALUE="0" SELECTED> in Normal order
      <OPTION VALUE="1"> in Version order
    </SELECT>
    Matching <INPUT TYPE="text" NAME="P" VALUE="*">
    <INPUT TYPE="submit" NAME="X" VALUE="Go">
</FORM>
```

IndexOrderDefault

Directory indexes are, by default, ordered by the names of the files. However, this default ordering can be changed with the IndexOrderDefault directive. This directive can specify which of the other fields you want to order by, and whether you want this ordering to be ascending or descending.

```
IndexOrderDefault Ascending Size
```

The first argument can be one of Ascending or Descending, and the second argument can be one of Name, Date, Size, or Description. When an option other than Name is chosen, the secondary key is always the filename. When the filename is the primary sort criterion, there is no ambiguity, as filenames are guaranteed to be unique.

If used in conjunction with the SuppressColumnSorting option, this directive will guarantee a particular ordering, no matter what the client asks for.

Examples

The following examples give a few ways in which directory index directives and options may be combined to provide customized directory index listings.

Example 1

```
<Directory /usr/local/apache/vhosts/apache/htdocs/apache-admin>
Options +Indexes
IndexOptions +IconHeight=20 +IconWidth=22
IndexOptions +FoldersFirst +SuppressLastModified +SuppressHTMLPreamble
HeaderName HEADER.html
AddDescription 'zip file' *.zip
AddDescription 'PDF format' *.pdf
IndexOptions +NameWidth=*
</Directory>
```

In the first line (the <Directory> directive) I specify that the directives here pertain only to the particular directory in which I am keeping these files, and any subdirectories thereof.

Next, I turn on Options Indexes so that the rest of the directives will be honored.

I specify a particular height and width for the icons to be displayed. This is the same as the default values for these sizes, but these sizes enable the browser to display the page before the images have loaded. I make the directories appear at the top of the directory listing, rather than scattered throughout the listing. I turn off the last modified column to give me sufficient room for the descriptions I add later. And I turn off the HTML preamble so that I can use the HTML header file specified in the next line with the HeaderName directive.

With two `AddDescription` directives, I add descriptions to the zip files and to Portable Document Format (PDF) files. Files with a .zip extension will be displayed with a description of "zip file", and files with a .pdf extension are displayed with a description of "PDF format."

Finally, with the `NameWidth` option, I make sure that the name field can expand to compensate for my tendency towards rather verbose filenames.

Example 2

```
<Directory /usr/local/apache/htdocs/manual>
Options +Indexes
IndexOptions +SuppressSize +SuppressLastModified +ScanHTMLTitles
HeaderFile header.html
ReadmeFile footer.html
</Directory>
```

In this example, you end up with a listing of your HTML files, with the title of each HTML document in the description field. This is very time- and CPU-intensive, but it is useful during the development of your Web site, showing you what files you have and whether they have well-formed and descriptive titles, and giving quick access to the various files without requiring that you navigate through the usual channels.

Indexing Security Concerns

In one sense, there is a security risk involved in permitting auto-generated directory indexes. People can see all the files in a given directory and download whatever files they want from that directory. If there are files in the directory that you did not explicitly link to from anywhere on your site, they can still get those files. However, assuming that people cannot download files from your site merely because you have not linked to them from anywhere is what I refer to as cosmetic security, or security through the advanced technique of "hoping nobody notices."[5] It is not real security, and if it gives you a false feeling of security, it is doing more harm than good. You should not put files that you don't want in the hands of the general public in any unauthenticated location on your public Web site.

Summary

The `DirectoryIndex` directive specifies a file to be displayed by default when a directory is requested without a particular file being requested.

---

[5] *Thank you, Scott Adams.*

11

Turning on `Options Indexes` enables the `mod_autoindex` module to automatically generate a directory index, with links to download each file. This listing is highly customizable with respect to the ordering of the files, which files are displayed, and what information is displayed about each file.

With these two sets of techniques, you can provide automatically generated file listings with a minimum amount of work, and provide users with an intuitive interface for downloading files.

Apache on Microsoft Windows

IN THIS CHAPTER

"Better run for your life!" cried the Mad Hatter
"Alright," said Alice..."I'm going back...
To the other side of the mirror"

Alice–The Other Side of the Mirror–Stevie Nicks

Apache 1.3a1 was released in July 1997. It was the first official version of Apache to run on Microsoft Windows. There were attempts prior to this to port Apache to Windows, some of them actually fairly successful. But this was the first official release from the Apache Group that you could download from `apache.org` and install on Windows.

However, throughout the 1.3 releases, the Windows documentation contained the following warning:

> Warning: Apache on NT has not yet been optimized for performance. Apache still performs best, and is most reliable on Unix platforms.

Earlier versions also contained this more ominous warning:

> Please note that at this time, Windows support is entirely experimental, and is recommended only for experienced users. The Apache Group does not guarantee that this software will work as documented, or even at all.

These warnings were hardly conducive to establishing trust and drawing in new users. But the fact is that Apache for Windows was done because the folks in the ASF realized that we needed Apache to run on Windows. As such, a lot of effort, even brute force when necessary, went into simply getting it working, with the understanding that after it was working, an effort would be made later to go back and do it right.

In version 2.0, Apache for Windows is done right. It takes advantage of Windows' internal API in ways that the 1.3 version never did. It is much faster, and much more stable.

The installation process is much cleaner in Apache 2.0, as it determines certain configuration directives for you based on your system configuration. For example, it will determine your hostname and make sure that you are not already running any service on port 80 that would conflict with Apache. Also, the code uses native NT networking calls for much improved performance.

Requirements

Apache for Windows is designed to work on the NT family of operating systems—Windows NT 4.0 and Windows 2000. Windows 95, 98, and ME are similar enough to Windows NT that Apache will also run there, but there are some features that don't quite work as desired. This is probably just as well, because you really should not be running production network services on an operating system that is designed to be a desktop OS, not a server OS. However, Apache runs well enough on Windows 9x that it is good for Web site testing before you move your site to a real server.

If installing on NT, it is recommended that you have Service Pack 6 installed. Service Pack 6 contains a variety of fixes to the TCP/IP stack. If running on Windows 95, you will need to install the Winsock2 upgrade in order for Apache to work at all.

Downloading

The installation files for Microsoft Windows are located on the Apache Web site at `http://httpd.apache.org/dist/httpd/binaries/win32/`. The distribution is available in several different packages. With the 1.3 version, Apache is available as an MSI (Microsoft Installer) package and as an InstallShield package. The MSI is the preferred distribution, as it makes it easier to track where files were placed, and thus easier to correctly uninstall the files if necessary.

If you are running Windows 95 or 98, you might need to install the Microsoft Installer, which you can get from the Microsoft Web site at `http://www.microsoft.com/downloads/release.asp?ReleaseID=17343`.

12

APACHE ON MICROSOFT WINDOWS

Installation

Because most Windows machines will probably not have a compiler installed, the Windows distribution comes as a batch of compiled binaries. Installing these binaries is very simple, and should be a familiar process to any Windows user. Simply click on the file that you downloaded and answer a few simple questions to have the necessary files installed in the appropriate places.

After the initial splash screen, you will be presented with three screens on which you will need to make configuration decisions. Figure 12.1 shows the first screen.

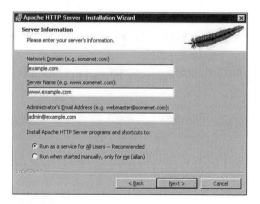

FIGURE 12.1
The Apache Installation Wizard

The first screen asks for the domain in which the server will be running (such as example.com), the hostname of the server (such as www.example.com), and the e-mail address of the server administrator (such as admin@example.com). You must also decide whether the server will be installed to run as a service (running with the privileges of the system account), or whether it should install only as the current user. The former choice (running as a service) is preferable, as it enables the server to start at system start time, whereas the latter choice requires that the server be started manually by the same user who is doing the installation.

The second screen (Figure 12.2) offers you the choice to install the complete package in the default locations, or to do a custom installation where you control more of the decisions. Choosing the complete installation is recommended for your first few times through this process.

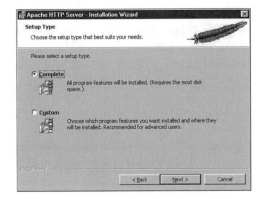

Figure 12.2

Choosing the setup type.

Finally, the last screen (Figure 12.3) asks you what base directory you want to put everything in. The default location is c:\Program Files\Apache Group, but you can put it anywhere you like.

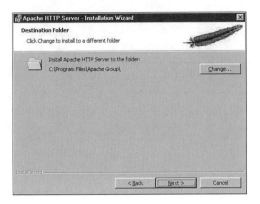

Figure 12.3

Picking a directory for installation.

After this screen, the installer will place the files in the correct locations for you.

Installing as a Service

Apache can be run as an NT service, or on Windows 95 or 98, as something that roughly approximates the same behavior.

An NT service is the equivalent of what is called a *daemon* in the Unix world. It is a process that is running in the background, rather than in a foreground window or console. You can communicate with the service with either command-line functions, or with the Windows control panel services dialog.

In order to install Apache as an NT service, you will need to use the following command, typed at a DOS prompt:

```
apache -i -n "Apache"
```

The program file apache will be located in the directory where you installed Apache, and you might need to either change into that directory to run the command, or provide the full path to the file.

The -i flag indicates that Apache is being installed as a service.

The -n flag enables you to specify the name of the service as you want it to appear in the services dialog. If you do not specify a service name, the default is Apache.

The -f flag is optional, and is used only if you want to specify the use of a configuration file other than the default file.

Other flags might also be used in this command to alter the behavior of Apache when started as a service.

You can alter the arguments supplied to Apache by the service with the -k config argument. For example, if you wanted to change the location of the configuration file, you could do so with the following command:

```
apache -k config -n "Apache" -f "\alternate\config.conf"
```

This will alter the configuration in the registry so that the next time that the service is restarted, it will be started with this alternate configuration file.

If you want to uninstall the Apache service, use the -u flag:

```
apache -u -n "Apache"
```

Starting and Stopping Your Server

After Apache is installed, you will start and stop the server in a somewhat different manner than described for the Unix version. The method of doing this will differ depending on whether you have the server installed as a service, and whether you are running on Windows NT or Windows 9*x*.

If Apache is installed as an NT service, you can start and stop your server in one of three ways. There are two methods that can be used from the command line, and one via the Windows graphical user interface.

From the command line, you can use the `apache` program itself to start the service, using the `-k` command-line flag:

```
apache -n "Apache" -k start
```

Likewise, to stop and restart you can also use the `-k` flag:

```
apache -n "Apache" -k restart
apache -n "Apache" -k stop
```

Note: Apache on Windows does not come with the `apachectl` utility mentioned earlier in this book. (`apachectl` is discussed in Chapter 3, "Starting, Stopping, and Restarting.")

You can also use the NT command-line tools provided to control services. These commands are the `NET START` and `NET STOP` commands:

```
NET START "Apache"
```

```
NET STOP "Apache"
```

Note that the quotes are only strictly required if the service name contains spaces. The `NET START` and `NET STOP` commands do not provide you with a method for passing additional arguments to the Apache server, so if you need to alter the behavior of the server from the defaults, you need to directly start and stop Apache yourself, rather than using the NT service tools.

Finally, you can use the NT services dialog. This dialog is accessible by opening the control panel and selecting the service icon. You can start and stop the service from this dialog. Windows 2000 also features a restart button that can be used to restart the service.

Note that Comanche will also run on Windows, and can be used as an administrative interface. See Chapter 5, "Configuration Utilities," for more information about Comanche.

Starting and Stopping in Win9x

There are two main ways to start Apache on Windows 9*x*—as a console application or as a service. (As of version 1.3.13, there is experimental support for starting it as a service.)

Running as a Console Application

From a DOS prompt, change into the Apache directory and start up Apache:

```
cd "\program files\apache group\apache"
apache
```

If you want to start Apache with a configuration file other than the one in the default location, you can specify the location of the configuration file with the -f flag:

```
apache -f c:\apache\conf\other.conf
```

Apache will run in this console window, and it must stay open as long as Apache is running. Closing this window will terminate the Apache server.

There is also a shortcut on the Windows Start menu labeled Start Apache As Console App that runs this same command line, starting Apache with the default configuration file. This too will launch a console (DOS prompt) that will need to stay open for as long as you want Apache to run.

Running as a Service

You can start Apache on Windows 9x as a service of sorts, in that it will run in the background rather than in a foreground window, as was the case until version 1.3.13. However, this is currently still labeled as experimental, and so is not guaranteed to work all the time, if at all.

After you have verified that Apache will run from the command line, you can use the following command to run Apache as a service from a shortcut on your desktop or start menu:

```
apache -n "service name" -k start
```

In order to stop Apache, you will need to run the following command, either from another DOS console or from a shortcut:

```
apache -n "service name" -k stop
```

Modules

Because everything is distributed as binaries, you have no compile-time options for adding and removing modules. Consequently, Apache for Windows is distributed with all the standard modules compiled as dynamic shared objects (DSOs), or, as they are called in Microsoft-land, dynamically linked libraries (DLLs). In your server configuration file, you'll need to specify which of these modules you actually want to load when your Apache server starts. This is done with the LoadModule directive, as shown here:

```
LoadModule speling_module modules/mod_speling.so
```

The LoadModule directive adds the named module to the active module list. The file path provided is relative to the ServerRoot, and because the file extension might vary from module to module, the full filename must be provided. The modules distributed with Apache have a .so file extension, while many third-party modules have .dll file extensions.

Differences Between Apache on Windows and Unix

For most purposes, Apache on Windows is exactly the same as Apache on Unix, and everything else in this book will apply. However, there are some important differences between Apache on Windows and Apache on Unix, and these are primarily in the area of configuring your server. There are, however, a few differences in other areas as well.

Threading Versus Prefork

Apache on Windows is multithreaded, as opposed to Apache on Unix, which is a single parent with multiple preforked[1] child processes. Consequently, the various directives that deal with the creation of new httpd processes are not relevant for Apache on Windows, and are replaced instead with several others that deal with the creation of threads.

The particular directives that are ignored by Apache on Windows in this context are MaxSpareServers, MinSpareServers, and StartServers, which specify the number of child processes that you have at any given time. These directives are discussed in more detail in Chapter 13, "Performance Tuning."

In their place, we gain the ThreadsPerChild directive, which specifies how many threads your Apache process should permit to be used. Note that because threads are roughly analogous to child processes in the Unix model, this number also limits the total number of simultaneous connections that will be permitted to your site at any time.

In Apache 2.0, we also get MaxSpareThreads and MinSpareThreads, which are directly analogous to the MaxSpareServers and MinSpareServers directives and govern the lower and upper limits on the total number of idle threads at any given time. These threads are in addition to any threads that are currently serving client requests, and are kept waiting in the wings to serve any additional incoming requests. Apache will create additional threads as the idle pool gets used up, and reap unused threads that exceed the configured maximum when load trails off.

Apache 2.0 greatly reduces the number of differences between the Windows and Unix versions of the server by introducing platform-specific *multi-processing modules (MPMs)*. These modules provide a variety of different ways to handle multiple processes serving incoming client requests. By choosing a different MPM, you can determine whether a threaded model, a prefork model, or some other model is used. The MPM for Windows NT, called mpm_winnt, is specifically written for Windows NT and takes advantage of specific Windows API calls that result in better performance and stability.

With Apache 1.3, this model is entirely determined by the platform on which you are running.

---

[1] *Preforked means that the processes are launched before they are needed, so that there are always several waiting in the wings for incoming requests.*

MaxRequestsPerChild

As mentioned previously, Apache on Windows is multithreaded. There is a single child process containing many threads, each of which serves requests.

The MaxRequestsPerChild, as the name suggests, is the maximum number of requests that a particular child process is permitted to serve before that child will be reaped. In the Windows single-child model, it is undesirable for the child process to ever be reaped, as this will take your server down. Of course, Apache will automatically launch a new child process to take the place of the one that was reaped, but this has two undesirable effects.

First, it means that you will have significant server downtime, from a few seconds to possibly a minute or more, depending on the number of modules you have loaded and the complexity of your configuration file.

Second, if you have made changes to your configuration file(s), but have not restarted your server to read in those new changes, these modifications will be read in and applied at this time. Restarting the only child process is equivalent to a complete server restart, and so the configuration files are re-read. This can have undesired or unexpected effects when a configuration changes and you had not intended to apply the changes yet.

Consequently, MaxRequestsPerChild should under no circumstances be set to anything but the default 0 on Windows. A value of 0 means that the child is never to exit, no matter how many requests it serves.

CGI Scripts

When running CGI scripts under Windows, there are two ways that you can indicate what interpreter is to process the script. (The term "script" is being used here in the traditional sense to indicate an interpreted program, rather than a compiled one.) The default behavior here tends to be rather unintuitive to users used to ordinary Windows behavior, and so generates a lot of questions on various mailing lists and newsgroups.

Microsoft Windows determines what type of file it is dealing with by the file extension—characters that appear at the end of the filename after a period. Thus, a file named index.html, which has a file extension of html, is known to be a HyperText file because of the extension. This information—the mapping between file extension and file type—is stored in the registry, which is a database of configuration variables stored in the Windows environment.

Unix variants, on the other hand, determine file type based on a variety of different criteria, which usually involves looking at the file contents and applying a series of rules to figure out what sort of file it is. For example, a file containing a GIF 89 header in the first part of the file is sure to be a GIF image file.

For our particular purposes, of utmost interest is figuring out what sort of file we are dealing with when asked to execute a script. The typical Unix way of doing things is to look in the first line of the file for a reference to the executable program that will be responsible for interpreting and executing the contents of the file. For example, if the first line of the file looked like

```
#!/usr/bin/perl
```

then the shell would know that the contents of the file are to be fed to the program found at the file path `/usr/bin/perl` for execution. The `#!` in this line, which is typically called the *shebang*, indicates to the shell that what follows is just such an instruction.

Apache employs a hybrid of these two approaches, using a variety of directives to map particular file extensions to particular MIME types (see Chapter 8, "MIME and File Types," for more details), but, in the case of CGI programs, employing the shebang line to tell it how to execute a particular CGI script.

On Microsoft Windows this is not a common practice, so a configuration directive is supplied to alleviate this confusion.

The `ScriptInterpreterSource` directive tells Apache whether it should look in the registry for a mapping from file extension to interpreter, or whether it should look in the first line of the file for a shebang line to determine this information.

Setting the value of the `ScriptInterpreterSource` directive to `registry` causes Apache to use the former method, while setting it to `script` tells it to use the latter method. The following examples show what each of these directives would look like. These directives go into your main server configuration file, or in a `.htaccess` file. It can be set on a per-directory basis by putting it into a `<Directory>` section.

ScriptInterpreterSource	*Values*
ScriptInterpreterSource registry	Look in the registry for file type mapping
ScriptInterpreterSource script	Look in the script for a shebang line

`.htaccess` Files

`.htaccess` files enable you to specify per-directory configuration options in a file located in the particular directory. By default, the name of these configuration files is `.htaccess`. However, you cannot create files with a dot as the first character of the filename in Windows.

The name of the file in which Apache will look for per-directory configuration changes is set by the `AccessFileName` directive, which can be set to something more friendly to the Windows[2] file system. The configuration file distributed with Apache for Windows has this directive set to `htaccess`—that is, the leading dot is omitted.

---

[2]*This is not entirely true—there are ways to do it—but it's not a particularly good idea.*

File Paths

File paths are specified differently from one operating system to another. In Microsoft Windows operating systems, you must specify what drive letter you are working on, and paths are specified with backslashes rather than forward slashes. On Unix operating systems, no drive letters are specified—everything is usually on one logical volume—and the past separator is a forward slash. This leads to differences in configuration files when file paths need to be specified.

When specifying file paths in configuration files, you can use either forward slashes, which are used in Unix and are used for examples in the documentation, or you can use the backslashes that are used by Windows. But you should be consistent, and forward slashes are preferred. The reason for this is that the documentation consistently uses the forward slash in those parts of the documentation that are not platform-specific. In order to be able to directly use the examples without modification and to avoid confusion, you will want to use forward slashes in your configuration files.

The `ServerRoot` directive must be specified with the drive letter so that Apache knows what drive to look on for the files. This will look something like the following:

```
ServerRoot c:/apache
```

If you are specifying other directives on the same drive as the `ServerRoot`, you do not need to specify the drive letter. Otherwise, you will need to provide the whole path.

If you need to specify a file path that has spaces in it, you will need to have the entire file path in quotes; otherwise, Apache will think that the file path ends at the first space:

```
Alias /pictures/ "c:/photo album/images"
```

Summary

Apache on Windows is very similar to Apache on Unix in most respects. After you have it installed and running, administering it will be almost identical to what you would need to do on Unix.

With Apache 2.0, efforts have been made to make Apache on all platforms almost identical, with a pluggable MPM to determine how the particular OS best handles multiprocessing—either via forking or threading, or some combination thereof. Management of the rest of the server is similar, with only this one layer differing in order to communicate with the underlying operating system.

12

APACHE ON
MICROSOFT
WINDOWS

Performance Tuning

IN THIS CHAPTER

"It's hard, this far into the revolution, to remember what you're fighting for."

Bill Hall, Jr.

When we're not implementing new features or fixing the old ones, my customers seem to be concerned about just one thing—how can we make it go faster? This chapter offers two possible solutions to this question, but it is important to understand that there is no silver bullet that will make your Web server run faster. The Apache team already makes every effort to ensure that your server runs as fast as possible as soon as you install it; any additional performance you can squeeze out of it is because of something unique to your particular situation.

In this chapter we talk about general performance tuning tips, which might improve the speed of connections to your Web site. Apache contains a number of performance-related directives that can be tweaked according to your particular needs, and what your site is doing.

Many of the things discussed here are interrelated. Modifications to one thing will give you more room to maneuver in another area.

Optimize the Right Thing

A common failing, when trying to improve the performance of some computer-based operation, is incorrectly identifying what needs to be optimized. Frequently, many hours are spent attempting to optimize things that do not need optimizing.

For most sites your bandwidth will be more of a bottleneck than any other consideration. The user on the other end of a 56K-modem connection will see your site at the same speed, no matter how much time and money you spend on improving site performance.

Similarly, if your performance problem is that your dynamically generated content is depending on a slow database server, then spending time optimizing your Web server configuration is unlikely to make any difference.

Benchmarking and profiling exactly what is going on is a tedious process, but will save you time and effort in the long run because you will be assured that your optimization effort will actually be directed to the portion of the equation that is actually causing the slowdown.

ApacheBench

ApacheBench is a utility that ships with Apache. You will find it in the `bin` directory of where you built Apache. The file is called ab, and you can get the command-line syntax by typing `./ab -h` while in that directory. ApacheBench enables you to benchmark how fast your Apache server runs. It is actually a client application, not closely tied to Apache itself, so you can run it against any Web server, not just Apache.

To run a test with ApacheBench, you can type a command such as the following:

```
./ab -n 50 http://www.apacheadmin.com/testing/url.html
```

This will fetch that URL 50 times and display a report of the process; giving times required to connect and to transfer the content, and the transfer rate.

The `-c` flag can be added to make several requests concurrently, to simulate a busy site where a number of users are requesting content at the same time.

```
./ab -n 500 -c 10 http://www.apacheadmin.com/testing/url.html
```

For CGI programs, you may want to simulate user behavior by posting form contents to the program. This behavior is invoked with the `-p` argument:

```
./ab -n 100 -p /tmp/formcontents http://www.apacheadmin.com/cgi-bin/example.cgi
```

In the above example, the specified file contains the data that you want posted to the given URL.

Profiling

Profiling, on the other hand, is much more difficult, and is somewhat beyond the scope of this book. Profiling means getting into your code—such as CGI programs, or mod_perl handlers, for example—and determining which part of the code is taking the longest. Or, more generally, how long each part of the code is taking. This permits you to determine which parts of the code are being the least efficient, and therefore could stand a little optimization.

Profiling techniques are very dependent on the particular programming language in use, but usually involve using a debugger of some variety. Most modern programming languages have a profiler of some description available for this sort of analysis.

Hardware Requirements

Getting a server (hardware) that will run your Web site fast enough is the same as getting a computer that will run anything fast enough. It depends on what you consider fast enough and how much you are willing to spend for it. There are, however, a few things that you should consider essentials.

Memory

You need enough memory (RAM) so that you never have to swap. If you run out of memory, and data has to be written to swap space, things will slow down substantially because disk access is orders of magnitude slower than memory.

Note that the more Apache children you have running at one time, the more memory you will be using. The `MaxClients` directive limits the total number of Apache child processes you can have running at any one time, and you should make sure that this is not set so high that you run out of memory.

Disk

Because most of your data will load off of a disk, you should try to get the fastest drive that you can. SCSI drives will, in general, be faster than the IDE alternative. They are also, of course, more expensive.

Placing drives in a RAID configuration, in addition to giving you data redundancy in the event of a hard-drive failure, will also (usually) give you improved data-access speed because the data can be loaded off of multiple drives simultaneously, improving the data throughout.

CPU

A faster processor will improve the performance of your Web server. This seems fairly obvious and will be even more the case if more of your content is dynamically generated in some fashion.

Apache Configuration

Apache offers a variety of directives for tuning performance to fit your particular needs. And there are some other directives that will have direct impact on your server performance.

HostnameLookups

Each time a request is made to your Apache server the access is logged in the server access log, (see Chapter 24). Part of the information that is stored is the address of the client accessing your site. This is, by default, just the IP address of that client. However the `HostnameLookups` directive, if set to `On`, causes Apache to log the full hostname of the client, rather than just the IP address.

```
HostnameLookups On
```

With this setting a DNS lookup will be performed each time a client requests a file from your site, which will cause Apache to pause until the hostname has been looked up. In the event that the client is connecting from a host that does not have a reverse DNS entry, which is increasingly common, you might have to wait through the entire DNS timeout before the file is served.

If you need to have host information in your logs, you should consider processing your logs in a separate process to convert the IP addresses into full hostnames. Apache provides a program that performs this process. It is called `logrotate`, and is located in the `bin` directory when you have finished building Apache. To use `logrotate`, copy your log file to a location other than where it was created, and run the command

```
/usr/local/apache/bin/logresolve < access_log > output_file
```

Note that this can take a very long time. It's a good idea to do this on some machine other than your production Web server machine, so that the DNS lookups don't interfere with server performance.

Symlinks

Symbolic links, or symlinks, are a feature of most modern file systems that permit a file (or directory) to be located in one location, but appear to also be in another location. Because Windows file systems do not permit symbolic links, this section really only applies to the *nix readers.

Most file operations make no distinction between symlinks and "real" files (or directories), so Apache actually has to do more work when you tell it not to follow symlinks. That is, using `Options +FollowSymLinks` causes a performance improvement because Apache does not need to check to see if the files are really symbolic links to files located elsewhere.

The exception to this rule is if you are using `Options SymLinksIfOwnerMatch`. In which case, not only does Apache have to check if they are symlinks, but it must also verify that the owner of the link is the same as the owner of the file. That requires a total of three file stats—one to see if it is a symlink, then, if it is one, it must check the owner of the file, and of the link. Note that Apache will have to check *every* file, and all the directories leading up to that file, to see if they are symlinks. And because this lookup is not cached, it has to do this for every resource that is requested.

For the best performance, always use `Options FollowSymLinks`, and never use `Options SymLinksIfOwnerMatch`.

Refer to Chapter 4, "Configuration Directives," for more information about the `FollowSymLinks` option and for information about the `SymLinksIfOwnerMatch` option.

AllowOverride and .htaccess Files

As was discussed in Chapter 6, ".htaccess files—Per-Directory Configuration," permitting per-directory configuration files, or .htaccess files, can cause a substantial performance degradation because every file access requires that the file .htaccess be looked for in the directory where the content is located, and all parent directories thereof.

Setting `AllowOverride off` disables the parsing of .htaccess files entirely, and will give you a performance improvement as a result.

Content Negotiation

Content negotiation results in a performance hit because Apache has to consider more than one option of files to serve, compare the available files to the preferences of the client, and choose the right file. However, the benefits of content negotiation outweigh the performance loss.

There are two ways in which you can improve performance while using content negotiation.

First, rather than using a wildcard `DirectoryIndex`, such as `index`, which will then get expanded to the possible variants of this file, explicitly list all the variants. For example, rather than using the directive

```
DirectoryIndex index
```

use a full listing instead, as in:

```
DirectoryIndex index.html.en index.html.es index.html.fr
```

Second, use a `type-map` file, rather than allowing `MultiViews` to figure things out for you. By taking the time to create the `type-map` file, and list the possible variants with their attributes, you can save Apache the time of figuring this all out for you. And because it has to do this each time a resource is requested the time investment to create the `type-map` is well worth your time.

Process Creation

Apache handles increased server load by creating new child processes to handle the additional incoming connections. And, when the number of connections dies down, Apache reaps those unused child processes. Starting up new processes can potentially be expensive, so you should set your configuration so that you usually have as many processes as you need and, therefore, don't need to start and stop processes frequently.

These settings are managed by the `MinSpareServers`, `MaxSpareServers`, and `StartServers` directives, which determine, respectively, the minimum and maximum number of child processes that should be kept waiting in the wings, and how many child processes are to be started when the server comes up in the first place.

The `MaxRequestsPerChild` directive is also related to this process. It determines how many requests a particular child process should be allowed to serve before it is reaped. The default value of this directive is 0, which means that there is no limit—a particular child should be allowed to run for the entirety of the life of the Apache process. Setting it to anything else causes Apache to kill a child process after it has served that many requests. If you have this set to some non-zero value, make sure that it is sufficiently high that you are not continually starting new processes.

On Microsoft Windows, `MaxRequestsPerlChild` needs to be set to 0. Because Apache under Windows is a single multithreaded process, and the directives mentioned previously have their analogies in `MinSpareThreads`, `MaxSpareThreads`, and `StartThreads`. Setting `MaxRequestsPerChild` to something non-zero in this threaded model causes that single process to get shut down, and restarted, taking all the threads with it, and causing momentary server outage while the process comes back up.

The `MaxClients` directive (or, in a threaded environment, the `MaxThreadsPerChild` directive) determines the maximum number of connections that will be possible to your server. This should be set high enough that clients will not ever have to wait, but not so high that this many child processes will consume all available memory and cause your server to swap to disk. A lot of experimentation is required to determine the appropriate numbers here. Examining the output of `mod_status` is very useful in determining these numbers.

Caching and Proxying

Caching is the practice of storing something for later use. In computer usage, it usually refers to storing a piece of information somewhere it can be retrieved from quicker than its regular location.

mod_proxy

Prior to version 2.0 Apache shipped with `mod_proxy`, which you could build into Apache, and configure as a caching proxy server to run with your Apache server. This has been removed from Apache 2.0 so that it could be developed independently of Apache. `mod_proxy` is being developed as a separate project under the umbrella of the Apache Software Foundation. Versions are available for Apache 1.3 and for Apache 2.0.

You can read more about `mod_proxy` in the Apache 1.3 documentation, but you should be aware that that documentation has not been updated for a long time. The latest version of the documentation can be seen in the CVS repository for the `mod_proxy` project, at `http://cvs.apache.org/viewcvs.cgi/httpd-proxy/docs/`.

`mod_proxy` performs two main roles—proxy and cache server. These functions are turned on with the following requests, respectively:

```
ProxyRequests On
CacheRoot /var/httpd/cache
```

Turning `ProxyRequests On` enables the proxying functionality, but does not enable caching because Apache will not know where to put the cached documents. The `CacheRoot` directive tells Apache where to put the cached content and, therefore, enables the caching part of `mod_proxy`.

A variety of further configuration tweaks can be made to mod_proxy to get it to do a variety of interesting things. What particular things you do with it will depend largely on your particular network configuration and user needs.

Squid

There are a number of alternate ways to do caching. The most popular of these is Squid. Squid, available from http://www.squid-cache.org/, is a caching proxy server. What this means is that it sits at the edge of your network and proxys either incoming, or outgoing requests, making those requests on behalf of the client.

Proxying outgoing connections from your network has two main effects—one immediate, and one longer term.

The first effect is that all outgoing requests from your network, through the proxy, appear to come from a single IP address. This hides the size and layout of your network from the outside world. Many other technologies perform this same task, NAT (Network Address Translation) and SOCKS, being two of the most popular, and provide services at the physical network layer. Squid provides caching at the protocol layer, proxying a variety of protocols including HTTP, FTP, SSL, and DNS.

The second way that Squid benefits your outgoing network connections is that it caches content. This becomes more useful the larger your organization is. The first time someone visits a Web site, Squid retrieves that content for the user, and stores it. The next user that gets that same content will get it from Squid, rather than from the actual Web site, resulting in a much faster retrieval of the content. Squid checks with the live Web site to see if the content has been modified because the last time someone looked at it, and if it has been, it will get the new content, rather than serving the now-stale cached content.

However, more to the point of this chapter is what happens when you use Squid to proxy incoming requests to your Web server. This looks similar to proxying outgoing requests, except that now it directly results in improved performance (or at least perceived improved performance, which amounts to the same thing) of your Web server.

Because Squid caches requests in memory, retiring them to disk after they have reached a certain age, the most frequently requested resources are always immediately available to be served and don't have to wait for a disk read. This frees up the Web server to serve only that content that is being modified—the dynamically generated content—and Squid serves the static HTML and image files from memory cache.

On the user end, this is directly seen as a faster load time. On the server side it is seen as a greatly reduced server load, and capability to focus processor time on generating the dynamic content, rather than spending time reading the same files from disk again and again.

You can read more about Squid, or download the program, at http://www.squid-cache.org.

Summary

In addition to the various hardware considerations common to any server performance optimization, Apache offers you a variety of configuration directives that enable you to tune your system performance based on your particular needs.

Also, consider using a caching proxy server, such as Squid, to balance some of the load of your server.

13

PERFORMANCE
TUNING

Dynamic Content

PART

III

IN THIS PART

Handlers and Filters

IN THIS CHAPTER

"His voice," thought Will, "I never noticed. It's the same color as his hair."

Something Wicked This Way Comes—Ray Bradbury

Although much of the content on a normal Web site will be static content such as HTML files, image files, and various other media files, some requests will need to be handled differently to generate some portion of the document. This is usually done with a *handler*. And, in Apache 2.0, it can also be done with a filter. In this chapter, we'll talk about seven standard handlers that are part of modules that come with Apache, and then we'll look at creating a custom handler of your own. Finally, we'll talk about filters, what they are, and how to use one.

Handlers

A handler is, simply stated, any process that is called when a particular resource is requested. Usually this process will do something to the resource before it is sent out to the client, although occasionally, a <Location> will be pointed directly at a handler, and there will be no actual file resource involved at all. A number of examples of will be described in this chapter.

Configuration

Handlers are configured primarily with the four directives Action, AddHandler, RemoveHandler, and SetHandler. Action is used to create a handler, and the other three directives are for using an existing handler. The Action directive will be discussed in section "Custom Handlers," and the other three will be described here.

AddHandler

The AddHandler directive is used to map a particular handler to files with a particular extension. The syntax of the directive is

```
AddHandler cgi-script .cgi
```

The first argument is the name of the handler, which is any of the handlers that will be described in the remainder of this chapter, or a handler that you have created using the Action directive, as described in the section "Custom Handlers."

The second argument is a file extension. For the duration of the scope of the directive all files with that extension will be processed by the specified handler, rather than being served verbatim to the client.

Note that the file extension is not case sensitive, and might be specified with or without the dot. See Chapter 8, "MIME and File Types," for comments about putting multiple extensions on a single file.

SetHandler

Although `AddHandler` associates a handler with a particular file extension, the `SetHandler` directive causes all files in a given scope (a `<Directory>` section, or a `<Files>` section, for example) to be served via the specified handler.

```
<FilesMatch "\.(pl|cgi|exe)$">
SetHandler cgi-script
</FilesMatch>
```

`SetHandler` can also be applied to a `<Location>`, so that the entire `<Location>` is served via that handler, and there is entirely no relation between resources served and the file system.

The `ScriptAlias` directive is equivalent to setting `SetHandler cgi-script` on the entire specified directory. Thus, the following block is equivalent to one `ScriptAlias` directive.

```
Alias /cgi-bin/ /usr/local/apache/cgi-bin/


<Directory /usr/local/apache/cgi-bin>
SetHandler cgi-script
</Directory>
```

RemoveHandler

As the name implies, the `RemoveHandler` directive negates the effect of a `SetHandler` directive. This is particularly useful if you want to use a `SetHandler` directive in one directory, but not in subdirectories thereof.

In this example, we're setting the `send-asis` handler to deal with all `.html` files in the directory `/usr/local/apache/htdocs/news`, but removing that association for the `stories` subdirectory.

```
<Directory /usr/local/apache/htdocs/news>
SetHandler send-asis .html
</Directory>


<Directory /usr/local/apache/htdocs/news/stories>
RemoveHandler .html
</Directory>
```

Action

The Action directive creates a handler. It tells Apache to map a particular handler name to a given program that provides the implementation for a handler by the same hand. We will talk more about custom handlers in section titled "Custom Handlers."

14

HANDLERS AND
FILTERS

default-handler

`default-handler` is, as you would expect, the default handler that is used by Apache to serve static content, such as HTML documents, image files, and other files which do not require preprocessing of any kind.

```
AddHandler default-handler html
```

Although you could use this syntax to add the default handler to HTML documents, it is not actually necessary because this is the handler that will be use by default.

send-as-is

The `send-as-is` handler tells Apache to serve the file as is, without adding the usual batch of HTTP headers on to it, such as the `Content-type`, but to use the contents of the file itself to provide these headers. This means that you need to make sure the file contains valid headers in the first few lines. A `send-as-is` file might look like:

```
Status: 200
Content-type: text/html

<html>
<head><title>send-as-is</title></head>
<body>
<h2>send-as-is</h2>

The <code>send-as-is</code> handler tells Apache to serve the file as
is, without adding the usual batch of HTTP headers on to it.

</body></html>
```

In order for this to be served as is you would use a directive like the following:

```
AddHandler send-as-is asis
```

This will cause every file with an extension of `.asis` to be served to the client in this manner.

Note that the file must contain a blank line after the HTTP headers to indicate that the headers have ended. Content after the first blank line is assumed to be the body of the document.

This would be used for files you want to set very specific HTTP headers for, as well as for files you don't want the server to add any of its own headers to. Note in the example that even the HTTP `Status:` header needs to be specified. This technique can be used, for example, to turn off caching (with the `NoCache` header), or to set a particular language mapping, without having to turn on content negotiation.

cgi-script

The cgi-script handler tells Apache to treat the file as a program, to execute it, and to send the output of the program to the client.

The following example tells Apache to treat all files with the .pl extension as CGI program.

```
AddHandler cgi-script .pl
```

Note that files that are already contained in a ScriptAlias'ed directory are automatically handled with the cgi-script handler. See Chapter 9, "URL Mapping," for more information.

CGI programming is covered in detail in Chapter 15, "CGI Programs."

imap-file

Almost all image maps are now implemented as client-side HTML image maps, but not very long ago all image maps had to be handled on the server.

Client-Side Image Maps

An image map, in case you don't know, is an image embedded in an HTML page, which is divided up into zones, so that clicking different parts of the image takes you to different URLs. This is usually handled by creating a <map> in your HTML file containing one or more <area> tags, which define the various zones in the image. This might look something like the following:

```
<map name="linkmap">
<area shape="rect" alt="A TAB" coords="12,14,12,14" href="#A" title="A TAB">
<area shape="rect" alt="B TAB" coords="43,5,47,7" href="#B" title="B TAB">
<area shape="rect" alt="C TAB" coords="84,5,118,29" href="#C" title="C TAB">
<area shape="default" nohref>
</map>
```

You would then use this map by linking an image to it:

```
<img src="/images/tab.jpg" USEMAP="#linkmap" border="0">
<br clear=all>
```

Because the image mapping is handled entirely within the browser, there is no need to contact the server to figure out the mapping from the image to the desired URLs.

This is now considered the preferred way to handle image maps because all GUI browsers released in the last two or three years contain the capability to understand these HTML client-side image maps.

14

HANDLERS AND
FILTERS

Server-Side Image Maps

Not so very long ago, however, there was a very real need to provide an alternative for those clients that did not know how to deal with client-side image maps. Widespread support for client-side image maps did not happen until about 1997.

There were a variety of different ways to deal with image maps, including several CGI programs that compared the coordinates of the click with a map file. I first implemented image maps using CGI code by Vivek Khera.

You can read more about the not-so-good old days of server-side image mapping at `http://hoohoo.ncsa.uiuc.edu/docs/tutorials/imagemapping.html`.

In Apache 1.1, however, a handler was introduced that would handle the mapping of image maps without involving CGI programs.

By using the `imap-file` handler, and creating a map file on the server to which an image is hyperlinked, you could implement image maps very easily.

A map file contains one or more lines that follow the general format

```
shape URL coordinates
```

For example,

```
rect http://www.serverop.com/ 10,10 75,112
```

Coordinates are measured from the top-left corner of the image, not relative to the Web page as a whole. When you have created a map file, you would use it by linking the image to it as follows:

```
<A HREF="/maps/imagemap.map">
    <IMG ISMAP SRC="/images/imagemap.gif">
</A>
```

With an appropriate `AddHandler` directive, Apache would know that the `.map` file should be handled as an image map file:

```
AddHandler imap-file .map
```

Because you are unlikely to use server-side image maps, and because this is not a book on HTML, more information is not provided here. If you want to learn more about image maps, client- or server-side read a book on HTML or the Apache documentation on `mod_imap`.

server-info

The `server-info` handler should be configured as a `<Location>` section. It displays detailed information about your server configuration. This handler is provided by the `mod_info` module. If you have this module built into your server you can activate its use as follows:

```
<Location /server-info>
SetHandler server-info
</Location>
```

Note that this is turned on with the SetHandler directive, which tells Apache to use the specified handler for all requests; not just those that match a particular file extension.

Accessing the URL /server-info on your server will give you

- A complete listing of the modules you have compiled into your module.

- The basic server settings, as well as the version number of the server build, and when it was built.

- The directives that each module offers followed by a list of the values each module has been given.

Please note that this information is loaded out of the server configuration file not out of the in-memory copy of the configuration, which was loaded when the server started, or restarted. Therefore, it is possible that the files have been modified since the server was started or restarted and, therefore, this information might be out of sync with the actual configuration in which the server is operating.

It is recommended, for security reasons, that you limit access to this handler to trusted hosts. This can be done by adding the following lines into the above <Location> section:

```
Order deny,allow
Deny from all
Allow from your.host.name
```

server-status

The server-status handler gives you a convenient way to display what the server is doing right now. It is, like the server-info handler, a handler that will be set up in a <Location> section, rather than being associated with a file type:

```
<Location /server-status>
SetHandler server-status
</Location>
```

Note that mod_status must be built into the server for this configuration to have any effect.

Visiting the URL you have created with this Location directive will provide you with a Web page that describes the current status of the server, including how long it has been running, how many children are currently active, and what state each one is in, among other things. If you set the directive ExtendedStatus On then you get more detailed information in the report.

With `ExtendedStatus` turned off, you will receive the following pieces of information. First, you'll see general information about your Apache server build:

```
Apache Server Status for buglet.rcbowen.com

Server Version: Apache/1.3.20 (Unix) mod_perl/1.26
Server Built: Jul 16 2001 21:34:30
```

This will be followed by general "uptime" information about the server. That is, when it was restarted and how long it has been up.

```
Current Time: Friday, 07-Sep-2001 23:02:08 EDT
Restart Time: Friday, 07-Sep-2001 22:56:32 EDT
Parent Server Generation: 1
Server uptime: 5 minutes 36 seconds
```

Following this, you will see a bird's-eye view of how many child processes are running, and what they are doing. A key that explains what each of the various characters means accompanies this. This is called the "scoreboard".

```
6 requests currently being processed, 7 idle servers

_WK_WKK_K___._.................................................
.................................................................
.................................................................
.................................................................

Scoreboard Key:
"_" Waiting for Connection, "S" Starting up, "R" Reading Request,
"W" Sending Reply, "K" Keepalive (read), "D" DNS Lookup,
"L" Logging, "G" Gracefully finishing, "." Open slot with no current process
```

Finally, you'll get an explicit listing of each child process by PID (process ID) and what state each is in.

```
PID Key:

    5742 in state: _ ,   5743 in state: W ,   5744 in state: K
    5745 in state: K ,   5746 in state: _ ,   5747 in state: R
    5748 in state: K ,   5749 in state: K ,   5756 in state: _
    5759 in state: _ ,
```

With ExtendedStatus turned on, you get just about the same information, with one exception. Rather than just getting a listing of PIDs and the state of that child, you get much more detailed information per connection. This information is arranged in an HTML table, divided into the columns shown in Table 14.1.

TABLE 14.1   Field in Server-Status Report

Fieldname	Explanation
Srv	Child Server number—generation
PID	OS process ID
Acc	Number of accesses this connection / this child / this slot
M	Mode of operation
CPU	CPU usage, number of seconds
SS	Seconds since beginning of most recent request
Req	Milliseconds required to process most recent request
Conn	Kilobytes transferred this connection
Child	Megabytes transferred this child
Slot	Total megabytes transferred this slot
Client	The address of the client
VHost	The virtual host from which the content was requested
Request	The actual request

For example, the following table shows typical values that might appear in one row of the table that server-status generates. Next to each value, I've indicated what that value means to you. Note that this data is just one row of a larger table, with one such row for each currently active connection to the server.

TABLE 14.2   Field Provided by Server-Status

Field name	Example value	Explanation
Srv	3-2	The third child process, in the second generation
PID	2520	This particular process is process ID 2520
Acc	10/41/41	10 accesses this connection, 41 total for this child, and 41 total for this slot
M	–	Waiting for connection
CPU	0.18	0.18 CPU seconds were used in processing this request
SS	9	9 Seconds since the beginning of the most recent request
Req	4	4 Milliseconds required to process the most recent request

14

TABLE 14.2 continued

Field name	Example value	Explanation
Conn	0.0	0.0 Kilobytes transferred this connection
Child	0.11	This child process has transferred a total of 0.11 Kilobytes
Slot	0.11	Child processes in this slot have collectively transferred a total of 0.11 Kilobytes
Client	209.152.205.5	Client IP address
VHost	www.apacheadmin.com	Virtual host name
Request		GET /index.html HTTP/1.0 Client requested /index.html with HTTP version 1.0

It is recommended, particularly if you have `ExtendedStatus` turned on, that you restrict access to the URL of this report. Note that it shows exactly what host is accessing your site, and what URL they are looking at. This could be considered an invasion of privacy to allow random Web users to view this sort of information. To restrict access to this handler to just yourself, you would add the following lines into the `<Location>` section in your configuration file:

```
Order deny,allow
Deny from all
Allow from my.host.name.com
```

server-parsed

`server-parsed` documents are documents that might contain SSI (Server-Side Include) directives. Associating them with the `server-parsed` handler causes Apache to parse these documents on their way out of the pipe, looking for these directives, and, if finding them, replacing these directives with the content that they generate.

For more information on SSI, see Chapter 16, "Server-Side Includes."

Please note that although the `server-parsed` handler has been superseded by the `INCLUDES` filter with Apache 2.0, it will in fact still work. Apache just silently replaces `server-parsed` with `INCLUDES` behind the scenes.

type-map

The `type-map` handler and `type-map` files were discussed in Chapter 10, "Content Negotiation." A `type-map` describes the various available representations of a particular resource that are available for content negotiation.

Custom Handlers

In addition to the handlers that are included in a standard installation of Apache, you can implement your own handler quite simply, providing you a way to process files as they are served out to the client.

This can be done, for example, by writing a CGI program to process your file, and creating a handler using the Action directive. In the following example, we'll implement an idea mentioned in the Apache documentation, which suggests that someone might create a handler to add a footer to HTML pages.

You would add these directives to your server configuration file:

```
Action add-footer /cgi-bin/footer.pl
AddHandler add-footer .html
```

The CGI program located at /cgi-bin/footer.pl would look like this:

```
#!/usr/bin/perl

print "Content-type: text/html\n\n";

my $file = $ENV{PATH_TRANSLATED};

open FILE, "<$file";
print while <FILE>;
close FILE;
print qq~

FOOTER GOES HERE
~;
```

This simple CGI program, and the previous directives, will add footer text to every .html file that is served out of your server. Unfortunately, it also means that every .html file that your server sends out requires that a Perl CGI program be run, which might cause a substantial performance hit on your server.

Filters

The concept of filters is added in Apache 2.0. A filter is a process that is applied to content as it is sent to the client or to data as it is received from the client.

The nice thing about filters is that you can chain them. That is, you can apply several filters to content as it is being sent out to the client, and specify the order in which they are applied, as opposed to only applying one handler to a particular resource. This solves a problem that is

14

frequently asked about on the various newsgroups pertaining to the Apache server. The question is "how do I evaluate Server-Side Includes embedded in the output of a CGI program?" The answer has always been "you can't." But with Apache 2.0 filters, now you can, by passing CGI output through the INCLUDES filter.

There are two types of filters that we'll be talking about, but there is very little difference between them, either in concept or in operation. Input filters intercept data coming in from the client—the HTTP request—and modifies it in some way before it reaches the request processing mechanism. Output filters intercept data as it leaves the server and modifies it in some way before it gets sent out to the client.

At the time of this writing, the INCLUDES filter is the only one distributed with Apache 2.0.

Configuration for Filters

Four directives are provided for specifying filters; they are AddInputFilter, SetInputFilter, AddOutputFilter, and SetOutputFilter. Additionally, there are two directives provided by the experimental module mod_ext_filter, which are used to specify external commands or programs to be used as output filters.

AddInputFilter

Like handlers, filters are mostly defined by file extensions. The AddInputFilter directive maps incoming requests to an input filter by the file extension of the requested file.

More than one filter can be specified in the order in which they are to be applied. The syntax of the directive is as follows:

```
AddInputFilterfilter1;filter2;filter3 ext1 ext2
```

filter1, filter2, and filter3 are the names of input filters to be applied to the incoming request, and ext1 and ext2 are file extensions to which the filter is to be applied.

No real example is given here because there are no input filters that ship with Apache 2.0 at this time.

SetInputFilter

Like AddInputFilter, SetInputFilter specifies an input filter that will be applied to requests. Rather than specifying a file extension, SetInputFilter works throughout a scope, such as a <Directory> or <Location> section.

The syntax looks similar to the AddInputFilter syntax, but without the file extensions.

```
SetInputFilterfilter1;filter2;filter3
```

This directive should be set within a section, such as `<Location>`, `<Directory>`, or `<Files>`.

No real example is given here because there are no input filters that ship with Apache 2.0 at this time.

AddOutputFilter

The `AddOutputFilter` directive associates one or more filters with resources with a particular file extension. This causes the filter to be run on the content as it is sent out to the client. Note that you can chain several filters in a row if you want:

```
AddOutputFilterfilter1;filter2;filter3 ext1 ext2
```

At this time, there is only one filter that is shipping with Apache 2.0, and that is the INCLUDES filter, which provides the same functionality as the `server-parsed` handler. This is enabled using the following directive:

```
AddType text/html .shtml
AddOutputFilter INCLUDES .shtml
```

This enables SSI parsing for files with a `.shtml` extension. You can read more about SSI in Chapter 16.

SetOutputFilter

The `SetOutputFilter` directive causes all resources in the scope to be passed through the specified output filter. This directive should be used within a carefully defined scope, as Apache will attempt to run the filter on files within the scope, even it if might not particularly make sense to do so. For example, if you attempt to run the INCLUDES filter on JPEG files, there is a possibility of corrupting those images, as well as the fact that passing binary files through a text filter will cause a substantial performance degradation.

```
AddType text/html .shtml
<FilesMatch "\.shtml(\..+)?$">
 SetOutputFilter INCLUDES
</FilesMatch>
```

Note that more than one output filter can be specified, by providing a list of the filters, separated by semicolons, in the order that you want to have them applied.

INCLUDES Filter

The INCLUDES filter, which ships with Apache 2.0, and is implemented in the module `mod_include`, provides for server-parsed HTML, and the capability to fill in values for various expressions embedded in the HTML. You can read more about SSI (Server-Side Includes) in Chapter 16, which is devoted to this topic.

Summary

Handlers provide a way to provide dynamic content, either by processing a file as it is sent out to the client, or by mapping a `<Location>` to a process for producing dynamic content, which is completely independent of any documents in the document directories. Filters are the Apache 2.0 way to provide this functionality. They have the added benefit that you can chain multiple filters together and have them run in turn on the content as it is sent to the client, or as it is being received from the client.

CGI Programs

IN THIS CHAPTER

It seems to me
As we make our own few circles 'round the sun
We get it backwards
And our seven years go by like one

Dog Years—Test For Echo (1996)—Rush

Since the very early days of the Web it was clear that static documents, as useful as they were, were just not going to cut it with the evolving roles that the Web was filling. The very first technology that was developed to address this limitation was the Common Gateway Interface, or CGI.

The CGI is a standard for communication between any program and a Web server. Ordinarily, this means some program that generates text output (specifically HTML) which is then sent to the client browser.

The CGI enables dynamic content to be generated, making a Web site into less of an electronic brochure, and more of a networked application.

The CGI specification itself is very simple. Basically, it describes a system whereby input from the client (HTML forms or arguments passed following a question mark in the URL) are passed to your program on STDIN (standard input). Your program is then supposed to do something with these and return some variety of content on STDOUT (standard output). This content is preceded by HTTP headers and includes a Content-type header, telling what sort of content is being returned.

The original CGI specification is available on the Web at http://hoohoo.ncsa.uiuc.edu/cgi/interface, and it has not changed much since it was put there in about 1992. But there is an effort to create an actual Internet RFC for the CGI specification, which has never been more than a set of general guidelines. Ken Coar, a member of the Apache Software Foundation, is heading up this effort. You can read more about it at http://cgi-spec.golux.com/.

NOTE

hoohoo.ncsa.uiuc.edu was the server where the NCSA HTTPd project was housed. It is a great resource for historical information about the World Wide Web, as well as a number of foundational documents, such as the CGI specification, some of the initial HTTP specifications, and other information about the HTTPd project, and the Mosaic browser. NCSA—the National Center for Supercomputing Activities, at the University of Illinois at Urbana-Champaign—was the incubator for Netscape, as well as producing the initial code on which Apache was based.

In this chapter, you'll learn how to configure your Apache server to permit CGI execution, and you'll learn how to write a simple CGI program. Finally, we'll talk about some of the limitations of CGI programs, and what you can do about them.

Apache Configuration

Before the rest of this chapter is useful you'll need to know how to tell Apache about your CGI programs, so that it knows to execute them, rather than allowing the user to download the program, which would not be very useful. There are a few different directives for doing this.

mod_cgi is the Apache module that implements the CGI and enables the execution of CGI programs. However, other modules provide most of the directives discussed in this chapter.

Options ExecCGI

The capability to execute CGI programs in a particular location is turned on with the ExecCGI option. This should be set either in a <Directory> section in your main server configuration file, or in an .htaccess file in the particular directory where you want this capability. Note that to use this directive in an .htaccess file, AllowOverride Options must be set for that directory.

For example, if you want to turn on CGI privileges for a particular directory, and you want to do this in your main server configuration file you would do the following:

```
<Directory /usr/local/apache/htdocs/scripts>
Options +ExecCGI
</Directory>
```

This is not sufficient, however, because although you have told Apache that you want to be able to execute CGI programs, you have not yet told it how to identify a CGI program. You need to tell Apache this using the AddHandler or SetHandler directive.

AddHandler cgi-script

As you saw in Chapter 14, "Handlers and Filters," the AddHandler directive associates a particular handler with a particular file extension. By associating the cgi-script handler with a given file extension, you are telling Apache (mod_cgi, to be specific) that the files are to be executed, and their output sent to the client, when that file is requested.

By default, Apache is not aware that any file type is a CGI program, so you have to tell it.

The following example associates the .pl and .cgi file extensions with the cgi-script handler, and therefore tells Apache to execute them. This, associated with the ExecCGI option, makes it possible to run CGI programs:

15

```
<Directory /usr/local/apache/htdocs/scripts>
Options +ExecCGI
AddHandler cgi-script .pl .cgi
</Directory>
```

SetHandler cgi-script

The SetHandler directive defines a particular handler that is to be used for all files that fall into the scope of the directive. Using it instead of an AddHandler directive saves you the trouble of having to name files anything special to get them to execute. Substituting the following configuration for the previous one, you can ensure that all files in the specified directory, regardless of name, are to be treated as CGI programs.

```
<Directory /usr/local/apache/htdocs/scripts>
Options +ExecCGI
SetHandler cgi-script
</Directory>
```

ScriptAlias

Fortunately, because you will always want to specify a directory in which CGI programs will be put, there is a single convenience directive that replaces the configuration in the previous example. This directive, the ScriptAlias directive, defines an Alias to map a particular URL to the specified directory, and also sets the necessary Options and handlers so that all files in that directory will be treated as CGI programs. The syntax of the ScriptAlias directive is as follows:

```
ScriptAlias /cgi-bin/ /usr/local/apache/cgi-bin/
```

The previous two directives (AddHandler and SetHandler) will therefore only be used for CGI programs, in most cases, when you want to execute CGI programs somewhere outside of a ScriptAlias'ed directory, which is not a great idea anyway. For reasons of content management (knowing where everything is) and security (being able to find CGI programs is a very important part of checking them for possible security problems), it is not recommended that you permit the execution of CGI programs outside of ScriptAlias'ed directories.

The Anatomy of a CGI Program

Any functioning CGI program performs the same three basic functions.

First, it retrieves any information passed in to them, if any, from the client. Second, based on that input, or based on some other criteria, it generates some variety of content. Finally, it sends that content, prefaced with the appropriate HTTP headers, back to the client.

Input

Input can come into a CGI program in two ways. Either from the environment—via environment variables—or via `STDIN` (standard input).

Environment Variables

CGI defines a set of environment variables for passing around information, much like your operating system environment variables, such as your path and login name. This information consists of things such as the server name, the username of an authenticated user, and the IP address of the client accessing the server. These environment variables are passed to each CGI program invoked by the server. Some variables are required, which means that a server must supply these variables to be considered CGI-compliant; other variables are optional. And finally, the server itself and the client (Web browser) are both at liberty to make up environment variables and pass these on to the CGI program.

Standard Environment Variables

The variables listed in Table 15.1 will return the same value each time a request is made of the server. The CGI specification calls these non-request-specific variables because they don't vary from one request to another.

TABLE 15.1 NonRequest-Specific Environment Variables

Variable	Meaning
SERVER_SOFTWARE	The name and version number of the Web server software that's answering the HTTP request. Example: Apache/1.3.9 (Win32).
SERVER_NAME	The hostname or IP address of the server. Example: www.mk.net.
GATEWAY_INTERFACE	The version of the CGI specification that's implemented on the server. Example: CGI/1.1.

Other variables will vary from request to request. Table 15.2 lists such variables.

TABLE 15.2 Request-Specific Environment Variables

Variable	Meaning
SERVER_PROTOCOL	The protocol, and version of that protocol, in which the content was sent to the client. Example: HTTP/1.1.
SERVER_PORT	The port number on which the client connected to the server to send the request. Example: 80.
REQUEST_METHOD	The method with which the request was made. This might be any one of GET, POST, PUT, or HEAD.

15

CGI PROGRAMS

TABLE 15.2   continued

Variable	*Meaning*
PATH_INFO	Additional path information can be passed on the end of the URL, following a slash. Example: `http://server/cgi-bin/script.pl/extra/info` has PATH_INFO of `/extra/info`, which is passed to the CGI program. This can be useful for passing additional arguments to CGI programs.
PATH_TRANSLATED	This probably doesn't mean what you expect it to mean. PATH_INFO is appended to SERVER_ROOT to produce a full-file system path. Example: In the example given for PATH_INFO, PATH_TRANSLATED would be `/usr/www/htdocs/extra/info`, if your SERVER_ROOT is set to `/usr/www/htdocs`. A common error is to assume that this variable contains the full path to the CGI program file.
SCRIPT_NAME	The virtual path to the CGI script being executed. Example: `/cgi-bin/script.pl`
QUERY_STRING	Any information appearing following a question mark (?) will be removed from the URL and placed into this variable. This is a good way to pass additional information to the CGI script. This can be used with PATH_INFO or by itself.
REMOTE_ADDR	The IP address of the client accessing the server. Example: `192.101.201.32`
REMOTE_HOST	The hostname of the client accessing the server. If the name can't be resolved, or if that function is turned off on the server, this variable should be left unset, and just the IP address will be put in REMOTE_ADDR. Example: `webslinger.databeam.com`
AUTH_TYPE	If the script is password-protected, this will contain the method of authentication that was used. See Chapter 21, "Authentication and Authorization," for more information. Example: `BASIC`.
REMOTE_USER	If the script is password-protected, this is the username with which the user authenticated.
REMOTE_IDENT	Almost never used, because very few clients pass anything meaningful in this variable. When set, this variable contains various identification information about the remote user, either from RFC931-type identification, or whatever the client chooses to pass in this variable. Browsers used to pass the user's e-mail address in this field until unscrupulous marketing types started harvesting that information to send out spam.
CONTENT_TYPE	If data is being passed with the request, such as with a PUT or POST request, this is the content type of that data. Example: `text/plain`.
CONTENT_LENGTH	The size of any data sent by the client to the server.

Other Environment Variables

In addition to the variables in the previous tables, any HTTP headers sent by the client to the server will be placed into the environment. These can be things such as the HTTP_USER_AGENT (the browser name and version), or any other information that the browser manufacturer wants to put in its headers.

Examples of variables that you are likely to encounter are

Variable	Meaning
HTTP_USER_AGENT	The browser name and version number. Example: `Mozilla/4.72 (X11; U; Linux 2.4.4 i686)`
HTTP_ACCEPT	The MIME types the client is willing to accept. See Chapter 10, "Content Negotiation," for more information. Example: `image/*, audio/wav`

Form Input

Most of the input to your CGI programs will come from HTML forms. HTML forms are a way for you to solicit input from users. Text input fields, select lists, check boxes, and radio buttons are presented for users to make selections and type their input.

HTML forms are created with the HTML `<form>` tag and can consist of the following elements:

Form Tag

A `<form>` tag starts the HTML form, and a `</form>` tag ends the form. The opening tag has the following attributes:

- Action—A URL that tells the browser where to send the form data when the submit button is clicked.

- Method—Either GET or POST. Tells the browser what method to use when sending the data to the server.

- Name (Optional)—Sets a name for the form. Used primarily for JavaScript.

- Target (Optional)—If the form appears on a framed Web page this tells the browser in which frame of the frame set it should display the response from the server.

The following is an example of the `<form>` tag:

```
<form action="/cgi-bin/process.pl" method="POST">
```

Inside the form, the following input fields are available.

Text Input

To get a simple line of input, use the following syntax:

```
<input type="text">
```

This displays a single-line text input field. Attributes are as follows:

- `type="text"`—This attribute is optional because text is the default type when using the `<input>` tag.
- `name`—The name of the input field. This will be sent to your CGI program for association with the value.
- `size` (Optional)—The width, in characters, that the input field should be in the browser window. The default will vary depending on which browser you are using. This number represents either characters or pixels, depending on which browser is displaying the form.
- `maxlength` (Optional)—The maximum number of characters permitted in this field. This is a good attribute to set if you are sending data to a database and need to limit values to a certain size.
- `value` (Optional)—The default value that should appear in the field when the page is loaded.

The following is an example of the text-input tag:

```
<input type="text" name="fname" value="Rich" size="15" maxlength="255">
```

Password Fields

The password-input field is used to get a text field, but not display what is being typed. `<input type="password">` displays a single-line text input field in which all typed text is displayed as asterisks (*) or otherwise obscured. Attributes are identical to those with `type="text"`.

CAUTION

Using `<input type="password">` is purely cosmetic security. The password is still passed over the network in plain text form. Don't use this for any serious security.

Radio Buttons

`<input type="radio">` displays a radio button. These are usually in a set of several and have the "select only one" behavior. Attributes are as follows:

- `name`—The name of the input field. This will be sent to your CGI program for association with the value. To create a set of several radio buttons, just give multiple radio buttons the same name.

- `value`—The value to be passed to your CGI program if this particular button is selected.

- `checked`—The button that will be selected by default.

In the following example, the AM button is selected by default:

```
<input type="radio" name="ampm" value="am" checked>
<input type="radio" name="ampm" value="pm">
```

Checkbox

`<input type="checkbox">` indicates a box that's either checked or not checked. Attributes are as follows:

- `name`—The name of the input field. This will be sent to your CGI program for association with the value.

- `value`—A value that will be passed to your CGI program if this checkbox is checked.

- `checked`—Indicates that the box will be checked by default.

The following is an example of a checkbox:

```
<input type="checkbox" name="paid" value="yes" checked>
```

Select List

A select list specifies a list containing one or more elements from which users can select one or more items. The select list starts with a `<select>` tag, and ends with a `</select>` tag. Items are enclosed in `<option>` tags that appear inside the set of `<select>` tags. Attributes are as follows:

- `name`—The name of the select list. Any items selected will be associated with this name.

- `multiple`—Indicates that more than one item can be selected from the list. If more than one item is selected, multiple name/value pairs are sent to your CGI program, with the same name.

- `size`—A particularly useful attribute if you have a multiple-item select list. It indicates how many items in the list are to be displayed in the select list. By default, only one is shown, in a drop-down list format.

- `<option>`—Defined a single option in a select list. This tag is followed by the text that should appear in the list, and, optionally, might contain a `value` attribute containing the value to be passed back to the server. If no value is set, the string following the `<option>` tag will be passed as the value.

The following is an example of a select list:

```
<select name="month>
<option value="01">January
<option value="02">February
<option value="03">March
<option value="99">etc.
</select>
```

Textarea

A textarea is an input box that can contain multiple lines of text. Text appearing between the `<textarea></textarea>` tags is the default text that will appear in the text area on the page. The attributes are as follows:

- `name`—The name of the input field. This will be sent to your CGI program for association with the value.

- `cols`—How many columns wide the text area should be.

- `rows`—How many rows high the text area should be.

- `wrap`—What wrapping behavior the text area should display. The options are `off` (the default), `virtual`, and `physical`. The latter two options provide different types of text wrapping within the text area. `virtual` wrapping just wraps the text as it appears on the screen, whereas `physical` wrapping inserts linebreak characters into the text as it is passed back to the server.

The following is an example of a text area:

```
<textarea name="bio" rows=3 cols=40 wrap="virtual">
I was born, I lived, and then I died</textarea>
```

Hidden Form Fields

`<input type="hidden">` enables you to pass a form variable that doesn't display on the page as something that users can change.

TIP

As with password fields, hidden fields provide only cosmetic security. You can't rely on the idea that the values will be what you set them to be in hidden fields. A user with a clue can download your page, edit the value of that hidden variable on his local copy, and post it back to your server with the altered values.

The available attributes are as follows:

- `name`—The name of the input field. This will be sent to your CGI program for association with the value.
- `Value`—The value that will be passed with the name.

Submit Buttons

A submit button, when clicked, sends the form contents to the `action` location defined in the `<form>` tag. When users click a submit button, that data is encoded and sent to the server either via a `GET` or `POST` HTTP request (as discussed in the following section). Attributes are as follows:

- `name`—The name of the input field. This will be sent to your CGI program for association with the value.
- `value`—The caption that will appear on the button. By default, this value is `"Submit"`.

For example:

```
<input type="submit" value="Add record">
```

Reset Buttons

A reset button, when clicked, resets the contents of the form to the default values. The attributes are the same as those of the submit button.

```
<input type="reset" value="Start over">
```

GET Requests

Most HTTP requests are `GET` requests. In a `GET` request, there is only one piece of information passed to the server—the resource that is being requested. However, additional information can be passed appended to the end of the URL. If the `action` specified in the `<form>` tag is `GET`, the form information is packaged into a single string and tacked onto the end of the URL, which is then sent to the server in a `GET` request.

Form names and values are URL-encoded, meaning that certain characters—mostly those that aren't alphanumeric—are converted to entities that can be safely passed in a string. Spaces are converted to plus signs (+), and other characters are converted to their ASCII representation in hexadecimal, preceded by a percent sign (%). The names and values are then combined into name-value pairs, with an equal sign (=) between the name and the value. Finally, these pairs are joined together with ampersands (&).

The resulting string is prepended with a question mark (?) and tacked onto the end of the URL specified in the `action` attribute of your `<form>` tag. So, for example, if your `action` attribute specified that the form contents were to be sent to `/cgi-bin/process.pl`, a typical URL generated by a `GET` form might look like the following:

`http://your.server/cgi-bin/process.pl?name=Rich\%20Bowen&occupation=author`

When this request reaches the server, everything after the question mark is placed into the environment variable `QUERY_STRING`, which is passed to the CGI program with the rest of the environment variables.

One main advantage of `GET` forms is that the user can see exactly what arguments are being passed to the CGI program, and can "hack" on these variables, perhaps substituting different values. Although this might seem undesirable, it does enable the user to get directly to the data that they want without having to figure out how to do this in the provided interface. For example, I can enter the following directly into the location field of my browser to do a Google search for the term Apache:

`http://www.google.com/search?q=apache`

By directly changing the string at the end of this URL, you can search for anything you like without having to fill out the search form.

Additionally, it's easy to bookmark the results of `GET` forms because all the information is contained in the URL.

There are also some disadvantages, such as the limits to a URL's length. The `LimitRequestLine` directive sets the maximum length of a URL. By default, it's set to 8190, which gives you a lot of room. However, other servers, and some browsers, limit the length more.

Because all parameters are passed on the URL line, items that were in password or hidden fields will also be displayed in the URL. Of course, neither method should be used for real security measures and should be considered cosmetic security at best.

NOTE

I use the term *cosmetic security* to refer to things that make information one step harder to get to but don't offer any real encryption or security. An example might be writing your ATM card PIN number on your card, but writing it backward. You have somewhat obscured the information from the casual glance, but anyone willing to spend more than five minutes on it would be able to figure it out. However, the person using your ATM card only gets three or four tries, someone trying to get into your Web site can try as many times as they like.

POST Requests

POST forms are handled similarly to GET forms, except that the data itself is sent to the server in the body of the HTTP request, rather than on the request line. It is then passed to the CGI program over STDIN. The length of this data is put into the environment variable CONTENT_LENGTH. You can get this data by reading CONTENT_LENGTH bytes from STDIN.

Because the data is encoded exactly the same way for POST forms as for GET forms, the rest of the decoding process will be exactly the same.

Decoding Form Data

Decoding form data is just a matter of reversing what was done in the form encoding process. Every available CGI-code library contains methods for parsing the form contents. You should not attempt to do this by yourself—not because it is particularly hard to get right, but because other folks have already done it. More importantly, other folks have thought about the possible ways Web users might attempt to circumvent security precautions by sending malicious data to the server, and have put in place safeguards to keep this from happening.

Consequently, you should use one of the many available CGI code libraries (there's one available in your favorite programming language), and use the form parsing routine in there.

For Perl, which is currently the most popular language for writing CGI programs there are a number of available CGI modules. The most popular of these is Lincoln Stein's module CGI.pm, which is part of the standard distribution of Perl. Another excellent module is the CGI_Lite.pm module, which, although it does not contain everything that is included in CGI.pm, contains the functions that you are likely to use on a regular basis.

For C, there are also a number of alternatives. Tom Boutell's cgic library, available at http://www.boutell.com/cgic/, is one such library, and is freely available.

Examples of decoding form data will be shown in the following example programs.

Output

After you have received your input from the user, and done some processing, all that remains is to return useful content to the client.

All content that is output to STDOUT (standard output) will be sent to the browser. What this means in most programming languages is that you just have to print content and it will go to the right place.

There is a prerequisite, however, that you send a Content-type header before you send your content. Because most CGI programs are going to output HTML content, this will usually look like

```
print "Content-type: text/html\n\n";
```

Note that the Content-type header is followed by two newline characters (that's what those slash-n characters are). This creates one blank line, which indicates that the HTTP headers are complete, and that everything following is the body of the response.

Following the header, just print content. Yes, it's really that simple.

What your content is, or how you generate it, is entirely up to your creativity, or whatever else motivates your CGI program. Generating that content is really the only interesting part of this process because it is the only part that requires any creativity.

Example Programs

CGI programming is best taught by example. However, you should be warned that there are a lot of very bad examples that you could learn from. You will find a large number of CGI archives of one description or another that offer a vast array of CGI programs for free download. Most of these are in Perl, and are largely responsible for the Perl's reputation of being unreadable. The fact is, one can write bad code in any language.

I would encourage you, if you plan to write CGI programs, to get a good non-CGI book about the language that you intend to use, and begin your learning there. This will give you a much more solid foundation in the language, and you will avoid the trap of cargo culting large quantities of bad code, and thinking that that's the right way to do things.

The following example is intentionally very simple, so that it illustrates CGI programming, but does not delve deeply into the intricacies of the particular programming language. Perl is the programming language used because (well-written) Perl code is fairly close to English prose, therefore, anyone with a modicum of programming experience should be able to follow it.

Simple CGI program—Perl

What follows is the source code for a Perl CGI program. After the code, I'll explain what you would then do with this program.

The Source

```
1   #!/usr/bin/perl -w
2
3   use CGI;
4   use strict;
5
6   my $cgi = CGI->new;
7   my @params = $cgi->param;
8
```

```
 9   print "Content-type: text/html\n\n";
10
11   print "<html><head><title>Form contents</title></head><body>";
12
13   foreach my $param ( @params ) {
14       print $param . " has a value of "
15           . $cgi->param( $param ) . "<br>";
16   }
17
18   print "</body></html>";
```

An Explanation

The previous code uses the CGI.pm module, which comes with Perl, so that you don't have to install any modules to get this program working. If you have Perl installed, this program should run for you.

It is important to note that the line numbers are not part of the program, but are provided solely for the purpose of referring to particular lines in the program.

Line 1 indicates to Apache where it should look to find the interpreter with which to run this program. If you are at all familiar with shell scripting you will recognize this as common notation for scripts, and Apache has adopted this notation with the same meaning.

Of course, CGI programs can also be binary executable files, same as compiled C programs.

Line 3 loads the CGI.pm module, which contains routines for CGI programming.

Line 4 tells Perl to be strict on syntax checking. In conjunction with the -w in Line 1, which turns on warnings, this will cause Perl to tell you when you are doing things that might cause problems, and to display errors on minor violations of syntactical rules that might otherwise just be allowed to pass. It is a good idea to use strict and -w (use warnings in Perl version 5.6 and later) to keep your code error free.

Line 6 creates a new CGI object, and Line 7 gets the list of form parameters from this object.

Line 8 prints the Content-type header. Line 11 prints the top portion of an HTML document. Note that these are just ordinarily print statements, and that the output is sent to the browser.

The loop in Lines 13-16 traverses the array of parameters that was loaded in Line 7, and for each one, displays the name of the form field followed by the value of that parameter, retrieved from the CGI object via the param function.

Finally, Line 18 closes the HTML document, and ends the program.

Getting It Working

To get this CGI program working, simply save the listed text in a file, and call this file `test.pl`. Put this file in the `cgi-bin` subdirectory of where you installed Apache. This is probably `/usr/local/apache/cgi-bin`.

Make sure that the file permissions permit execution by the user `nobody`, or whichever user you have configured the server to run as. This will usually be accomplished by typing the command:

```
chmod a+x test.pl
```

You should now be able to access your CGI program in one of three ways.

First, you should be able to load it directly in a browser, by typing the URL `http://servername/cgi-bin/test.pl`. This will load a blank page, but you should see the text `Form contents` in the title bar as the page title.

Second, you can provide arguments directly to it on the URL, by typing the URL `http://servername/cgi-bin/test.pl?this=is&an=argument`. You should now see text that reads:

```
this has a value of is
an has a value of argument
```

Third, you should be able to create an HTML form containing one or more input fields, and direct this form at your program by putting in the `<form>` tag the attribute `action="/cgi-bin/test.pl"`. The contents of your form will be displayed in name/value pairs on the generated HTML page.

CGI Programs on Microsoft Windows

Under Windows, the `ScriptInterpreterSource` directive tells Apache whether it should determine how to execute a CGI program from the program itself or search the Registry for a mapping between the file extension and some executable. For example, you might have a mapping in the Registry between a `.pl` file extension and the program `\perl\bin\perl.exe`. The syntax of the directive is

```
ScriptInterpreterSource [registry|script]
```

and the default value is

```
ScriptInterpreterSource script
```

If you have `ScriptInterpreterSource` set to script (or if it doesn't appear in your configuration file at all), the location of the Perl executable (or other script interpreter) should be indicated in the first line of the program code, preceded with `#!`:

```
#!/perl/bin/perl
```

You can use forward slashes or backslashes, and you only have to specify the drive letter if it's other than the drive on which `ServerRoot` is located.

Troubleshooting Common Problems

When your CGI program doesn't work, you should check several things first.

First, always check the error logs. They will very likely contain useful information that will tell you exactly what went wrong. If that doesn't work check the following.

Permissions

After you put your CGI program in the correct location, you need to make sure that the file has the correct permissions. Remember that the server runs as some user which, hopefully, has very limited permissions on your server.

Because the owner of the CGI program and the user who runs the program aren't the same user; the user as whom the server runs might not have permission to run the CGI programs that you have put on your server. A common symptom of this problem is that users can run the CGI program from the command line, but when they try to run it from a browser, they get an error message.

The simplest way to make sure that the server can execute your CGI programs is to change the permissions on the file so that anyone can execute it. You do this with the Unix `chmod` command:

```
chmod a+x example.pl
```

Note that this discussion of file permissions and ownership is aimed at Unix users. File permissions and ownership are handled rather differently on Windows, and so this usually isn't a problem for Windows users.

Make sure that any file that you are trying to open for reading or writing also has permissions on it so that the server can access them. You can use `chmod` to give the server permission to read from and/or write to your file. If possible, it's sometimes a better idea to change the ownership of the file to the server user, and then just enable that user to have access to the file. This prevents other users on the same system from tinkering with the file.

Syntax Errors

Make sure that your CGI program runs from the command line before you try to run it from a browser. By doing so, you can see whether a lot of cryptic error messages about misconfigurations and internal errors result, and then you can fix any problems. If the program doesn't run from the command line, it probably won't run from a browser unless it specifically relies on some CGI environment variables.

Invalid Headers

Make sure that you've outputted the necessary HTTP headers and included that blank line after the last header. Without this line, the server thinks that the rest of your output is just a continuation of the headers.

Asking a Newsgroup for Help

If you don't know what else to check and still can't get it working, consider posting your question to a Usenet newsgroup or a mailing list. If you are planning to do this, make life a little easier for the folks who are being generous enough to read your questions and suggest solutions. By following these simple recommendations, you can avoid getting flamed and increase your chance of a useful answer:

1. Check the FAQ and the list archives first.
2. Mention what server software and version you are running.
3. Mention the language that your code is written in and, if applicable, the version number of that language.
4. Include the source code of the program that's failing, if at all possible.
5. Include any error messages that appear in the browser window, in the error log, or at the command line when you run the program.

One main Usenet newsgroup, `comp.infosystems.www.authoring.cgi`, is dedicated to CGI programming, and this is where you should post any questions that you might have.

Limitations of CGI

CGI is slow. This is simply a consequence of the mechanism. When a CGI program is requested by a Web client, the CGI program is loaded from the disk, compiled and run, and the output is sent back to the Web server. This is inefficient and time consuming. This startup period usually also includes the startup of the script interpreter, such as Perl, Python, or some other very heavy table.

You can optimize your CGI program all you want, and the bottleneck will still almost certainly be the CGI program itself, not your program code. 75–90% of the time spent executing a CGI program is actually spent on things other than executing the program. So, you will get a little performance enhancement by writing your program in C rather than in Perl, for example, but this will be dwarfed by the startup time, and the end-user will not actually perceive any difference.

A variety of other technologies are available to avoid this limitation, and the next two chapters will discuss two of these alternatives—mod_perl and PHP. There are, of course, many others, including FastCGI, ColdFusion, and Active Server Pages. This book has attempted to cover the technologies in the widest use on Apache servers, but this in no way is intended to indicate that these are the only options. You are encouraged to research the alternatives and choose the one that most closely matches your skills and needs.

Summary

CGI is by far the most common way of generating dynamic content on your Web site. This is because it is simple and can be written in any language. Development is therefore fast and a project can go from concept to functioning code in a short period of time.

This is offset by CGI's slowness and the overwhelming tendency to write sloppy code when given the opportunity to roll something out quickly.

Make sure you give adequate consideration to alternate technologies when choosing a technique for generating your dynamic content.

Server-Side Includes

IN THIS CHAPTER

Don't clarify things I already understand. It only confuses me.

Mary Cook

Server-side includes (SSI) are directives written directly into HTML pages that the server parses when the page is served to the browser. Rather than pass the page directly to the requesting client, the server opens and reads through the document, looking for SSI directives. If it encounters one, it replaces it with whatever content is produced by that directive.

SSI would be the right choice if, for example, you have an existing HTML page that needs a small amount of dynamically generated text inserted. SSI changes things such as the day's date, or when the document was last updated, and you don't have to change the document every day, or remember to update a date every time you make a change to the document.

In this chapter, you will learn how to enable SSI on your server and how to use the various directives available to you. You'll learn how to use server-side includes to add a small amount of dynamic information to an otherwise static HTML page.

You can accomplish various things with SSI directives: External text files can be included, CGI programs can be called, and environment variables can be accessed. And a simple, flow-control (if/else) structure is even available in Apache Version 1.2, so you can display content based on simple conditions.

The SSI directives are defined in the `mod_include` module, which is part of the standard batch of modules installed with Apache. Much of this functionality was already in the NCSA code when the Apache project began. Some of it, such as the flow-control portions, was added later.

The choice of when to use SSI and when to use CGI programs should be considered carefully, particularly for heavily loaded Web sites, because there are performance considerations either way. You might want to do some actual benchmark testing to see what your best approach is.

The decision whether to use SSI or CGI to accomplish a particular task isn't always clear-cut. Generally, you use CGI when the page is more dynamic rather than static and SSI if there's more static than dynamic.

Configuration for SSI

The default Apache configuration files don't enable SSI for any files. There are a variety of reasons for this ranging from security to performance. There are a number or reasons for *not* using SSI, and these will be discussed later in this chapter. Make sure that you enable SSI only for those portions of your site for which it is actually necessary.

The following sections show three ways to enable a particular document to be parsed for SSI directives. Whichever option you choose you must also enable the `Includes` option with the `Options` directive:

```
Options Includes
```

This might be set in the main server configuration file or an .htaccess file and can be config-ured for your whole server, a directory, or for a virtual host.

Enabling SSI by File Extension

The most common way to enable SSI processing is to indicate that all files with a certain file-name extension (typically .shtml) are to be parsed by the server at the time they are served. This is done with the AddHandler directive, as we discussed in Chapter 14, "Handlers and Filters."

In the configuration file httpd.conf you will find the following lines, if you are running Apache 1.3:

```
# To use server-parsed HTML files
#
#AddType text/html .shtml
#AddHandler server-parsed .shtml
```

Or, if you are running Apache 2.0, you'll find lines that look more like this:

```
# To use server-parsed HTML files
#
#<FilesMatch "\.shtml(\..+)?$">
#    SetOutputFilter INCLUDES
#</FilesMatch>
```

To enable all .shtml files for server-side parsing, simply uncomment those lines. For Apache 1.3, they should look like this:

```
# To use server-parsed HTML files
AddType text/html .shtml
AddHandler server-parsed .shtml
```

The AddType directive tells the server that all files with the file extension .shtml are to be served with a MIME type of text/html. The AddHandler line tells the server to enable the han-dler server-parsed for those same files. The server-parsed handler is also provided by mod_include module, and tells the server to parse these files for SSI directives.

For Apache 2.0, you should have

```
# To use server-parsed HTML files
#
<FilesMatch "\.shtml(\..+)?$">
    SetOutputFilter INCLUDES
</FilesMatch>
```

Note the directive that comes with Apache 2.0 makes an allowance for files with multiple extensions. By using the `FilesMatch` directive, this directive not only applies to files with a `.shtml` extension, but also to those with, for example, a `.shtml.en` extension.

There are two reasons not to use this approach of enabling SSI. First, you might need to change the name of all your files. Secondly, it's generally considered a bad idea to expose the mechanism that is working behind the scenes.

Changing Filenames

If you want to add SSI capability to an existing site, you would have to change the names of all files to which you wanted to add SSI directives and, consequently, change all links in other pages that referred to these pages. This is clearly a huge hassle. Additionally, you don't necessarily control all the pages that have links to your Web site, because they might be on other sites.

Some folks have addressed this hassle by simply SSI-enabling all files with the extension `.html`, in addition to `.shtml` files. This isn't recommended, but would be accomplished with the additional directive:

```
AddHandler server-parsed .html
```

The reason this is not a recommended solution is because this means that every HTML file served by a server in this configuration would have to be parsed for SSI directives. This slows down the process of serving content greatly because rather than just sending the file to the client Apache now has to examine every line of that file on its way out.

Don't Expose the Mechanism

A second reason not to enable SSI parsing on files by extension is one of philosophy rather than one of technology. In building a Web site, you should think of your user. One aspect of this is making URLs "guessable." If users are looking for some specific information on your site, they should be able to guess at a URL and get to the information they're looking for. If you have `.shtml` filenames (or something equally nonintuitive, such as `.asp`), it makes it less likely that users will correctly guess a URL containing the information they came for.

More importantly, exposing the mechanism by way of the filename—that is, using `.asp` or `.jsp` filenames, for example, locks you into that technology. If, at some later date you want to change from using ASP to using PHP you would need to once again change the names of all your files and break any links and bookmarks to your site. By using names with no particular mechanism associated with them, there is no need to make this kind of change later.

Using the XBitHack Directive

Fortunately, the XVitHack directive offers an alternative to these problems.

Although the name XBitHack seems to imply that this is a hack, and thus somewhat less desirable than other techniques, this is a widespread method for enabling SSI in files. The XBitHack directive enables server-side parsing for all documents on which the user-execute bit is set.

This feature is not available for Windows, because Windows NT doesn't have the concept of marking a file executable.

The XBitHack directive can appear in the server configuration file (httpd.conf) or an .htaccess file, and can be configured for the entire server, a directory, or a virtual host. The directive can be given one of three possible values:

- on—All files with the user-execute bit set are parsed for server-side includes, regardless of file extension.
- off (Default)—Executable files aren't treated specially. Use this to turn off the directive for a subdirectory where it's undesirable. Remember that directives specified for a directory also apply to all subdirectories.
- full—The same as on, except that the group-execute bit is also checked. If it's set, the Last-modified date is set to the last-modified time stamp on the file itself. If the group-execute bit isn't set, no Last-modified date is sent to the client, which allows the page to be cached on the client end or by a proxy server.

For Example:

```
XBitHack on
```

Using XBitHack has two main advantages:

- You don't need to rename a file and change all links to it simply because you want to add a little dynamic content.
- Users looking at your Web content can't tell by looking at the filename that you are generating a page dynamically, so your wizardry is just that tiny bit more impressive. More importantly, the filename is easy to guess at, so a user can jump directly to the portion of your site that they are interested in.

Using SSI Directives

SSI directives look rather like HTML-comment tags. This is nice if you happen to have SSI directives in a page, but have SSI parsing turned off because these directives then don't display in the browser.

The syntax of SSI directives is the following:

```
<!—#element attribute=value attribute=value ... —>
```

The element can be any one of `config`, `echo`, `exec`, `fsize`, `flastmod`, `include`, `printenv`, `set`, `if`, `elif`, `else`, or `endif`.

config

The `config` element enables you to set various configuration options regarding how the document parsing is handled. Because the page is parsed from top to bottom, `config` directives should appear at the top of the HTML document, or at least before they are referred to. You can change a configuration option several times in a page, and it will apply to the portion of the following page, until the next time it is changed.

There are three configuration variables that can be modified with the `config` element.

errmsg

`config errmsg` sets the error message that is returned to the client if something goes wrong while parsing the document. This is usually [an error occurred while processing this directive], but can be set to anything with this directive. For example, you can place the following in your HTML document:

```
<!—#config errmsg="[It's broken]" —>
<!—#directive ssi="Invalid command" —>
```

Because the second directive is not valid the error configured in the `config` directive will be displayed in the location where the output from the directive should have been put, if it were a valid directive.

sizefmt

`config sizefmt` sets the format used to display file sizes. You can set the value to `bytes` to display the exact file size in bytes, or `abbrev` to display the size in kilobytes or megabytes. In the first of the two following examples, file sizes will be displayed as the exact number of bytes in the file, whereas in the second example, it will be rounded off to the nearest kilobyte or megabyte.

```
<!—#config sizefmt="bytes" —>
<!—#config sizefmt="abbrev" —>
```

See the `fsize` element for further examples of what this does.

timefmt

`config timefmt` sets the format used to display times and dates. The format of the value is the same as is used in the `strftime` function used by C (and Perl) to display dates, as detailed in Table 16.1:

TABLE 16.1   Date Formats

Template	Meaning	Range
%A	Weekday name	'Sunday'–'Saturday'
%a	Abbreviated weekday name	'Sun'–'Sat'
%d	day of the month (leading zero)	01–31
%e	day of the month (leading space)	` '1'..–'31'
%B	month name	'January'–'December'
%b	Abbreviated month name	'Jan'–'Dec'
%m	month as a decimal number	01–12
%Y	year with century	1970–2038
%C	Century number	00–99
%y	year without century	00–99

TABLE 16.2   Time Formats

Template	Meaning	Range
%H	Hour (24-hour clock)	00–23
%I	Hour (12-hour clock)	01–12
%M	Minute	00–59
%S	Second	00–61
%Z	Time zone name	"EST", "EDT", "GMT", and so on.
%p	locale's equivalent of either	'AM' or 'PM'

TABLE 16.3   Shortcut Date and Time Formats

Template	Meaning	Range
%r	The time in AM/PM notation	%I:%M:%S %p
%R	The time in 24-hour notation	%H:%M
%T	The time with seconds in 24-hour notation	%H:%M:%S
%D	the date	%m/%d/%y

TABLE 16.4   Locale-Dependent Representations

Template	Meaning
%x	locale's appropriate date representation
%X	locale's appropriate time representation
%c	locale's appropriate date and time representation

> **NOTE**
>
> The locale is the combination of such things as the language, country, timezone, and other things relating to the location of the server which affect, among other things, how date and time information are displayed. Other locale-dependent things are language, character set, and currency, for example.

TABLE 16.5   Other

Template	Meaning	Range
%j	day of the year	(001–366)
%w	weekday as a decimal number	0–6, where 0=Sun,6=Sat
%u	weekday as a decimal number	1–7, where 1=Mon,7=Sun
%U	Week number	counting with the first Sunday as the first day of the first week
%V	Week number	counting with the first Monday as the first day of the first week
%t	the tab character	
%n	the newline character	
%%	the percent symbol (%) character	

For example, you can place the following text directly into your HTML document:

```
<!—#config timefmt="%B %e, %Y" —>
```

See the following `flastmod` element for an example of this in action.

echo

The `echo` element will display the value of any variable. The variable can be any one of the variables displayed in Table 16.6, any environment variable, or variables that you define yourself with the set element, which we will see shortly. Times are displayed in the time format specified by timefmt, and file sizes are displayed in the format specified by sizefmt. The variable to be displayed is indicated with the var attribute.

TABLE 16.6 Built-In Variables

Variable	Definition
DATE_GMT	The current date in Greenwich Mean Time.
DATE_LOCAL	The current date in the local time zone.
DOCUMENT_NAME	The filename (excluding directories) of the document.
DOCUMENT_URI	The (%-decoded) URL path of the document.
LAST_MODIFIED	The date and time on which this file was last modified.

For example:

```
<!—#config timefmt="%B %e, %Y" —>
Today's date is <!—#echo var="DATE_LOCAL" —>.
```

exec

The exec element executes a shell command or a CGI program depending on the parameters provided. Valid attributes are cgi and cmd.

cgi specifies the URL of a CGI program to be executed:

```
<!—#exec cgi="/cgi-bin/unread_articles.pl" —>
```

The URL needs to be a local CGI, not one located on another machine. The CGI program is passed the QUERY_STRING and PATH_INFO that were originally passed to the requested document (see Chapter 15, "CGI Programs," for an explanation of these terms) so the URL specified can't contain this information. It is recommended that you use the include virtual syntax, rather than using exec cgi.

cmd specifies a shell command to be executed. The results will be displayed on the HTML page. Example:

```
<!—#exec cmd="/usr/bin/ls -la /tmp" —>
```

In your configuration files (or in .htaccess) you can specify Options IncludesNOEXEC to disallow the exec directive because this is the most insecure of the SSI directives. Be especially cautious when Web users can create content (such as in a guest book or discussion forum) and these options are enabled! Users could potentially include SSI directives containing arbitrary commands that would be executed the next time the page was loaded.

fsize

The `fsize` element displays the size of a file, which is specified by either the `file` or `virtual` attribute. Size is displayed as specified with `config sizefmt`.

Using the `file` attribute specifies the file system path to a file, either relative to the root if the value starts with `/`, or relative to the current directory if not.

Using the `virtual` attribute specifies the relative URL path to a file. That is, it specifies the file path relative to the document root, if the value starts with `/`, or relative to the current directory if not.

For example:

```
<!—#config sizefmt="bytes" —>
/etc/passwd is <!—#fsize file="/etc/passwd" —> bytes.
```

flastmod

The `flastmod` element displays the last modified date of a file. The desired file is specified in the same manner as with the `fsize` directive. That is, you can specify the location of the file with either the `file` or `virtual` attribute. See the explanations of these attributes in the details of the `fsize` element.

In the following example, the directive shown will display the time and date when I last received e-mail:

```
<!—#config timefmt="%r" —>
You last received email at
<!—#flastmod file="/var/spool/mail/rbowen" —>.
```

NOTE

On Unix systems, the `/var/spool/mail` directory contains the mail files for each user.

Although this can be used for any file on the system, it is most frequently used to display the date the particular document you are looking at was last modified. When used this way, it is equivalent to using the following:

```
File was last modified <!—#echo var="LAST_MODIFIED" —>
```

include

The `include` element includes the contents of the specified file or URL into the HTML document. The file is specified with the `file` and `virtual` attributes, as described with `fsize` and `flastmod`. If the URI specified by the `virtual` attribute is a CGI program, and `IncludesNOEXEC` isn't set, the program will be executed and the results displayed. This is the preferred method of including the results of a CGI program, rather than using `exec cgi`, because you can pass a `QUERY_STRING` argument to the CGI program, for example.

```
<!—#include file="/etc/aliases" —>

<!—#include virtual="/cgi-bin/login.cgi?user=bob" —>
<!—#include virtual="/themes/header.html" —>
```

printenv

The `printenv` element is primarily useful for testing. It displays all defined environment variables.

```
<pre>
<!—#printenv —>
</pre>
```

The directive should be enclosed on HTML preformat tags because the output is in plain text, not in HTML.

Listing 16.1 is the output when the previous directive was put in an HTML page on my server.

LISTING 16.1   Output from the `printenv` Directive

```
DOCUMENT_ROOT=/usr/local/apache/htdocs
HTTP_ACCEPT=image/gif, image/x-xbitmap, image/jpeg, image/pjpeg, image/png, */*
HTTP_ACCEPT_CHARSET=iso-8859-1,*,utf-8
HTTP_ACCEPT_ENCODING=gzip
HTTP_ACCEPT_LANGUAGE=en
HTTP_CONNECTION=Keep-Alive
HTTP_HOST=rhiannon.rcbowen.com
HTTP_IF_MODIFIED_SINCE=Sun, 30 Sep 2001 01:23:49 GMT; length=1190
HTTP_PRAGMA=no-cache
HTTP_USER_AGENT=Mozilla/4.72 [en] (X11; U; Linux 2.4.4 i686)
PATH=/usr/local/sbin:/usr/local/bin:/sbin:/usr/sbin:/bin:/usr/bin
REMOTE_ADDR=127.0.0.1
REMOTE_PORT=39082
SCRIPT_FILENAME=/usr/local/apache/htdocs/testing.html
SERVER_ADDR=127.0.0.1
SERVER_ADMIN=rbowen@rhiannon.rcbowen.com
```

LISTING 16.1   continued

```
SERVER_NAME=localhost
SERVER_PORT=80
SERVER_SIGNATURE=<ADDRESS>Apache/1.3.20 Server at localhost Port 80</ADDRESS>

SERVER_SOFTWARE=Apache/1.3.20 (Unix) mod_perl/1.26
GATEWAY_INTERFACE=CGI/1.1
SERVER_PROTOCOL=HTTP/1.0
REQUEST_METHOD=GET
QUERY_STRING=
REQUEST_URI=/testing.html
SCRIPT_NAME=/testing.html
DATE_LOCAL=Saturday, 29-Sep-2001 21:38:44 EDT
DATE_GMT=Sunday, 30-Sep-2001 01:38:44 GMT
LAST_MODIFIED=Saturday, 29-Sep-2001 21:37:17 EDT
DOCUMENT_URI=/testing.html
DOCUMENT_PATH_INFO=
USER_NAME=nobody
DOCUMENT_NAME=testing.html
```

Variables and Flow Control with SSI

The directives described so far enable you to display existing values. Although this is very useful, sometimes you want to define your own variables and do some limited scripting on an HTML page. Various other products offer server-side scripting embedded in HTML pages, and this shouldn't be thought of as rivaling those because it's very limited. However, it does enable you to do some simple functions without resorting to a third-party product.

The two aspects to this programming are variables and conditional statements. Variables are provided with the set directive and conditionals with an if/else flow control statement.

The set directive sets the value of a variable. Attributes are var and value. For example:

```
<!—#set var="animal" value="cow" —>
```

This example defines a variable called animal, and gives it the value of "cow".

When referenced in other SSI directives, the variable will be distinguished from plain text with the $ character. In this case, $animal can be used in place of any text in any SSI directive.

Within an echo directive, the var value is understood to be a variable, and the $ isn't required.

In a larger string, where the variable might run up against other text, curly brackets ({}) are used to delimit the variable from the rest of the string:

```
<!—#set var="basepath" value="/home/rbowen/public_html" —>

Basepath = <!—#echo var="basepath" —><br>

index.html was last modified
<!—#flastmod file="${basepath}/index.html" —><br>
<!—#config sizefmt="bytes" —>
test.html is <!—#fsize file="${basepath}/test.html" —> bytes<p>
```

Variables can be used, as in the preceding example, to define a string that will be used later in several other directives. This is useful for one-location configuration changes; it also saves you a lot of unnecessary typing.

By using the variables set with the set directive along with the various environment and include variables, you can use a limited flow-control syntax to generate a certain amount of dynamic content on server-parsed pages.

Conditional flow-control is implemented with the directives if, elif, else and endif.

The syntax of these conditional functions is as follows:

```
<!—#if expr="test_condition" —>

<!—#elif expr="test_condition" —>

<!—#else —>

<!—#endif —>
```

The test condition can be a string, which is considered true if non-empty, or various comparisons of two strings. Available comparison operators are =, !=, <, <=, >, and >=. If the second string has the format /string/, the strings are compared with regular expressions. Multiple comparisons can be strung together with && (AND) and || (OR). Any text appearing between the if/elif/else directives will be displayed on the resulting page. An example of such a flow structure follows:

```
<!—#set var="agent" value="$HTTP_USER_AGENT" —>

<!—#if expr="$agent = /Mozilla/" —>

Mozilla!

<!—#elif expr="$agent= /MSIE/" —>

Internet Explorer

<!—#else —>
```

```
Something else!
<!—#endif —>
```

This code will display `Mozilla!` if you are using a browser that passes Mozilla as part of its `USER_AGENT` string, and `Something else!`, otherwise.

Security Considerations

The security considerations involved in using server-side includes have been mentioned throughout the chapter, and are just summarized here.

Whenever possible, use the `IncludesNoEXEC` argument to `Options`, rather than using `Includes`, so that arbitrary commands cannot be executed from within Web pages.

Make sure that `Includes` is not turned on if there is any chance that Web users might be able to create content that is part of an HTML document, such as with a guest-book application, or a discussion forum of some variety. This could potentially enable them to execute arbitrary commands on the server.

If you have `AllowOverride Options` turned on you should be aware that the user can then put `Options +Includes` in their `.htacess`. Before you turn on any of the `AllowOverride` options you should consider all the various ways in which that freedom might be used.

Summary

Server-side includes were extremely popular in the early days of the World Wide Web for things such as hit counters and cute little messages that told you what time it was and where you were visiting from. Fortunately, the appeal has worn off, although you still see them on some beginner sites. However, SSI can still be used for some genuinely useful things, particularly now that the `if`/`elsif`/`else` flow-control directives are available. They provide for dynamic content that can be calculated at runtime without having to fork off an entirely new CGI process.

This chapter covered configuring your server to permit SSI and went through the available SSI directives and their uses.

There's a good article about SSI on the Apache Week Web site at `http://www.apacheweek.com/features/ssi`, which covers most of the same material but offers different examples.

mod_perl

IN THIS CHAPTER

"These then, were the mountains, which the Lutherans believe they can remove with their faith. I greatly doubt it."

The Monk and the Hangman's Daughter—Ambrose Bierce

As we discussed in the Chapter 15, "CGI Programs," CGI has a lot of problems. Primarily, it boils down to one thing—it's slow. mod_perl addresses most of the problems that cause slowness in CGI programs. There are some tradeoffs, but most of them are acceptable, given the benefits.

What Is mod_perl?

mod_perl is an Apache module that embeds a Perl interpreter into the Apache process. This enables you to do a number of rather cool things. Perhaps most importantly, it gives you access to the entire Apache API from within Perl.

First, it enables you to run CGI programs written in Perl without having to launch the Perl interpreter. Because launching the program is the primary cause for slowness in most CGI programs, this results in a speed improvement of as much as 3000% for unmodified CGI programs.

Secondly, because the Perl interpreter is inside the Apache process, you can have persistence of state within the Perl interpreter. This means that your code can compile once, and never have to be compiled again. Perl is, contrary to common belief, a compiled language. It just compiles immediately before runtime, rather than compiling once and being stored as a binary file for later execution.

When Perl programs are executed under mod_perl, the program is cached in its compiled state so the next time the program is invoked, the compiled form of the program is already in memory, and just has to be executed. Because the compilation of your CGI program is the other major place where time is spent in CGI execution, you can see that this is another source of speedup.

Thirdly, and most importantly, mod_perl enables you to write Apache modules in Perl. Writing Apache modules might seem like a rather daunting task to the Apache beginner, and mod_perl makes this functionality available to anyone who knows a little Perl. (Of course, it has to be *good* Perl. More details later).

How Does It Work?

This will be something of an oversimplification because it is not necessary that the full details of mod_perl be explained for the purposes of an Apache administrator. But some points made in this chapter will make more sense if you understand something about the way mod_perl works.

mod_perl embeds a Perl interpreter in the main parent Apache process. Each Apache child then contains its own memory space that is used in conjunction with the Perl interpreter to execute Perl code. This means that data (and code) that is in the main Perl interpreter can be used by all the child processes. However, data that is only in one child process is not accessible to the others.

Installation

Installing mod_perl is simple in most cases, if you are not installing Apache with an unusual assortment of modules. If you are only going to be using modules that come with the default distribution of Apache, you should be able to follow this procedure.

The "Simple" Form

First, download the latest Apache distribution, and the latest mod_perl distribution. You will find these at http://httpd.apache.org/ and http://perl.apache.org/, respectively.

Unpack these distributions somewhere convenient. /usr/src is a recommended location, so that you'll know where all your installed packages live.

Change into the mod_perl directory, and type something like the following:

```
perl Makefile.PL \
APACHE_PREFIX=/usr/local/apache \
APACHE_SRC=../apache-1.3.20/src \
DO_HTTPD=1 \
USE_APACI=1 \
EVERYTHING=1 \
APACI_ARGS='—enable-module=rewrite,—enable-module=speling'
```

Note that those backslashes at the end of each line are continuation characters. That means that you can either type them, if you like, or just type the entire command as one single line.

After this has finished doing things, you should then type:

```
make && make install
```

The Gory Details

To back up a little, here's a blow-by-blow of what that long command line did.

The first line, perl Makefile.PL, is the command that starts the process that builds and installs mod_perl and Apache on your server. Perl comes with a set of utilities that assist in the generation of makefiles, which are scripts that automate a build process. Makefile.PL is a Perl program that generates a makefile.

When running `Makefile.PL`, a number of arguments can be passed in, which affect the behavior of the build.

The first such argument is `APACHE_PREFIX`, which is the location Apache is to be installed. This is the equivalent to the `-prefix` argument that we used when building Apache earlier in the book.

`APACHE_SRC` gives the location of the Apache source code, which you have presumably unpacked in the same directory where you unpacked the `mod_perl` code. In the given example, we are building with Apache version 1.3.20, and so the source code for Apache is in the directory `../apache-1.3.20/src` relative to the current location.

The `DO_HTTPD` argument tells `mod_perl` to build and install Apache when it builds itself. By default, it will just build the `mod_perl` portion, but not rebuild Apache.

`USE_APACI` causes the build process to use `APACI` to configure and build Apache. This was discussed in Chapter 2, "Acquiring and Installing Your Apache Server," and is the Apache autoconf tool.

`EVERYTHING=1` tells `mod_perl` to build and install everything that came with it, including all the Perl modules and support programs.

Finally, perhaps the most important part of the command, the `APACI_ARGS` argument lists the arguments that we want passed on to `APACI` to build Apache. This is where you put all the arguments that you would have passed to `./configure` if you were building Apache without `mod_perl`. In my example, I have added the modules `mod_rewrite` and `mod_speling` by using the `-enable-module` argument, which is passed directly to the Apache configuration.

Typing `make && make install` compiles the `mod_perl` and Apache source code into binary form, and installs it in all the correct locations, as we discussed in Chapter 2.

Start It Up!

After you have typed the previous commands, you can restart your Apache server with the `apachectl` utility. Using this procedure, you can have a new Apache installation in place in just a few minutes. If you already have Apache installed and configured, the build and installation process will preserve your existing configuration files, and just install the various binaries over the ones that are already there. Consequently, unless you are *removing* modules that you had installed before, you should be able to install a new Apache and continue using your existing configuration files with no ill effects.

Configuration

You won't be configuring mod_perl in the same manner that you have configured other modules that we have talked about. mod_perl provides some additional functionality, as well as a plethora of configuration directives, but we will be using them in slightly different ways than you are used to. Additionally, we'll be putting actual Perl code into configuration, which might strike you as rather odd the first time through. You should bear in mind that mod_perl is not a traditional module, but an interface between Apache and Perl.

Consequently, most of the configuration information that I'll be giving is in the specific context of particular examples.

PerlRequire

The PerlRequire directive specifies the location of a Perl script that is to be run when the server starts up. Because the Perl interpreter is in the main Apache parent process, and any Perl code that is cached in that parent process is available to all child processes, Perl code executed at server start time is always available to the child processes.

So, any code that is run by the server at run time will be cached in the parent process, and available to the children.

PerlRequire should be used to load modules or constants that will be used by all the child processes. This will save memory because it is loaded into memory only once for the parent process, rather than having one copy in memory for each child process.

For example, in your main server configuration, you might have the following:

```
PerlRequire /usr/local/apache/vhosts/clueful/conf/preload.pl
```

Then, in the file preload.pl you would have the following:

```
use Apache::DBI;
use DBI;
use CGI qw(:Standard);
use MyCompany::Utils;
1;
```

Any child process that tries to load DBI will get it from the parent Apache process, rather than having to load it from a disk each time.

Note that the file loaded by PerlRequire needs to return a true value to tell Perl that it was successfully loaded. This is accomplished by putting a 1; as the last statement of the file. This is a no-op, but returns a true value.

Actually, DBI is a special case. mod_perl comes with a special-purpose module called Apache::DBI, which is a wrap-around DBI and provides persistent database connections. The first time you make a connection to a database, Apache::DBI intercepts calls to DBI and caches that connection so that all future database connections are made through the connection that is already open. This results in yet another enormous performance improvement, as you never have to wait for a database connection except for the first time. You will still make your DBI calls exactly as before, and Apache::DBI will automatically take over as needed.

> **NOTE**
>
> DBI is the Perl DataBase Interface, which provides a uniform API (Application Programmer Interface) to just about any database you might ever encounter.

Make sure that your PerlRequire script has Apache::DBI in it before DBI. You might also want to add a call to connect_on_init, which establishes the database handle during server startup, so that all the Apache children can share the database connection. It will look like this:

```
Apache::DBI->connect_on_init( $database, $username, $password );
```

The arguments $database, $username, and $password are the same as in the DBI connect method. See the DBI documentation for additional details.

CGI Under mod_perl

The most common usage of mod_perl, although not the most useful, is to run CGI programs under mod_perl, to get the speed benefits of mod_perl without actually rewriting any code.

There are two ways to run CGI programs under mod_perl—Apache::Registry and Apache::PerlRun. Although the former is the better of the two, the latter is good if you have existing CGI code that works fine as CGI, but is not written well enough to survive under the stricter requirements of Apache::Registry.

Apache::Registry

Apache::Registry is the preferred of the two methods, because it gives you all the benefits of using mod_perl, and removes all the things that make CGI unpleasant.

Apache::Registry works by compiling your CGI program once, the first time that it is run, and then storing that compiled form for future reference. The next time that the resource is requested, mod_perl loads it out of the cache, and executes the version that it has already compiled, saving the two most expensive parts of CGI execution—launching Perl in the first place, and compiling your CGI program. The first person to request the resource after a server restart (or after a new Apache child has been spawned) will get CGI-speed performance, but everyone after that will experience the speedup.

Configuration

All you have to do to run CGI programs as Apache::Registry is set up a PerlHandler for a particular directory and put CGI programs in it. Most of the time, what you want to do is point this at the place where you already have your CGI programs. This enables you to run the programs either in CGI mode, or in Apache::Registry mode, by just changing the URL.

This configuration will look like the following:

```
Alias /perl/  /usr/local/apache/cgi-bin/

<Location /perl>
  SetHandler  perl-script
  PerlHandler Apache::Registry
  Options +ExecCGI
</Location>
```

All files located in the directory /usr/local/apache/cgi-bin/ will be executed through Apache::Registry if accessed via the URL /perl/. So, for example, to access a CGI program called test.cgi located in that directory, you would access the URL
http://your.server.name/perl/test.cgi

Yes, that's really all there is to it. Almost.

Caveats

One of the problems with CGI, which was not mentioned in the CGI chapter, is that CGI enables you to get away with really bad code. This might be viewed as an advantage for the beginner who wants to write a working CGI program in a few minutes, but in the long run it's a real problem because you end up with a lot of CGI programs that are difficult to maintain. Additionally, you end up with enormous Web sites containing thousands of terrible CGI programs, which not only teach very bad programming style to beginners, but they give Perl a bad name.

For our purpose the important thing to know is that bad Perl code will run just fine as CGI, but when run under mod_perl it causes problems. The reason for this is in the very thing that makes mod_perl useful—its persistence. It is common (but bad) practice for CGI programmers to use global variables, for example. Using them in a mod_perl environment causes that variable to be visible not only throughout the current execution of the CGI program, but throughout all executions of the program under the same child process. Consequently, if you modify that variable during one execution that change will be seen the next time the program is invoked. This can be particularly problematic if the variable contains information that you distinctly don't want shared across multiple instances of the program, such as a username, or a count, for example.

Careless Perl CGI programs running under `mod_perl` can have two unpleasant side effects. As alluded to previously, you can end up with unexpected values of variables because of that variable getting modified in another instance of the program. An even more dangerous side effect is that you can end up leaking memory if you are using variables in an unsafe manner. Because the lifetime of a CGI program (under `mod_cgi`) is very brief, the program runs and goes away immediately, and the leaked memory is immediately reclaimed. However, under `mod_perl`, the leaked memory is permanently lost—at least until Apache is restarted. The symptom that you will see is that the various Apache child processes will grow in memory usage until all your available resources are consumed and your server grinds to a halt or swaps excessively.

The solution is simple—don't write bad code. Or, stated more pragmatically, make sure that all your Perl code runs using `strict` and `-w` (or, in Perl 5.6, `warnings`). That is, make sure that every one of your Perl CGI programs starts with the lines

```
use strict;
use warnings;
```

Or, under versions of Perl prior to 5.6, append `-w` to the end of the `#!` line at the start of your program. This should look something like

```
#!/usr/bin/perl -w
```

Any code that runs under these conditions without printing warning messages should be fine under `Apache::Registry`.

Additionally, you should read the document at `http://perl.apache.org/dist/cgi_to_mod_perl.html` for more tips on migrating your Perl CGI programs to `mod_perl`.

Apache::PerlRun

If you have existing Perl CGI programs that work under `mod_cgi`, and you really don't want to spend the time to make them work under `mod_perl`, there is a halfway solution. `Apache::PerlRun` gives you some of the benefits of `mod_perl`, but without having to make sure that your code is `strict` safe.

This is only recommended as an interim solution while you whip your CGI programs into place, or for programs that you have acquired from some other source and don't really understand where you can make modifications.

Configuration

Configuring Apache to use `Apache::PerlRun` looks very much like the configuration for `Apache::Registry`. And, you can run CGI programs with all three methods (`mod_cgi`, `Apache::Registry`, and `Apache::PerlRun`) out of the same directory at the same time, even running the same program all three ways, if you like.

The configuration for `Apache::PerlRun` looks like the following:

```
Alias /cgi-perl/  /usr/local/apache/cgi-bin/

<Location /cgi-perl>
  SetHandler  perl-script
  PerlHandler Apache::PerlRun
  Options +ExecCGI
  PerlSendHeader on
</Location>
```

Now, a file called `test.cgi` located in the directory `/usr/local/apache/cgi-bin/` can be accessed via the URL `http://your.server.name/cgi-perl/test.cgi` and will be run through `Apache::PerlRun`.

The `PerlSendHeader` directive is added here because, by default, `mod_perl` does not send the HTTP headers `mod_cgi` provides for you.

What It Does

Rather than getting the full benefit of `mod_perl`, all you get is the benefit of having the Perl interpreter resident in memory, when you use `Apache::PerlRun`. Your CGI programs are still loaded from disk and compiled each time when they are requested, so anything nasty that is being done with global variables, or other unpleasantness, will have short-term affect, and then the program will go away, releasing any memory that it might have leaked.

Note that any modules you are using will be cached by `mod_perl`, so they will not have to load and compile each time.

Comparing Performance

With the configurations previously shown, and with a `ScriptAlias` directive also pointing at the same directory, you can do a direct head-to-head comparison of performance on the same CGI program. The URLs `http://your.server.name/cgi-bin/test.cgi`, `http://your.server.name/cgi-perl/test.cgi`, and `http://your.server.name/perl/test.cgi` should all be pointing to exactly the same CGI program, but executed in three different ways, and executed in progressively better time, in the order listed here. The exact performance improvement will depend on the complexity of the code, but you should see a noticeable improvement.

It is important to note, as discussed in more detail in the "Common Problems" section that follows, each Apache child will have to cache the CGI program before you start seeing an improvement in performance. So, if you have 10 Apache child processes running, you will have to hit reload 10 times (on average) before you start seeing a child that has the code cached and gives you better performance.

Apache Handlers with `mod_perl`

Although by far the most common use of `mod_perl` is for CGI programs, it is actually much more powerful when used to write Apache handlers in Perl. Doing this enables Apache to do a lot of the things that CGI programs have to do for themselves. You don't have the startup cost associated with CGI programs, and, your programs are called directly by Apache, rather than second-hand through `mod_cgi`. And, because most of your programs will call methods directly out of the Apache API, for things such as printing headers, doing redirects, and writing to the log files, you gain an additional speed improvement over using either `Apache::Registry` or `Apache::PerlRun`.

`mod_perl` gives you access to the full Apache API, so that you can do useful things that are difficult or impossible with CGI.

Writing a `mod_perl` Handler

A `mod_perl` handler is an Perl module that contains a `handler` method. This method gets called by Apache, and passed an `Apache::Session` object. The method is expected to generate content that is sent to the client.

> **NOTE**
>
> "Method" is just a fancy name for a function. It is the common terminology used in object-oriented programming. However, you don't necessarily need to know anything about OO programming to write a `mod_perl` handler.

The `Apache::Session` object, which is passed to your method, is useful for things such as cookies, environment variables, authentication information, and so on—the sorts of things that you got from the environment when using CGI. It can also be used to make calls directly to the Apache API. This can be used to get form contents, to redirect to another location, or for a wide variety of other tasks.

This chapter does not attempt to be comprehensive with regard to mod_perl, so you should check out some of the resources listed in section "Where to Get More Information" to get more details.

Example mod_perl Handlers

As in Chapter 15, we'll start with a very simple example to show you what a mod_perl handler looks like. The following code example displays the text mod_perl in your browser window.

Note again that the use warnings; should be removed if you are running a version of Perl earlier than 5.6.

```
package ApacheAdmin::ExampleOne;
use strict;
use warnings;

sub handler {
    my $r = shift;
    $r->content_type('text/html');
    $r->status(200);
    $r->send_http_header;

    print "mod_perl";
}
```

When Apache calls your handler it loads the module and calls the handler method, sending any output to the browser.

The argument passed in, which is referred to in this example as $r, is the Apache::Session object. It is traditionally represented as $r because it is usually a request or response object. Also, the Apache code itself always refers to the Apache session object with the variable r, you will see it represented this way in many examples as well as a lot of the documentation.

Also note that the line use warning; will not work if you are using a version of Perl earlier than 5.6. You are encouraged to upgraded to at least that version of Perl.

Installing the Example mod_perl Handler

mod_perl handlers are Perl modules, and are found by mod_perl in the same way that Perl finds modules. That is, it looks through directories listed in the special variable @INC, which is a list of directories where Perl can find modules.

So, to install your new mod_perl handler, you need to either put it in a directory listed in @INC, or put it's location into @INC. For the moment, we'll do the latter.

The name of our module is `ApacheAdmin::ExampleOne`. When Perl looks for this module, it will look for a file called `ExampleOne.pm`, in a directory called `ApacheAdmin`, a subdirectory of one of the directories listed in `@INC`.

Perl provides an easy way to add directories to `@INC` with the `use lib` pragma. The syntax of this function is as follows:

```
use lib '/path/to/directory';
```

Save the example Perl code in a file called `ExampleOne.pm`, and put it in a directory called `ApacheAdmin`, in some convenient location. For example, you might place this in your home directory, so that the full path to the file is `/home/rbowen/ApacheAdmin/ExampleOne.pm`.

Then, in the file that you have noted in your `PerlRequire` directive add the following directive:

```
use lib '/home/rbowen/';
```

This directive added the specified directory to `@INC` so that Perl knows to look there for Perl modules, and therefore can find your module. Now you're ready to configure `mod_perl` to run your handler.

Configuring the `mod_perl` Handler

Now that you have the handler installed so that Perl can find it, you need to tell Apache how to use it. As with other handlers, `mod_perl` handlers are configured via a section directive in the main server configuration file. Because these handlers are not related to file-system resources, they will be configured with a `Location` section. You just need to tell Apache what module to call when asked for the particular resource.

This configuration will look like the following:

```
<Location /apacheadmintest>
    SetHandler perl-script
    PerlHandler ApacheAdmin::ExampleOne
</Location>
```

If you want to call a function in your module that is called something other than `handler`, you will need to specify this explicitly in the configuration, as shown here:

```
<Location /apacheadmintest>
    SetHandler perl-script
    PerlModule ApacheAdmin::ExampleOne
    PerlHandler ApacheAdmin::ExampleOne::other_method
</Location>
```

This enables you to have several different locations fielded by several different functions within a single module.

An Example That Is a Little More Useful

The previous example did not actually do anything useful. The example that follows, although it does not do much more, contains a useful element that will be part of most handlers that you write—the capability to acquire the contents of a form that was sent to you. Rather than having to rely on a CGI library to get this content, you can request it directly from mod_perl, as shown here.

```
package ApacheAdmin::ExampleTwo;
use strict;
use warnings;

sub handler {
    my $r = shift;

    my %form = $r->method eq 'POST' ? $r->content : $r->args;

    $r->content_type('text/html');
    $r->status(200);
    $r->send_http_header;

    foreach my $key ( keys %form ) {
        print $key . ' => ' . $form{$key} . '<br>';
    }
}
```

This rather inelegant example prints to the browser the contents of either any form posted to it or any arguments passed on the URL command line via the ?key=value&key=value syntax. See Chapter 15 for more information about the format of this syntax.

For further discussion of the code shown here, please see Appendix D, "mod_perl Example Code."

Common Problems

There are a number of mistakes that every beginner mod_perl programmer makes at least once, and several of them are listed here. More of them can be found in Stas Bekman's tutorials, which you can find at http://perl.apache.org/.

Don't Exit!

Perl programs have a tendency to call exit when they are done. This indicates where the program ends, and nothing more is to be done. The exit function causes the Perl interpreter to stop immediately.

Remember, however, that the entire point of mod_perl is that the interpreter does not stop, ever. Consequently, calling exit is a very bad thing. The Perl interpreter exits, causing the particular mod_perl child to lose its mind. This has a number of results. The client does not get a complete document most of the time, because the Apache child never gets a message that the generated content is complete. And typically, that particular child becomes useless for future mod_perl-generated resources, often serving the same content (whatever it saw last) repeatedly, until the child is killed, or the Apache server is restarted.

So don't use exit in your handlers, for any reason.

Restart the Server

When you change a handler that you are working on, your changes will not be seen immediately because they are with CGI programs. Because mod_perl loads the modules into the Perl interpreter memory, and caches them there forever, your new version of the module will not be seen until the server is restarted.

Note that you usually will have to stop the Apache process, and start it again, rather than just doing a restart, to actually get all the cached modules reloaded.

You can overcome this with the directive PerlFreshRestart on in your main server configuration file. With PerlFreshRestart on all modules will get reloaded on a server restart. This will generate a lot of function was redefined warnings in your error log on server restart. This is normal, and should not unduly concern you.

Where Did You Get That Value?

If you find that some values are unexpected sometimes, you might be using global values carelessly. Remember that all global values are shared across all accesses to a given Apache child process.

This problem can be rather elusive if you are not very careful in testing. Because a normal Apache server will have many child processes at a time you need to make sure to test a condition sufficiently after a server restart. You should go through all the server children at least once, so that you are actually using a child that you had used before. It is a good idea to set MinSpareServers, MaxSpareServers, and StartServers very low for testing purposes so that you are dealing with a very small server pool and problems related to reusing child processes will show up more rapidly.

mod_perl on Windows

Running Apache with mod_perl on Windows is not recommended, but can be done. The documentation shipping with mod_perl states that "mod_perl is considered alpha under NT and

Windows9x." Development on mod_perl for Windows has been slow because of a lack of Windows expertise on the mod_perl team.

However, if you want to run mod_perl on Windows, it can be done in two ways: build it yourself from source, or install a binary distribution.

To build it yourself you will need to follow the detailed instructions in the file INSTALL.win32, which you will find in the top-level directory where you have unpacked your mod_perl distribution. Microsoft Visual C++ 5.0 or later is required for this.

To find a binary distribution, see http://perl.apache.org/distributions.html, which lists binary distributions of mod_perl, including those for Microsoft Windows.

Note that it is also possible to build mod_perl under Cygwin.

Where To Get More Information

If you need more information about mod_perl there are a number of sources that you should look at. I don't attempt to be comprehensive on the topic of mod_perl in this chapter, and if you are going to be doing a lot with it, you need to make sure that you familiarize yourself with some of these other resources.

First and foremost, http://perl.apache.org/ is *the* definitive source for information about mod_perl. It contains an enormous amount of documentation, including numerous examples, and is the first place that you should go in your quest for mod_perl understanding. In particular, you should read the mod_perl guide, by Stas Bekman, which you will find at http://perl.apache.org/guide/. Anything that you want to do is likely to be covered in there.

Bekman also has an excellent series of articles on the *Apache Today* Web site, starting at http://apachetoday.com/news_story.php3?ltsn=2000-12-07-002-06-NW-HW-PL, about mod_perl performance tuning.

Secondly, there are a few (very few) excellent books on the issue. The most useful book is *Writing Apache Modules With Perl and C* ("The eagle book") by Doug MacEachern and Lincoln Stein. This book covers, as the title suggests, Apache module development, with a particular emphasis on mod_perl. And Andrew Ford has written the very excellent *mod_perl Pocket Reference,* which covers the basics of mod_perl usage, and is a great reference to have on your desk when you are actively working with mod_perl applications.

And, of course, there is the mailing list. You can get on the mailing list by sending an e-mail to modperl-subscribe@apache.org. Make sure you peruse the archives before you start firing off questions because most of what you will encounter in your first few months with mod_perl are things that have been discussed before. You will find the archives at `http://forum.swarthmore.edu/epigone/modperl/`, as well as at a number of other places listed on the Web site.

Summary

`mod_perl` embeds a Perl interpreter in the Apache process, and solves most of the problems associated with using CGI for dynamic content generation. It demands a higher-quality of Perl code for CGI code. `mod_perl` enables you to write Apache handlers using only Perl.

PHP

IN THIS CHAPTER

"Programming is an art form that fights back."

Tc Wilson

PHP is a popular Web-development language that works with a variety of Web servers. This chapter will teach you

- The main features of PHP, its strengths, weaknesses, and how it compares to other Web-development languages. This will help you decide whether PHP is an appropriate solution for your development needs.
- How to build and install PHP and common extensions for database connectivity, graphics, and PDF document generation.
- How to configure PHP to accommodate the performance or security needs of your installation.
- Where to find popular extensions and frameworks that can be added to your PHP installation.

This chapter concentrates on administration and installation. It will not teach you how to program in PHP, but it will provide you with a good overview of the language. You can find links to books and online resources at the end of the chapter where you can learn more about this exciting language.

What Is PHP?

PHP is a server-side scripting language that can be embedded in HTML pages. A simple PHP page looks like the following:

```
<h1><?php echo "Hello World!"; ?></h1>
<?php $program="PHP 4"; ?>
Welcome to <?php echo $program; ?>
```

If a client requests this page from the Web server it gets processed before being sent back. Usually, this is done by a PHP module that is part of the Web server, although PHP can be installed and used in CGI mode. The PHP engine parses the file, the code gets executed, and the result substituted. The resulting page is shown here:

```
<h1>Hello World!</h1>
Welcome to PHP 4
```

The concept is similar to that of JSP (JavaServer Pages) and Microsoft ASP (Active Server Pages).

This was a simple example. A typical Web application might need to connect to databases, LDAP directories, or perform complex operations in the server before returning a page. PHP provides an impressive amount of extensions to ease these tasks.

PHP History

The original author of PHP is Rasmus Lerdorf. He designed the language as a replacement for typical CGI development so that users could add dynamic features to their own pages without having to know too much about programming. He named his creation PHP (Personal Home Page). He made it freely available on the Internet and soon people from all over the world starting using it and submitting patches and suggestions for improvement. Rasmus continued development on PHP and eventually Zeev Suraski and Andi Gutmans made a complete rewrite and created PHP version 3. The current version of PHP is PHP4, which is built on top of the Zend scripting engine. At the time of this writing PHP is an incredible success by all measures—it runs on more than seven million sites and is installed on more than 40% of all Apache Web servers, making it the most popular Apache module. More than 50 books in many languages cover PHP and the developer and user community keeps growing daily.

PHP Architecture

PHP is a modular, extensible language. Figure 18.1 describes the PHP architecture.

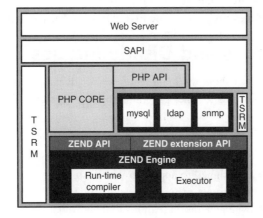

FIGURE 18.1

PHP architecture

PHP is implemented on top of the Zend scripting engine. The Zend engine is open source under the Q Public License (QPL) and designed to be embedded and used in a variety of scenarios.

> **NOTE**
>
> Please refer to the links at the end of the chapter to learn more about the Zend engine. You can learn more about the QPL at
> `http://www.trolltech.com/products/download/freelicense/license.html`

Extension writers have access to PHP and Zend via well-defined APIs. Many of those extensions are wrappers around existing C libraries. The extensions make the features provided by these libraries available to PHP developers, thus extending the capabilities of PHP. Database and directory connectivity, SNMP, graphic generation and manipulation, and so on are some extension examples. This chapter covers many of the available extensions and how to build and integrate them into your PHP installation.

The SAPI (Server API) provides an abstraction layer that enables PHP to be embedded in a variety of Web servers, not only Apache.

TSRM (Thread Safe Resource Manager) is a layer that provides thread-safe access to global-data structures. This is necessary to integrate PHP into threaded Web servers.

PHP Advantages and Disadvantages

In this section you will learn about the main features and advantages, as well as disadvantages, of PHP and how PHP compares to other programming languages.

Advantages

- **Easy to learn:** PHP has a short learning curve and programmers can quickly become productive. PHP was designed to appeal to Web designers and HTML coders, and they appreciate the ability to freely mix HTML and PHP. PHP allows them to easily and gradually add dynamic page generation features to their Web sites.

- **Open Source:** PHP is distributed under an Apache-style license that allows for both commercial and non-commercial use and development. This means that you can use it freely, without paying any licenses fees for machine, CPU, and so on. Also, there is a worldwide network of talented developers continuously improving and enhancing PHP. You can fix bugs or customize the software to your specific needs (or pay someone to do so) because the source code is available. This is not possible with commercial, off-the-shelf products.

- **Community:** PHP has a large base of users and developers. It is easy to find programmers fluent in the language. Many online resources are dedicated to PHP (Web sites, mailing lists, and so on) that provide valuable information and support.

- **Database support:** PHP provides extensive database support. It supports ODBC, open source databases such as MySQL and PostgreSQL, as well as commercial ones such as Microsoft SQL Server, Oracle, and Sybase.

- **Multiplatform support:** PHP runs on a variety of platforms and Web servers. PHP runs in most flavors of Unix and Windows as well as other OS such as Mac OS, OS X, or OS/2. PHP supports a wide variety of Web servers, ranging from the popular Apache, Microsoft IIS, and Netscape servers to less-known ones such as thttpd or AOLserver. This allows you to standardize on a common development language across a heterogeneous environment of systems and servers. You can build a solution with PHP on a specific platform/server/database combination and then migrate to a different combination gradually, replacing one component at a time. You can develop your code on a Windows workstation running IIS and deploy it on a Unix server running Apache with little or no changes.

- **Extensions:** PHP has a great number of available extensions and source code for everything from XML manipulation to directory access. Programmers can leverage this body of existing code to quickly put together advanced applications.

- **Safe mode:** PHP allows execution of code in restricted environments. This option is very attractive to ISP and Application Server Providers, which can offer PHP to their clients without compromising security. These providers often want to serve multiple customers using a shared infrastructure.

- **Session support:** Most Web applications require you to keep and manage state between requests. PHP offers native session management and an extension API so users can provide their own backend storage mechanisms.

- **Rapid development:** PHP gets compiled to an special bytecode format before getting executed. That step is completely transparent to programmers and users. Developers can make changes to a PHP page and see the results immediately in their browsers. By comparison, Java servlet development requires compile cycles and careful configuration of things such as class loaders, and so on.

- **Commercial support:** Several companies provide support and services around PHP, or bundle PHP as part of their server solution. Please refer to the resources at the end of this chapter to learn more about these companies. You should consider their services if you are using PHP in an enterprise environment, a mission critical Web site, or need custom features added to the language.

- **It's Fun!** PHP is an exciting language to program in. You can leverage existing extensions and code to quickly and easily put together great Web sites.

18

PHP

Drawbacks of PHP

You have learned about some of PHP's strong points such as its open source nature, its ease of use, and the availability of a great number of extensions. PHP has also some weak points:

- **Code maintenance**: Web developers like the quick development cycle and the ability to mix PHP and HTML code. The short learning curve attracts people without a previous programming background. The result is that as the functionality of the Web site expands the architecture can easily grow, without a clear structure, into a mess of code and HTML. Therefore, maintenance becomes a nightmare (also known as *spaghetti code*).

- **Not fully object-oriented:** Language wise, PHP is lacking the full object-oriented capabilities of other languages such as private variables, multiple inheritance, and so on.

- **Stability and interdependences:** Although PHP has a great number of extensions, they are in different stages of development and maturity. Even if these extensions are distributed with PHP and kept up to date with PHP releases, they still depend on external libraries for database connectivity, and so on. Hunting down which library version goes with which one and making sure that different extensions work together can be a time-consuming task. Commercial vendors are starting to offer ready-to-run PHP distributions, often in conjunction with open source databases and the Apache Web server.

- **Corporate acceptance:** PHP is quite popular in the open source world and technically superior to many of it its commercial counterparts. It still lacks important momentum and mind share in corporate and enterprise environments. That means that if you work in a corporation and want to use PHP you might be either unable to do so, or you'll need to do significantly more explanation than if you chose to go with Java or C++. Zend Technologies and other PHP-centric companies are working hard evangelizing PHP. They are building the support and products necessary to make PHP a viable choice for enterprise customers.

Language Comparison

Many other languages and technologies are used to create dynamic Web sites. These include Java, ASP, ColdFusion, Perl, Tcl, Python, and others.

Java

Java uses servlets and JSP (JavaServer Pages) to create Web content. Servlets are the Java equivalent of CGIs and JSP allow embedding Java code in HTML pages. Tomcat is a servlet engine from the Jakarta project (http://jakarta.apache.org) that also provides JSP support.

Java is widely accepted as an enterprise development language and Java application servers provide environments for creating complex, transactional applications that connect to a variety of enterprise data sources. Java is more difficult to learn than PHP and uses significantly more resources. Java was not originally designed to be a Web-development language and lacks the rapid development and string manipulation capabilities of scripting languages. You might want to encapsulate your backend logic and legacy systems integration in Java and access that information from a PHP frontend, which provides a fast, feature-rich, template environment. PHP allows you to either embed PHP in a servlet environment or add Java support directly to PHP.

Perl

Perl (http://www.perl.org) is a scripting language with great support for extensions and string processing. Perl gained popularity as the language of choice for CGI development. Modperl (http://perl.apache.org) is an Apache module that integrates a Perl interpreter with the Apache Web server, as you learned in Chapter 17, "mod_perl." This allows access from Perl to the Apache API and the development of template engines based on Perl, such as Mason (http://www.masonhq.com/), which are similar to PHP. Perl is more difficult to learn and master than PHP, but it is also more mature and can be applied in more scenarios, whereas PHP's primary focus and strength is in Web development.

As with Java, it is possible to integrate Perl and PHP. For more on that project you can go to http://freshmeat.net/projects/phpperl/

ASP

ASP, or Active Server Pages, is a framework developed by Microsoft to provide dynamic page generation. It supports different languages (including Perl) but the most common is Visual Basic Script. Commercial vendors provide Java environments with support for the ASP environment, thus making it possible to use ASP on non-Microsoft platforms. ASP is easy to use and comes bundled as part of Microsoft server solutions. ASP has also comprehensive development tools and vendors providing third-party solutions. PHP is regarded as faster and more stable, and supports a greater number of different Web servers and OS platforms.

Downloading and Installing PHP

This section will teach you the steps necessary to get a basic installation of PHP version 4 up and running and tested on Apache 2.0.

NOTE

At the time of this writing PHP 4 on Apache 2.0 is completely unsupported on the Windows platform. Please visit http://www.php.net to download the Windows version when it is released.

Installing Binary Packages

If you are using the Apache that came with your Linux or Unix distribution, chances are they also provide a PHP module. Use your package manager to find out if PHP is installed, and if not, go to your distribution Web site and download and install the package. If you are using a RPM-based distribution (such as Red Hat, Suse, or Mandrake) you can install the downloaded package with the command line rpm tool:

```
rpm -I mod_php*.rpm
```

You will need to become root to install the package (use the su command or log in as root). In most distributions installing the package simply copies the binary libraries to the appropriate directory, so you might still need to edit the configuration files to fully configure PHP.

Installing PHP from Source Code

This section describes all the steps necessary to get a working PHP installation using the PHP source code distribution.

Getting PHP

The PHP source code can be downloaded from http://www.php.net. The file you need will likely be called php-4.x.y.tar.gz, where x,y is the particular version of PHP. After you have downloaded the tarball, uncompress it, and cd into the created directory.

```
# gunzip < php-4*.tar.gz | tar xvf -
# cd php-4*
```

> **TIP**
>
> We only cover PHP installation as an Apache module. You can also compile PHP as a CGI script that will bring a performance penalty but allows for greater security in certain setups.

The PHP directory structure contains the following important directories:

TABLE 18.1   PHP Directory Structure

Directory	Description
TSRM/	Tread Safe Resource Manager.
Zend/	This is the code for the Zend scripting engine.
build/	Builds related scripts and makefiles.

TABLE 18.1 Continued

Directory	Description
ext/	This directory contains the extensions bundled with PHP for database access, XML manipulation, and so on. Each one of the subdirectories contains a makefile and most of them have a README file that explains the purpose of the extension.
libs/	This is the directory where PHP Apache module shared library will be placed when built.
main/	This contains the core of PHP code.
modules/	Where additional modules and shared libraries will be placed.
pear/	PHP—PHP Extension and Application Repository contains a collection of reusable library code similar to Perl's CPAN.
regex/	This contains regular expression library code.
sapi/	This contains the server extension abstraction layer. Here you can find modules to interface PHP to Microsoft IIS, Netscape, and of course, Apache.
scripts/	Misc. scripts used by PHP developers.
tests/	Test suite.
win32/	Windows platform-specific code.

Compiling PHP

PHP, like many other open source projects, uses autoconf and automake tools to ease portability. The build scripts are able to find out by themselves most of the information they need to compile PHP, but certain parameters you need to pass explicitly.

The rest of this section assumes that you have installed apache 2.0 in /usr/local/apache2 and that you have root privileges. Apache needs to have been compiled with loadable module support enabled (−enable-so option). We will install PHP under /usr/local/php4. If you want to build Apache and PHP as a regular user you need to change the following paths to paths you have write permissions to.

Type the following in the directory created when you uncompressed the php4 tarball:

```
./configure --with-apxs2=/usr/local/apache2/bin/apxs --prefix=/usr/local/php4
```

You will see a rapid succession of messages while the configure script checks for the libraries it needs in your system and creates the makefiles necessary for the build system. If everything goes well, and configure finishes without throwing any errors, you can type the following to build PHP:

```
make
```

After the build finishes you will have a `libphp4.so` file in the `libs/` directory.

To install the files type

```
make install
```

This will do the following:

- Install the shared library `libphp4.so` into the `/usr/local/apache2/modules` directory.
- Add a `LoadModule` directive to `/usr/local/apache2/conf/httpd.conf`.
- Install PHP-header files, binaries, and the PEAR libraries into `/usr/local/php4`.

The PHP module for Apache 2 is built as an Apache filter. To test it you need to enable PHP for the files containing the PHP code. Add the following to `/usr/local/apache2/conf/httpd.conf`.

```
<Files *.php>
SetOutputFilter PHP
SetInputFilter PHP
</Files>
```

Now create a file called `test.php` in the `/usr/local/apache2/htdocs` directory with the following contents:

```
<?php phpinfo(); ?>
```

Restart your Web server.

Connect to your Web server and retrieve the URL `http://127.0.0.1/test.php`, it should look similar to the page in Figure 18.2.

Congratulations! You successfully installed PHP and created your first PHP page.

If you get an error or get an empty page, the first place to look is the Apache error file `/usr/local/apache2/logs/error_log`. It will provide you with valuable information about what might have gone wrong. By far the most common issue is permissions—make sure that the file `test.php` is readable by the user Apache is running as.

Also, make sure that Apache was built with loadable module support. You can do so by issuing the following command:

```
/usr/local/apache2/bin/httpd -l
```

and looking for `mod_so.c` in the output. Make sure PHP is being loaded by checking for the appropriate `LoadModule` directive in `httpd.conf`.

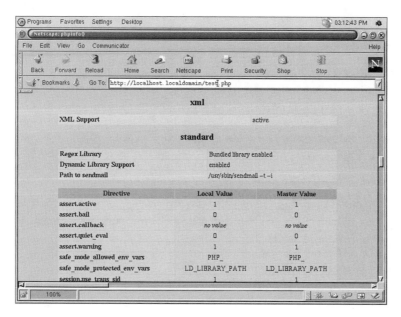

FIGURE 18.2
PHP test page

PHP Extensions

In the previous section you learned how to build PHP into an Apache module and how to configure it to work with your Apache installation. That was a basic installation. The configure command enables many more flags to be passed to enable different language features and extensions. We describe a selection of them now. You can get a complete list by typing

```
./configure --help | more
```

General Options

—prefix=/*some*/*path*

Enables you to specify the path where to install PHP.

—with-apxs2=/*path*/*to*/*apache2*/*bin*/*apxs*

Build shared Apache 2.0 module. If no path is provided it defaults to apxs.

—enable-debug

Enables the debug symbols. It's useful for troubleshooting.

—without-pear

18

PHP

Do not install PEAR.

—enable-safe-mode

Enables the restricted safe mode by default. If you use this option you will also be interested in —with-exec-dir, which specifies the executables allowed in safe mode.

—with-openssl

Include openssl support. Openssl is a library that provides SSL support. You can learn more about openssl at http://www.openssl.org

—with-curl

Include curl support. Libcurl is a library that provides client-side support for a variety of protocols, including HTTP/HTTPS, FTP, Telnet, and so on. You can learn more about curl at http://curl.sourceforge.net/.

—enable-ftp

Enables FTP support.

Graphics Support

—with-gd=/*path*/*to*/*gd*/*install*/*dir*

GD is a library that enables programmatic image creation and manipulation. It is useful for generating on-the-fly images and logos. You can learn more about GD at http://www.boutell.com/gd/.

The previous command line will build gd as part of PHP. If you want to create a shared library you need to pass the command line as

—with-gd=shared,/*path*/*to*/*gd*/*install*/*dir*

GD depends on additional libraries to support certain graphic formats. Associated configure options are

—with-jpeg-dir=/path/to/jpeg/install/dir

libjpeg support

—with-png-dir=/path/to/libpng/install/dir

libpng support

—with-xpm-dir=/path/to/libxpm/install/dir

libXpm support

—with-t1lib=/path/to/t1lib/install/dir t1lib

Adobe Type 1 fonts support

GD enables the use of TTF (True Type Fonts) to add text to images:

`—enable-gd-native-ttf`

Enables TrueType string function in gd.

`—with-freetype-dir=/path/to/freetype2/install/dir`

Freetype 2 support

`—with-ttf=/path/to/freetype/install/dir`

Includes Freetype 1.x support.

There is an additional PHP module that provides improved graphic manipulation using the imlib graphics library. You can find more information at `http://mmcc.cx/php_imlib/`.

Flash Animation

PHP provides Shockwave Flash support via two libraries: SWF and Ming.

`—with-swf=/path/to/swf/install/dir`

The SWF library can be found at `http://reality.sgi.com/grafica/flash/`.

`—with-ming=/path/to/ming/install/dir`

The Ming library provides support for Flash generation and includes a PHP binding. It can be found at `http://www.opaque.net/ming`.

PDF Generation

PHP supports on-the-fly generation of PDF documents via the clibpdf and pdflib libraries.

`—with-pdflib=/path/to/pdflib/install/dir`

PDF support via the pdflib library, which requires a license for commercial usage. You can learn more about pdflib at `http://www.pdflib.com/pdflib/index.html`.

`—with-cpdf=/path/to/clibpdf/install/dir`

PDF generation support via the clibpdf library. You can learn more at `http://www.fastio.com/`.

Database Support

PHP supports a variety of database backends.

`—with-mysql=/path/to/mysql/dir`

Support for the MySQL (http://www.mysql.com) database. MySQL is a popular open-source database. If this switch is not specified, PHP includes built-in support.

—with-pgsql=/path/to/pgsql/dir

Support for the PostgreSQL database (http://www.posgresql.org).

XML Support

—with-dom=/path/to/libxml/install/dir

Includes DOM support via the libxml library. Libxml is a C-based, XML-processing library distributed under the LGPL and the W3C IPR licenses. You can learn more about libxml at http://xmlsoft.org/.

—disable-xml

Disables built-in expat XML support (it is on by default).

—enable-xslt

Enables XSLT support.

—with-sablot=/path/to/sablotron/install/dir

Provides support for the Sablotron XSLT transformation engine. You can learn more about Sablotron at http://www.gingerall.com/.

—with-expat-dir=/path/to/expat/install/dir

The expat library is required by Sablotron; you can find expat at http://www.jclark.com/xml/expat.html.

—with-qtdom

XML DOM support via the qt library that can be found at http://www.trolltech.com/products/qt/.

—enable-wddx

Enables wddx support, which is used when programming Web services.

Session Support

—enable-trans-id

Enables transparent id propagation of session information (this can be done via cookies).

--with-mm

Enables shared-memory support for session storage via the mm library. You can learn more about the mm library at: http://www.engelschall.com/sw/mm/.

This section presented you with the several configuration options to give you an idea of the capabilities of PHP. Many more provide support for additional databases, SNMP, corba, calendar functions, IMAP, Unicode, Java, LDAP, encryption, and so on. You can get a comprehensive description of supported language features at http://www.php.net/manual/en/.

You can find additional extensions and PHP Web applications in Freshmeat (http://freshmeat.net), and in the Sourceforge PHP foundry (http://sourceforge.net/foundry/php-foundry/).

For example, the Vagrant charting extension http://vagrant.sourceforge.net provides support for programmatic generation of graphic charts. Examples of Web applications in PHP are Phorum (http://phorum.org/) for Web discussion boards, IMP (http://www.horde.org/imp/) a Web-mail program, and Nuke (http://phpnuke.org/) and Midgard (http://www.midgard-project.org/) for content management/Web portal systems.

PHP Configuration

PHP can be configured either via the php.ini file located in /usr/local/php4/lib/ or from inside the Apache configuration file. You can copy the file php.ini-dist from the build directory to /usr/local/php4/lib/php.ini. The php.ini consists of key value pairs. The same settings can be specified in the Apache configuration file with the use of these directives:

```
php_value name value
```

This sets the value of the specified variable.

```
php_flag name on|off
```

This is used to set a boolean configuration option.

There are certain options, admin options, which must be specified in the main Apache configuration file. They can be set using php_admin_value and php_admin_flag. These options are usually security related, such as open_basedir or safe_mode_exec_dir.

Some of the configuration options are relevant to PHP and some are used by PHP modules. The following is a selection of the available configuration options.

PHP Language

You can modify the way PHP can be mixed with HTML tags with the following directives, which can be included in the httpd.conf configuration file.

```
short_open_tag boolean
```

To include PHP code you usually need to surround it with `<?php` or `<script>` tags. This enables you to use `<?  ?>` tags in your code, although PEAR coding practices encourage you to use the `<?php` format.

`asg_tags` *boolean*

Enables use of ASP-style tags `<% %>` and constructs (`<%=$varname %>` to include the value of a variable.

`max_execution_time` *integer*

`memory_limit` *integer*

These two directives set the maximum amount of memory in bytes that a script is allowed to allocate and the maximum time in seconds a script is allowed to run before the script is terminated by the PHP engine. This helps protect the server resources from poorly written scripts.

`include_path` *string*

Specifies a list of directories where certain PHP functions (for including other files, and so on) look for files.

Error Manipulation

`display_errors` *boolean*

This determines whether errors should be printed to the screen as part of the HTML output or not.

`error_log` *string*

Name of the file where script errors should be logged. If the special value `syslog` is used, the errors are sent to the system logger instead.

Output Manipulation

Apache transmits to the network the content created by the PHP script as it is being generated. You might want to add specific headers to a response but are unable to do so because you already sent part of the content. If you enable output buffering, PHP will cache the page, enabling you to set headers. PHP also provides hooks so the content generated can be filtered or changed. As an example, PHP provides support for compressing the output of a script if the browser allows for it, thus minimizing download time. PHP also provides the capability to append or prepend headers or footers to all generated pages, thus easing the task of creating a consistent, site-wide look and feel.

`auto_append_file` *string*
`auto_prepend_file` *string*

PHP makes it possible to append or prepend files to every page served. These files are parsed and interpreted as PHP scripts. If the name of the file is none then auto-prepending or appending is disabled.

`output_buffering` *boolean*

Enables or disables output buffering.

`output_handler`

Allows the specification of an output handler such as `output_handler` = `ob_gzhandler`, for compression.

Security

It is possible to configure PHP to enhance the security of the installation, especially in environments with multiple users or where you do not fully trust them. PHP allows a safe-mode operation, which restricts the PHP/system functionality the scripts can access, such as limiting access to only certain files or directories. It is possible to configure PHP to run as a CGI. This has advantages and risks from a security standpoint, such as the capability to use the Apache `suexec` wrapper. Many of the security issues need to be handled or complemented at the PHP level with safe coding practices. You can learn more at
`http://www.php.net/manual/en/security.php`.

`safe_mode` *boolean*

Whether to enable PHP's safe mode.

`safe_mode_exec_dir` *string*

System calls executing external programs will only work with binaries in this directory.

`open_basedir` *string*

If present, it will limit the files that can be opened by PHP to the specified directory path.

Dynamic Extension Support

As previously described, PHP supports extensions. You can either compile these extensions in the PHP executable or you can choose to compile the extensions themselves as shared objects and load them from within PHP.

`enable_dl` *boolean*

Enabled by default, this directive restricts the capability to load shared library code into PHP. The main reason to disable dynamic loading is security. Dynamic loading is not available when using safe-mode.

`extension_dir` *string*

Tells PHP what directory it should look for dynamically loadable extensions.

`extension` *string*

Tells PHP which dynamically loadable extensions to load when it starts up.

Resources

This section contains pointers to additional resources related to PHP.

PHP

The official PHP Web site is `http://www.php.net`. Here you will be able to download PHP and find related documentation. The PHP user guide provides installation and configuration instructions as well as a comprehensive language reference guide.

Netcraft (`http://www.netcraft.com`) and Security Space (`http://www.securityspace.com/s_survey/data/index.html`) provide figures on Apache and PHP usage.

Support

You can access PHP development and user mailing lists at `http://www.php.net/support.php`. Before asking your question, research the existing documentation and the Frequently Asked Questions document. If you still cannot find an answer, consider posting to the mailing list, including as much detail as possible about your problem, what you tried and which errors you got, operating system, server, and PHP versions. This will greatly increase the chances of getting a response and will help reduce the noise in the mailing list.

PHP Books

A comprehensive book list can be found at the PHP Web site `http://www.php.net/books.php`. The following provide a good companion for learning the language:

PHP Fast and Easy Web Development (Prima Publishing, 2000), by Julie Meloni is a good introduction to the language.

PHP Developer's Cookbook (Sams Publishing, 2000), by Sterling Hughes and Andrei Zmievski, is packed with useful practical examples.

PHP and MySQl Web Development (Sams Publishing, 2001), by Luke Welling and Laura Thompson is another good language tutorial that explains PHP alongside with MySQL, a popular open-source database, commonly used with PHP.

Web Sites

The following are popular Web sites that provide information on PHP:

`http://www.phpbuilder.com`

`http://www.zend.com`

`http://www.phpwizard.net`

`http://www.devshed.com/Server_Side/PHP/`

PHP GTK

Use PHP to program your GUI application!

`http://gtk.php.net/`

Commercial Vendors

Several vendors provide products based around PHP or include PHP as part of their server offering:

- **Zend—`http://www.zend.com`:** Founded by members of the core PHP team; Zend provides enterprise support and services around PHP. They also provide a development IDE and useful addons to the Zend engine for improved performance, source hiding, and script caching.
- **Covalent Technologies—`http://www.covalent.net`:** Offers PHP as part of their Apache server solutions.
- **Synop—`http://www.synop.com/`:** Provides products around PHP, including a development IDE, content management, and site development solutions.
- **Nusphere—`http://www.nusphere.com/`:** Provides Internet server solutions that include PHP, Perl, MySQL, and Apache.

Summary

PHP, as most other open-source projects, is driven by the needs of the users and developers, which program PHP on a daily basis for their own projects. These projects range from personal home pages to high-profile financial sites.

PHP usage and the number of extensions continue to grow. The language itself continues to evolve and it is starting to find applications outside the Web-development field as a general-purpose scripting and embeddable language.

Version 2.0 of the Zend engine will include improved object-oriented support, exceptional handling, and internationalization support.

18

PHP

Security and Auditing

PART

IV

IN THIS PART

Apache Security

IN THIS CHAPTER

Probably the last man who knew how it worked had been tortured to death years before. Or as soon as it was installed. Killing the creator was a traditional method of patent protection.

Small Gods—Terry Pratchett

One of the strengths of Apache is that its developers are very security conscious. Open source projects are sometimes criticized for having too many security holes. Amazingly, the opposite appears to be true with Web servers. In September of 2001 the Gartner Group, a research organization, recommended that companies switch from Microsoft's Internet Information Server to Apache, among other Web servers, because there are fewer security risks (`http://www.gartner.com/DisplayDocument?id=340962`).

At times this chapter might seem excessively draconian in its recommendations. To quote Andy Grove, co-founder of Intel, "Just because you are paranoid does not mean they are out to get you." When it comes to security you can never be too paranoid. Implementing many of the suggestions in this chapter might cause riots among your users, and that is fine, you can use that as a divining rod for measuring the success of your security policy. The sweet spot in security is somewhere between several flaming e-mails from users and the users lined up outside of your office door with voodoo dolls and pitchforks. Unfortunately, in this world of script kiddies and hacker wars, a restrictive security policy is necessary.

When discussing Apache security, there are four areas you need to think about:

- The Apache program
- The external security risks
- The internal security risks
- The vendor security issues

The source code is probably the least of your worries. The Apache source code is tested and retested for security holes and potential security holes. As of this writing, the last time a security hole was found in the source code was in 1998.

External security risks are problems that arise from someone attacking your server. These problems can range from a denial of service attack, to someone trying to exploit a security hole in a piece of software you have installed. They are best dealt with as part of a broader security strategy, which will be discussed later in this chapter.

Internal security risks are by far the biggest problem that Apache administrators face. Generally, these are not attacks, as much as misconfigured CGI scripts, poorly written modules, and other issues that can cause a server to crash, or worse, leave your valuable data exposed.

Vendor security issues are another big problem. When you purchase or download an operating system that includes Apache as part of the base installation, you do not know what configuration changes the vendor has made to Apache. You also do not know what type of security bugs might have been introduced during the installation process. Most vendors are good about posting updates, but it is important to stay abreast of any security holes that the vendor reports.

The focus of this, and the next, chapter is external and internal security problems. These two security problems are the ones you have the greatest control over, and the ones you can most easily prevent from turning into full-fledged crises. They are also the easiest problems to prevent. As with any other security issue, it simply requires careful planning.

A Web server presents a unique security challenge that almost no other networked server faces. A Web server needs to be accessible to anyone on the Internet, yet it needs to be protected from potential damage that can be inflicted by one of these remote users.

To better understand the challenges faced in securing a Web server contrast the security policies needed for a Web server versus a mail server. A mail server is similar to a Web server in that it needs to be publicly accessible; otherwise you will not be able to receive mail. It is also a potential target of attacks because other people can use a mail server to send Unsolicited Commercial E-mail (UCE), more commonly known as spam, to thousands or even millions of people.

So, a mail server administrator is left with this problem—keep the mail server publicly available, but don't allow anyone, except for trusted users, to send mail through it. The solution to this problem is relatively simple. A mail server administrator can create an access list of hosts that are allowed to send mail, or relay, through the server. The mail server stays public, but only trusted users can actually relay mail.

Unfortunately, the same sort of panacea does not exist for Web servers. As we will discuss in this chapter, the majority of the security problems associated with Web servers are caused by the fact that the servers have to provide access to everyone.

Developing a Security Strategy

A Web server does not operate in a vacuum. It is an integral part of your business, and your network. Therefore, a security strategy for your Web server has to include discussion of a broader network and server strategy.

The best way to develop a security strategy is from the outside in. The strategy has to include the network, the server, the operating system, Apache itself, and finally the individual Web sites. This is outlined in Figure 19.1.

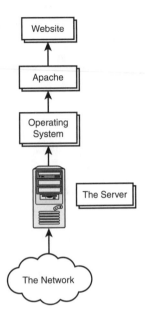

FIGURE 19.1

A security strategy has to involve the entire network.

The first security decision you need to make is whether you want to host your server in house, or collocate it with a hosting vendor. From a security perspective hosting a server in house forces you to add a layer of complexity to your network, which we will discuss later in this chapter. However, collocating your server in a remote data center means that you will lose a level of control because you will not be able to administer or monitor the remote data center networking devices. The in house versus collocation debate is discussed in greater detail in Chapter 1, "Getting Started."

If you decide to host the site on an internal network you will need to create a Demilitarized Zone (DMZ) for the server. A DMZ is a firewall term used to describe an area between the Internet and the protected portion of your network. The DMZ is still part of your network, but it is more open than the rest of the network, with a less restrictive ruleset, and, therefore, more vulnerable to attacks.

If you have a database driven Web site, especially one with confidential customer information, another layer of complexity is added to your network. Obviously, your database server has to have very strict access restrictions, which means it will have to reside the behind firewall, but it still has to be reachable by the Web server. Your firewall will have to be configured to allow the Web server access. It is also a good idea, whenever possible, to encrypt the transactions between the Web server and the database server, providing your customers with the maximum amount of protection.

The next decision you need to make is what services, in addition to HTTPD, you are going to run on that server. The temptation, especially for smaller companies, is to run as many services as possible on a single server. If possible, this is something you should resist. Adding additional services, such as mail, DNS, and NNTP to a server increases the number of open ports, and, therefore, increases the potential for security holes to be found.

You might be asking yourself why it is so important to separate services. After all, if someone were going to break into the server why would it matter if there were one service or many?

The answer is simple. The most common form of external attack is called a root exploit. A root exploit is an attack where a remote user takes advantage of a security hole in a program and uses it to gain root access to a server. If an attacker were to take advantage of a root exploit in Sendmail, a very common mail program, that attacker would then have the ability to deface your Web site, or access your customer database. Conversely, if an attacker were to find a root exploit in Apache she would now be able to read mail stored on the server, modify DNS zone files, and more.

One of the most common internal security problems is poor programming. A runaway CGI script, or a poorly written program, can consume all the memory on a server and render it virtually useless. Obviously, you do not want a poorly written CGI script to knock your mail and DNS servers offline. Nor would you want to have a Sendmail module develop a memory leak and crash your server.

By separating your services you are providing an extra level of protection for your network, if one server, or service, is compromised it does not impact other services.

After deciding on a server, and where to locate it, the next step is to secure the operating system. Although securing an operating system is beyond the scope of this book, there are several excellent resources detailing ways to protect your operating systems. One title that is particularly comprehensive is *Sams Maximum Security, Third Edition.*

There are, however, some general guidelines for securing any Web server. To start, disable any ports that are not in use. In this case, a port is shorthand for port number, which is a numerical value mapped to an application on the server. The server is always listening on open, or active, ports. When it receives a packet with that port number it activates the proper application. By disabling unused ports you will decrease the likelihood that someone performing a port scan against your server will discover a security hole you were not aware existed.

It is also useful to remove any unnecessary user accounts from your server. For instance, many flavors of *nix include a games account. The account is used to record high scores for games on a shared user system. Hopefully you will not be using your Web server to play Unreal Tournament, so it can be deleted.

19

It is important to be as restrictive as possible with system files. Any file that could cause irreparable damage to the server, or worse someone else's server, should have the tightest security permissions and only the root or Administrator account should have access to it.

Finally, don't use telnet. This was touched on briefly in Chapter 1, but it bears repeating. Sending passwords over the Internet in clear text is a very bad thing, especially if it is your root password. Both telnet and FTP send passwords in clear text, and should be avoided. SSH provides you all the benefits that telnet does, and it encrypts your connection.

This chapter has moved from the general to the specific. Starting with the location of the server and migrating to the server configuration. The rest of the chapter focuses on operating system and Apache security. These are the aspects of your Web server over which you will exert the most control and that deserve the most attention.

Understanding *nix File Permissions

To fully understand how to secure the Apache server, and individual sites, it is necessary to understand how *nix file permissions work.

The best way to visualize *nix file permissions is as a matrix. Along the side of the matrix are the three levels of access to the file:

- Read—able to view the file
- Write—able to make changes to the file
- Execute—able to run the file as a program

At the top of the matrix are the three users or groups that might want access to the file:

- Owner—the user who owns the file
- Group—the group to which the owner of the file belongs
- World—everyone else

*nix file permissions are set by assigning a value of read, write, or execute to each of the three groups. This is displayed from the command line by requesting a long file list:

```
[allan@ns1 conf]$ ls -l
-rw-r—r—    1 root      root        348 Oct 18  2000 access.conf
-rw-r—r—    1 root      root      46467 Sep 29 23:56 httpd.conf
-rw-r—r—    1 root      root        357 Oct 18  2000 srm.conf
```

Setting file permissions is a matter of arithmetic. Each permission type is assigned a numerical value. Read permission has a value of 4, write permission is assigned a value of 2, and execute permission has a value of 1. 0 indicates no permission to access the file. To combine permissions add the numbers together. For example, to assign the read and write permissions, for the file owner, to the access.conf file you would add 4 and 2 together for a permission value of 6.

Permission settings are set using the chmod command. So, to assign read and write permissions to the file owner, read only permissions to the group, and read only permissions to other users for the access.conf file you would type the command

```
[allan@ns1 conf]$ chmod 644 access.conf
```

Similarly, if you wanted to set the permissions so that all users had read, write, and execute permissions (never a good idea) you would use the command

```
[allan@ns1 conf]$ chmod 777 access.conf
```

As an administrator of a Web server you should strive to enforce 644 permission settings for all text, non-CGI, files. There is no reason to have these files with execute permissions. You also do not want to risk having the files overwritten by someone who does not have permission.

The only exception to this rule are files updated by multiple users in the same group (we will discuss groups further in the next section). In cases where multiple users need to update a file, make sure all the users are in the same group and set the permissions to 664.

As with any security concerns, you should always err on the side of caution when setting file permissions. If you need to loosen the file permissions to make the site usable, it is a simple matter to adjust them. It is better to be cautious then to have to recover from an attack that was expedited because of inappropriate file permissions.

Users and Groups

*nix and Windows both use "users" and "groups" to track file ownership, and limit the capability to access critical operating system files. A user is an individual login, whereas a group is one or several users that have the same level of access to the server.

Let's take a look at the long file list we used earlier:

```
[allan@ns1 conf]$ ls -l
-rw-r—r—    1 root     root           348 Oct 18  2000 access.conf
-rw-r—r—    1 root     root         46467 Sep 29 23:56 httpd.conf
-rw-r—r—    1 root     root           357 Oct 18  2000 srm.conf
```

The third column is the username that owns the file, and the fourth column is the group to which the user belongs. In the previous listing the access.conf file is owned by the user root and the group root.

For some flavors of *nix the default setting for a new user is to create a group with the same name. This provides some level of protection because it prevents users from one group from editing files owned by someone in another group, assuming good permission settings are practiced. However, if you have multiple users that need to have access to the same set of files, it is better to put those users in the same group. This allows all users in the group to edit the file and upload it to the server.

Another level of user and group security you can enhance is restricting access to which users can become root.

Unless your version of *nix ships with enhanced security settings, any user who finds the root password can become root and make changes.

You can prevent this by only allowing certain users to become root. The settings for the su command are stored in the file /etc/pam.d/su. You can edit the file to only allow users from the "wheel" group to become root. Depending on your operating system, there are several ways to do this. For example, if you were running RedHat 7.1, you would type the following:

```
auth      sufficient    /lib/security/pam_wheel.so trust use_uid
auth      required      /lib/security/pam_wheel.so use_uid
```

Wheel is a special *nix group that is designed specifically for the purpose of creating a special group of administrative users.

Superuser do (sudo) is another option for granting limited privileges to certain users. Sudo is maintained by Todd Miller and can be downloaded from the sudo Web site http://www.courtesan.come/sudo/.

In a traditional su environment a user who becomes root has the same privileges as root, and all commands are logged as if a single root user performed them. Sudo allows a server administrator to restrict access to certain commands. When a user becomes root, a sudo shell is invoked, as opposed to the normal root shell. The user can only execute the allowed commands, and all information is logged. If something goes wrong, the server administrator can quickly determine what happened, and hopefully, how to fix it.

Sudo also limits the idle time in a session to five minutes before timing out. If the five-minute idle limit is reached, the user is forcibly logged out, and has to restart the session.

The Apache User

Apache is shipped with fairly tight security measures. However, if you are using a preinstalled binary, it is a good idea to double-check some of the security permissions.

It is especially important to know which user is running the Apache process. There are several ways to do this. You can look in the httpd.conf file for the User/Group variables; another way is to run the top command. If the Apache httpd executable is running you should see an entry similar to this:

```
PID    USER      PRI  NI SIZE RSS   SHARE STAT  %CPU %MEM  TIME COMMAND
22071 apache     14   0 9680 9680  7812  S      3.5  1.8   0:01 httpd
```

As you can see on this system, Apache is running as the apache user. Apache should always run as an unprivileged user, usually `apache` or `nobody`.

If you notice that your server is running Apache as root, you should definitely change to a different user, one that has no other function on the server.

Although the Apache process should be run as an unprivileged user, the configuration files for the Apache should be well protected. As in the previous example, the files should be owned by root, and have as many restrictive permissions as possible.

User Permissions

Depending on the type of server you are running you will either have multiple users updating files on the same Web site, or multiple Web sites, each with a different user.

There are many levels of access you can assign to users depending on what role they will be playing in terms of updating the Web site. Of course, before determining the role a user has in developing the Web site, the first thing that needs to be determined is the level of access a user has to the server.

In Chapter 1, the four main types of access to a Web server were discussed—Telnet, FTP, SSH, and SCP. Telnet and SSH are redundant as are FTP and SCP. In an ideal world you would not want to use either Telnet or FTP because both programs send passwords in clear text. Unfortunately, using SCP can be confusing to some people. If you do have control over how users access the servers, such as in an enterprise environment, then you should consider permitting primarily SCP access and enabling SSH only when necessary, and never enabling Telnet or FTP access.

You might be wondering how you can grant access to SCP and not SSH because SCP runs over a SSH tunnel. There are a couple of ways to do this, but the most common is to change the login shell for the SCP-only user, so that it will only run the SCP program. The user still makes a connection using SSH, but the only program she can run is SCP.

Limiting a user to a SCP-only connection enables you to limit the number of people who are making shell connections to the server, and making file changes directly on the server. It also limits the number of mistakenly deleted or accidentally overwritten files that you will have to restore from backup. Presumably, if a user is forced to upload files, that user will have local copies of all the files that are being changed.

If you do allow files to be changed and modified directly on the server, you should consider using a version control system, such as rcsedit. A version control system requires users to check out files, edit them, summarize the changes made, and then check them back in. This type of version control has two advantages. The first is it keeps track of who edited a file, so if a mistake is made you will know who did it. The second advantage is that an archive of the file is kept. If something goes horribly wrong with the file, it can quickly be reverted to an earlier version.

In addition to access and version control, you also have to worry about user permissions. If you are not going to personally monitor all the files on a server, you should be as restrictive as possible with file permissions.

The best permissions for non-CGI files on a Web server are 644. Again, this enables the user to read and write to the file, but no one else to write to it. CGI scripts, which generally have permissions of 755, should all be quartered in a special directory. Although it is useful to be able to have executable files in all directories, it is not very secure.

If you are very paranoid about security permissions, you can create a cron job that will check file permissions nightly and save a list of files in violation of your permissions to a file. You can then either investigate the files or change the permissions yourself.

A cron job is a task that an administrator tells to perform at regularly scheduled intervals, ranging from once a minute to once a month.

The cron job would use the find command to search for permissions in the root directory of the Web site or sites. Assume the content of your Web site is stored in /home/website/httpd/. The find command you ran would look something like this:

```
find /home/website/httpd -type f -perm -ga=wx > /root/badfiles.txt
```

This command looks for all files that are writable and executable by the group and everyone in the /home/website/httpd directory, as well as its subdirectories. If it finds a match, it will write the filename to a file called badfiles.txt.

You can make your life even easier by making the change automatically, like this:

```
find /home/website/httpd -type f -perm -ga=wx  | xargs chmod ga-wx
```

This will automatically remove write and execute permissions from the files that are found in violation of your permissions policy. Be warned, this might cause angry users to call you and tell you their site no longer works.

Another solution is to install a program that will monitor these changes for you. Tripwire (http://www.tripwire.com and http://www.tripwire.org) is a program that runs on *nix systems and monitors file system integrity. When you initialize Tripwire you tell it what files or directories to watch, and what changes you want to generate alerts. For example, you may want check file permissions for every file in your root web. Feed this information into Tripwire's database, it encrypts it, and checks the specified files. If it notices a problem, it alerts you, so you can take appropriate action.

Limit Modules

The modular nature of Apache is one of the reasons that it is so popular. You can install a myriad of modules, or even write your own.

From a security perspective each module presents an additional security risk.

This risk is exasperated by precompiled binaries of Apache. Most often these binaries include modules, aside from the standard Apache modules that the developer thinks you will need. Most often these are modules that incorporate Perl, mod_perl, PHP, and MySQL into Apache. That is great if you are going to use these features, but if you are not going to use them they do present a security risk, however slight it might be, to your server.

Before installing Apache, you should consider what Web site enhancements you intend to use right away, as well as enhancements you intend to use within six months, and what you plan to use in a year. If you are unsure, ask your developers what enhancements they would like to add.

Even if you do not intend to add any enhancements you will want to review the standard modules, and decide if you need them. You can view a list of currently installed modules by appending the -l flag to the httpd command, like so:

```
[root@ns1 allan]# /usr/sbin/httpd -l
```

You can also review the installed modules directly in the httpd.conf file.

To remove a module from being compiled when Apache is first started simply comment it out in the httpd.conf file. Make sure that you comment it out both in the Dynamic Shared Object Support section and the AddModule section of the httpd.conf file.

If you are not sure if you need a module, you can review what the module does on the Apache Modules Web site at http://httpd.apache.org/docs/mod/. If, after reading the description, you are still not sure if you need it leave it in rest assured that the standard modules have been repeatedly tested and used by, literally, millions of administrators, so they are fairly secure.

Do You Really Need FrontPage Extensions?

Chances are, if you run a large Web site with a lot of users, or a Web server with a lot of sites, someone will tell you they need to have FrontPage Extensions installed.

If at all possible, try to avoid doing this. FrontPage is notorious for its security holes, and although each version of the software has gotten more secure, there are still fundamental security problems with it.

The biggest problem, and one that is integral to the way FrontPage works, is that when FrontPage publishes files to your Web site it does so using an HTTP connection. As with telnet and FTP your password is sent as clear text, so it is readable by anyone with a sniffer.

Older versions of the FrontPage software stored the usernames and passwords for the site and the sub webs as plain text files within the main directory. This meant anyone who knew where to look would be able to find the password.

A FrontPage enabled Web site also uses significantly more storage space than a site that does not use FrontPage. FrontPage makes copies of all files that are part of the Web site, and stores them in private subdirectories. It also has executables that enable the file transfer, and the FrontPage bots (CGI programs that are built into FrontPage). These bots sit on the server, even if they are not being used. Again, this means that anyone who knows where the executables are kept might be able to exploit them and break into your server.

There are many other programs, such as Dreamweaver (for more information check out *Sams How to Use Dreamweaver and Fireworks 4*), that provide the same type of functionality as FrontPage without the associated security holes.

Cautious Server-Side Includes Usage

Server-Side Includes (SSI) are a great way to enhance a Web site. They enable users to embed CGI scripts, other files, and Unix commands into a regular HTML file. More information about SSI can be found in Chapter 16, "Server-Side Includes."

Unfortunately, SSI can also be a nightmare to a server administrator. The same problems inherent in CGI script security are now exacerbated by the fact that the scripts can be called any non-executable document. Which means that even documents that you have secured with 644 permissions can still be used to cause problems on the server.

If you are going to use SSI, there are things you can do to lessen the potential security risks.

One of the best things you can do is only enable SSI on a per-directory basis. If a directory does not need SSI there is no reason to enable this feature. You can do this by disabling SSI for the server and selectively enabling it for certain directories.

When you do enable SSI for a directory, make sure the server-parsed documents end in `shtml`, or some suffix that is not `htm` or `html`, the standard HTML file extensions. SSI forces Apache to parse every file in that directory every time it is requested. If your site is filled mostly with non-SSI enabled files you are placing an unnecessary burden on Apache by forcing it to parse the non-SSI files.

In addition to limiting the location and type of files that can contain SSI executables, it is a good idea to limit what can be executed in the file.

You can limit the types of files that can be executed by adding the IncludesNOEXEC flag to the Includes directive. So, it would look something like this:

```
<Directory "/home/website/httpd">
    AllowOverride None
    Options IncludesNOEXEC
</Directory>
```

This will disable the exec command within SSI documents. You can still execute CGI scripts using the "include virtual" tag. Any scripts referenced by the "include virtual" tag will need to be in a directory defined by the ScriptAlias directive (discussed in Chapters 9, "URL Mapping," and 15, "CGI Programs").

Cautious .htaccess Usage

There are two different reasons for using .htaccess files. The first, and most common is to setup password protection, the second reason is to overwrite the Apache system-wide settings.

Although password protection is, technically, a way of overwriting Apache system-wide settings it is the most popular use of .htaccess and deserves special attention.

As with any optional Apache setting, you do not have to enable the use of .htaccess files.

If you do decide to enable the use of .htaccess, you should do it selectively. Start with a very restrictive level of user control:

```
<Directory />
AllowOverride None
Options None
Allow from all
</Directory>
```

This creates a default setting that is very restrictive; you can then pick individual directories that will have system override enabled.

In addition to selecting which directories will have override capabilities you will need to determine which directives you will allow to be overwritten.

There is a temptation when enabling the use of .htaccess to just enable all directives to be overwritten:

```
<Directory />
AllowOverride ALL
Options None
Allow from all
</Directory>
```

19

APACHE SECURITY

For some directives, such as `ErrorDocument`, which enables a user to change the default error document, this is no problem. However, other directives, such as `Includes` can cause problems by enabling them.

For example, if you have disabled SSI for a directory and you leave the `AllowOverride` directive set to all, a user will be able to enable SSI, without letting you know.

Deciding which directives you will enable is a matter of choice. However, it is something you should carefully consider, enable selectively.

Password Protection

As mentioned earlier, `.htaccess` is most commonly used for password protection. It is a good way of handling password protection, and it is secure.

Unfortunately, there are some fairly common practices, implemented by users, which diminish the effectiveness of this tool.

One common mistake made by users is to put the file that contains the usernames and passwords in the same directory as the `.htaccess` file, or in the root Web directory. This file should not be in a publicly accessible directory. Keep it in the root directory of the user, or some other directory that they have write access to, but is not accessible through the Web site.

Another common request is to use the system password file to handle authentication. This is obviously a bad idea. One of the nice features of `.htaccess` is that it creates virtual users, with no permissions on the server. If you query the system password file, you are taking that advantage away, and by creating more system users, some of which will undoubtedly have very simple passwords; you are increasing the security risk to the server.

Finally, make sure that your `httpd.conf` file has the following lines:

```
<Files ~ "^\.ht">
    Order allow,deny
    Deny from all
</Files>
```

This will prevent site visitors from reading the contents of your `.htaccess` file. It also prevents site visitors from reading `.htpasswd` files, which are commonly used to store the username password combinations (of course you won't have to worry about that because your users will not have their `.htpassword` files in Web accessible directories).

Using a Staging Server

So far we have discussed ways you can tighten the security of your server, and of Apache in general. Although these suggestions are great in a perfect world controlled by system administrators, they are not always practical in a corporate environment.

One way to combine the security you, as an administrator, desire with the enhancements that your users demand is to setup a staging server.

A staging server is a server that is a mirror of your Web server. It has the same operating system, the same version of Apache, with all the same modules, the same version of PHP, Perl, and so on. New content is published to the staging server, tested, and then published to the live server. The staging server enables users to test code in a near production environment before making it live.

There are several advantages to running a staging server.

At a minimum forcing users to publish to a staging server enables you to close off unnecessary ports on your production server. As an example, although it might not be practical to force users to use SCP versus FTP, you can force all connections from the staging to the production server to be SCP. Which means you can disable FTP on the production server.

A staging server provides you with a testing ground for software upgrades. If you are worried that an upgrade might cause problems on your server, you can perform the upgrade on the staging server, giving yourself some room for error. If the installation is successful, perform it on the live server. Otherwise, determine what went wrong and try the installation on the staging server.

Having a staging server also enables you to lock down your server and tightly control what addresses can connect to the live server. On most variants of the *nix operating system this type of control is done through the `hosts.deny` and `hosts.allow` files. As the names suggest, the `hosts.allow` file determines who to allow access to selected services on the server, although the `hosts.deny` file lists addresses and services that are denied access to the server. The files can contain multiple lines, each one representing a different rule and the `hosts.allow` rules overwrite the rules in the `hosts.deny` file.

The `hosts.allow` and `hosts.deny` files are formatted in the same manner: service, hosts, and command. The service column is the service, or services (a comma-delimited list)—expressed as the services daemon—represented by a given rule. The hosts column is also a comma-delimited list of hosts to which the rule applies. The command column is a special command, executed by a query to the port, to which the rule applies.

In this case, you are trying to create as restrictive an environment as possible, so you would want to create a `hosts.deny` file that looks like this:

```
# /etc/hosts.deny
#
# Disallow all hosts.
ALL: ALL
```

19

APACHE SECURITY

This will block all traffic, on all ports to the server. Very secure, but not very practical. To compliment this restrictive `hosts.deny` file, you can create a `hosts.allow` file that looks something like this:

```
# /etc/hosts.allow
#
# Allow all traffic from the server.
ALL: LOCAL
#
# SSH traffic is allowed from the staging server and the
# local network
sshd: staging.domain.com, 10.10.100.
```

This enables the server to access all services, for sending mail, and other Web interfaces to services on the machine. It also enables all incoming traffic to the Web server, but blocks SSH traffic from all hosts, except the staging server and the local network.

Notice the local network is listed as `10.10.100`. The server interprets this to mean that any address from `10.10.100.1` through `10.10.100.254` is allowed to make a SSH connection. If you wanted to be more restrictive you could specify individual workstations that are allowed SSH access to the server.

Of course, this does not prevent a nefarious user from using a CGI exploit, or another security that can be accessed through the `httpd` server, but it does prevent them from accessing a security exploit on any ports you might have forgotten to close.

An important consideration with a staging server is the level of control you are going to allow the users of the server to have. There are two different models of staging server security. The first model enables users to upload their content to the staging server, test it, and then push it to the live server themselves, using staging tool servers you install. The second method is to have users upload content to the staging server, test it, and then send the server administrator, or group of administrators, an e-mail asking to have the documents published to the live server.

The second obviously provides tighter security control, however it makes a lot more work for the server administrator. It is important to determine how much time you are able to devote to managing content before deciding on a staging server strategy.

The placement of the staging server is an important consideration. Because you are, essentially, leaving this server wide open it is a good idea to place it behind a firewall. This will enable users from your network to access it, but no one from the outside. The live server can then be placed in a DMZ, between the firewall and the Internet, as shown in Figure 19.2, or placed in a collocation facility.

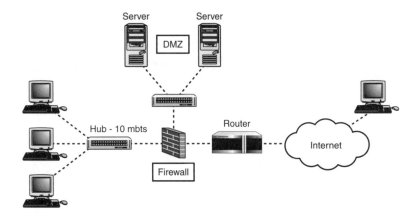

FIGURE 19.2
A Web server residing in a firewall DMZ.

Special Issues for Virtual Hosts

If you administer an Apache Web server for a hosting company, especially a shared server, you might have read this chapter and thought, "There is no way I am going to be able to implement and track these security guidelines for 200 different sites on a server."

The truth is, many of the more restrictive suggestions in this book are difficult to implement across the board for small hosts. Inevitably a customer will demand to have a feature enabled that you know is a bad idea. The quandary then becomes do you risk losing the revenue from that customer to maintain tighter security, or do you make an exception to your security policy?

Generally speaking, the same rules that apply to a multiuser single site also apply to servers with multiple Web sites:

- Restrict shell access to the server.
- Only allow SSI and .htaccess when necessary.
- Don't enable modules that you are not going to use.
- Make file permissions as tight as possible.

Fortunately, there are many control panels on the market that aide in maintaining site and system settings, while still giving you full control over Apache.

Control panels come in two varieties: open source, such as Webmin (http://www.webmin.com), and commercial, such as Plesk's Server Administrator (http://www.plesk.com). These control panels allow you to control more than just Apache.

But their Apache control is exceptional, letting you set default directives that are enabled for each account, as well as making exceptions for each individual account.

Special Issues for Windows and Apache

Repeated security issues with Microsoft's Internet Information Server have caused many Windows-based Web server administrators to abandon it and switch to Apache.

Apache is certainly an excellent choice on any platform, but there are some special security issues to be aware of when running Apache on the Windows platform.

If possible, run Apache on Windows 2000 versus Windows NT. Windows 2000 has more secure default system settings, which means you will be running more secure right out of the box.

As with a *nix installation you should be as restrictive as possible with file and directory permissions. Only providing write and execute capabilities when necessary.

It is also important to maintain a secure "user" and "group" structure so users cannot access the files of other users or groups.

Disabling ports and services that you are not using is also important. Windows 2000 does a good job of not running unnecessary services, or leaving unnecessary ports open, but you might have to manually make these changes in Windows NT.

Unlike a *nix systems, Microsoft recommends putting a Web site's root directory in a separate partition or on a different disk. Segmenting the site from the system files will prevent a user from accessing the system files, by changing directories to the server root.

You might have requests from users to access the Web server through a GUI interface such as PCAnywhere, or Terminal Server. Windows does not have the same type of control that *nix does, so if a user has access to the desktop, she can access all files on the server. In other words, this is not a good idea on a shared server.

If you do have a dedicated server, and don't mind giving users access to it, use Windows Terminal instead of PCAnywhere whenever possible. Windows Terminal connections are secure and encrypted. Everything in PCAnywhere is sent in plain text.

Finally, as with any operating system, it is important to keep up with the latest security patches and service packs. Microsoft does a good job of updating users when a new patch is released, but you also have to review and install the patch.

Summary

Hopefully reading through this chapter made you feel more paranoid about the security of your Apache installation.

You should not live in constant panic that your site is being attacked, but you should be aware of security issues, and take reasonable steps to ensure the security of your server.

The basic steps that can be taken to help secure Apache on any server are

1. Limit access to the server.
2. Only allow the root user to access the configuration files.
3. Maintain strict user and group rules.
4. Restrict the Apache features you enable to only those you need.
5. Keep up with operating system and Apache security patches.

If you follow these guidelines, you should have no trouble maintaining a secure Apache installation.

Security in Dynamic Content

IN THIS CHAPTER

"Some people are heroes. And some people jot down notes. Sometimes they're the same person."

The Truth—Terry Pratchett

The Common Gateway Interface (CGI) is an integral part of most Web sites today. Dynamic content allows a site owner to gain a better understanding of what visitors to the site are looking for, and it allows site users to communicate better with the owner of the site.

Unfortunately, CGI, and other types of dynamic content, also open up many more security holes than a site with plain HTML. This leaves a server administrator with a quandary: How do you protect the server and still allow site owners to interact with their site visitors?

CGI scripts are always going to present an inherent security risk. Any file that is executable, or interacts with files that are executable has risks associated with it. There are ways to minimize these risks.

By following good programming practices, strict file permission settings, and carefully monitoring your server you can severely diminish the potential for attacks.

There are two types of security concerns associated with CGI and dynamic content. The first is the potential to exploit the script or program to either break into your server, or take advantage of the resources on your server, such as your mail daemon. The second security risk is that a badly written program will use up an inordinate amount of system resources (RAM, Disk Space, or CPU). This can slow down your server, or worse, cause it to become completely unresponsive and crash.

This chapter focuses on both types of security risks, and gives you some pointers about how to lessen the risks and make your server run smoother. Most of the suggestions in this chapter will work whether you are running a single site on a server or multiple sites on a shared server.

Understanding Security Risks in Dynamic Content

Most server administrators do not take security risks seriously until something happens to their server. After all, there are literally millions of servers on the Internet, what are the chances that someone would attack yours?

Believe it or not the chances are pretty good. The Code Red worm was the first wake up call for many server administrators. In early August 2001 messages started appearing in hosting message boards all over the Internet asking what the following requests were:

```
"GET /default.ida?NNNNNNNNNNNNNNNNNNNNNNN"
```

They were, of course, part of the Code Red worm, which was spreading through the Internet very quickly and compromising many servers in the process. Those servers in turn infected other servers.

You are probably thinking to yourself, "That's fine, I am running Apache, Code Red only affected Windows servers running IIS. So it wouldn't have affected me."

That's not entirely true. You have to pay for bandwidth, especially if you collocate your server. Which means that the thousands of extra hits caused by a security hole within a dynamic content framework—Microsoft's Index Server—might have cost you money.

If you are still not sure, let's use an example that might be on your server. If you have a Web site, you probably have a contact feedback form, or perhaps several, that customers can use to send you messages.

Contact feedback forms are a great convenience to both you and your customers. You can direct traffic where you want it to go, and you can ensure the message has the information you need in it.

Feedback forms and other form processing scripts are so popular that there are Perl libraries written just to parse the data.

If your form processing script is written in Perl, it probably has code similar to this:

```perl
#!/usr/bin/perl
require 'cgi-lib.pl';

print &PrintHeader;

$subject = "FORM Data Received";

$mailprog = "/usr/sbin/sendmail";

&ReadParse;


$recipient = $FORM($recipient);

open(MAIL, "|$mailprog -t");
print MAIL "To: $recipient\n";
print MAIL "Subject: $subject\n";

foreach $key (keys(%FORM)) {
        print MAIL "$key = $FORM{$key}\n";
}
```

```
close(MAIL);

print <<EOF;

<html>
<body>
<h2>Your form has been sucessfully submitted</h2>
</body>
</html>
EOF
;
```

This script uses the `cgi-lib` Perl library (`http://cgi-lib.berkeley.edu`). `cgi-lib`, and other Perl libraries, are written to make some of the more repetitive Perl tasks simpler. Rather than type 10 lines of code to process the form data, a simple call to `cgi-lib.pl` provides a programmer with the same results.

The recipient of the e-mail is specified in a hidden field in the form. This means that anyone with a little knowledge of how CGI works can use your form, and server, to mass e-mail other users. To make matters worse you would have no idea because it would not get logged in Sendmail, or in the server records (except you would notice a lot more hits to that file).

As you can see, security has to be a concern for everyone who uses dynamic content.

Compiled Versus Parsed Dynamic Content

CGI Scripts fall into two different categories: Compiled and Parsed. A compiled script is a script that is able to run by itself without the need of an interpreter. Compiled scripts are similar to Windows executable files, double-click it and it runs.

A parsed script is a script that requires an interpreter to run. Perl scripts are great examples of parsed scripts. At the top of every Perl script is a line that identifies the Perl interpreter. It usually looks something like this:

```
#!/usr/bin/perl
```

Shell scripts are another example of parsed scripts.

Some programmers will tell you that, for security reasons, you should always use compiled scripts instead of parsed scripts. The truth is that parsed scripts can be as secure as compiled scripts.

The reasons people feel compiled scripts are safer than parsed scripts are twofold. The first has to do with the nature of compiled scripts. You can compile a script in binary format, which prevents potential intruders from obtaining the source code. If they cannot get the source code, it is harder for them to find weaknesses in the script.

The second reason some prefer compiled scripts is that it is more difficult to make system calls in compiled scripts. For example, if you are writing a shell script that outputs domain information, it is very simple to install a "whois" binary and create a system call to that command and output the information. This is a lot more difficult to do with a compiled script, so if you are writing a "whois" CGI Script in C, you will probably program the entire sequence from scratch, or even more likely, from borrowed code.

Of course, there is nothing wrong with using borrowed code, or current libraries. Many C/C++, Perl, and PHP Libraries perform routine, laborious tasks, and save time for programmers. Generally, these libraries have been thoroughly tested and are secure. But, never trust others to do your security checks. No matter how often a piece of code, or library has been used, it never hurts to review it for security holes.

Although these are compelling reasons to think that compiled scripts are safer than parsed scripts, the truth of the matter is that most modern parsed scripts provide programmers with many of the same security capabilities that compiled scripts have.

So, with good server security and good programming practices, a parsed script can be as secure as a compiled script.

Writing Safer Dynamic Content

There are many programming languages that are used to create CGI Scripts. When it comes to Apache, the three most popular languages, by far, are Perl, PHP, and C/C++.

To `cgi-bin` or Not

One of the most common questions asked by server administrators is whether or not they should put CGI Scripts in a `cgi-bin` directory.

The answer is that there is no inherent advantage to putting scripts in a specific directory. The same potential for security risks exists whether the scripts are in one place or spread over the server.

That being said, the advantage you get by having CGI scripts located in one place is that it is easier for you, as the server administrator, to monitor them for potential problems. It is also easier to maintain uniform permission standards across all directories and sites.

Common Mistakes

Although there are specific issues with each language, there are also some common guidelines, which should be followed by all CGI programmers.

Make sure you validate all input. Never accept user information without verifying it. This includes watching out for buffer overflows. A buffer overflow occurs when a fixed length is set for an input variable, and data is sent that is greater than that variable length. The excess characters can be used to execute a system command or cause other problems. Most modern languages, such as Perl, JAVA, and PHP have safeguards against buffer overflows. Unfortunately, neither C nor C++ have these safeguards.

As mentioned previously, limit system calls as much as possible. Only call to system programs when necessary, and as with other variables, validate input to ensure the calls are behaving as you expected them to.

If there is an error with a script, avoid providing too much information regarding the error. Follow the example set by Apache—if a user requests a document that is not available, Apache returns the 404 Error, and simply states that the file is not found. The simpler your error messages, the less likely someone will be to use that information to exploit your server.

In general, it is a good idea to avoid giving too much information out about the server configuration.

Perl

Perl is the programming language most closely associated with CGI. It's flexibility and power has made it popular with Web developers for years.

The downside to this popularity is that literally hundreds of thousands of inexperienced programmers write or edit Perl scripts that are available for download. These scripts are a great convenience, but are often riddled with security holes similar to the example used in the beginning of this chapter.

There are several steps you can take to secure Perl scripts. Some of these steps will apply to other parsed languages, whereas some are Perl specific.

Always run Perl with the -T and -w tags enabled. The -T tag tells Perl to run in taint mode. Taint mode assumes that all variables received from the command line, STDIN, or the users environment variables are unsafe, and will not pass these variables to anything outside of your program.

If you enable taint mode you will, at a minimum, need to do to things to run your scripts. First you will need to set your path:

```
ENV{'PATH'} = '/bin:/usr/bin:/usr/sbin';
```

Or whatever directories you want to ensure are included in your path.

You will also need to untaint any variables, that are going to pass data to another program. A common example of this is taint checking an e-mail address before passing it to Sendmail. You can untaint an e-mail address like this:

```
$email =~ /(\w{1}[\w-.]*)\@([\w-.]+)/ or die "not a valid e-mail address";
$email = "$1\@$2";
```

These lines parse the variable $email to make sure the e-mail address contains valid character constructs. Note, this is not the same as ensuring the e-mail address is valid. If the address appears to be okay, the variable information is removed and replaced by $1 and $2. Although this is simply a copy of the original variable, it is now clean and can be passed onto other programs.

Any Perl variable that will be passed to another program should pass through this type of taint check. Of course, if your variable is already tainted, your results will become tainted.

In addition to the taint flag, Perl scripts should have the -w flag enabled. The -w flag tells Perl to run in warn mode. This means that Perl will warn you about potential problems or obsolete commands within a script.

The taint and warn flags will increase the security of your scripts, but you should also follow secure programming practices.

Again referring to the script at the beginning of this chapter, one way it can be secured is by specifying which referrers are allowed to access the script:

```
if (($ENV{'HTTP_REFERER'}) &&
($ENV{'HTTP_REFERER'} !~ /^http:\/\/test.example.com/)) {
print "Content-type: text/html\n\n";
print "Sorry, you are not able to access this script\n";
exit 0;
}
```

These lines check the referring page. If it is not within the test.example.com domain an error message is printed and the program is exited. You can be even more specific and set the referral to certain pages (such as, test.example.com/form.html).

This security precaution should not be used alone. The HTTP_REFERRER field can be easily faked. It is, however, part of a good programming strategy.

You can also use environmental variables to limit GET requests:

```
if($ENV{'REQUEST_METHOD'} eq "GET"){
print "Content-type: text/html\n\n";
print "Sorry, you are not able to access this script\n";
exit 0;
}
```

Finally, you can also limit the e-mail addresses that are allowed to use a form:

```
@mailto = ('^allan@example.com','^roseanne@example.com');
```

This creates an array that includes my wife and my e-mail addresses. This array can be used to limit the valid e-mail addresses to which the script can send information.

For more information about securing Perl scripts, you might want to read *Sams Teach Yourself Perl in 24 Hours, Second Edition.*

PHP

PHP is a relatively new scripting language, but its ease of use, cross-platform capabilities, and Web integration has quickly made it a favorite among Web developers.

There are two ways in which PHP scripts can be run: As part of an Apache module or as CGI scripts.

For security reasons, you are better off running PHP as an Apache module. When run as an Apache module, PHP derives security settings from Apache, which is already secure.

When you run PHP as an Apache module, the PHP environment settings are taken from the PHP configuration file called `php.ini`. By securing your `php.ini` file you are able to diminish the security risks posed by PHP scripts.

One of the easiest changes you can make is to enable the `safe_mode` variable in the `php.ini` file. Because of additional security concerns, when you enable `safe_mode` you should do it in conjunction with run `suEXEC` (discussed later in this chapter).

When `safe_mode` is enabled PHP compares the owner of a file that is requested by a script with the owner of the script. For instance, if you were to put this script on your server:

```
<?php
 readfile('/etc/passwd)';
?>
```

Anyone who accessed it would be able to read the contents of your `passwd` file. Enabling `safe_mode` will prevent that script from being successfully executed, and an error will be generated.

In conjunction with `safe_mode`, you should also limit PHP script access to the Apache root document directory. You can do this by enabling the `doc_root` variable. The `doc_root` variable defines the location of the Web server root, so users cannot use PHP scripts to access server files outside of that realm. The variable is simple to set, simply point it to the root Web directory:

```
doc_root = /home/httpd/
```

Finally, you can also limit the types of system calls that a user can make by using the `disable_functions` variable. `Disable_functions` operates independently of `safe_mode` and is a comma delimitated list of function names:

```
disable_functions = fwrite();
```

C and C++

As Perl and PHP have grown in popularity C and C++ have diminished as CGI scripting tools. However, there are still many C and C++ CGI scripts used on the Web today, and it is important to understand what type of security risks are involved.

The biggest security concern with C and C++ is that they are very susceptible to buffer overflows, as described earlier.

You can prevent buffer overflows from occurring by dynamically setting the buffer size. The World Wide Web Consortium recommends the following in their Security FAQ:

```
char* read_POST() {
    int query_size=atoi(getenv("CONTENT_LENGTH"));
    char* query_string = (char*) malloc(query_size);
    if (query_string != NULL)
        fread(query_string,query_size,1,stdin);
    return query_string;
}
```

This reads the data from a form, and assigns the sets the size of the incoming data to the size of the CGI environment variable `CONTENT_LENGTH`. In other words, it sets the size of the buffer to the size of the incoming data.

In addition to dynamically setting the buffer size, you should use standard library functions that defend against buffer overflows. For example, instead of using the library calls `strcpy` and `strcat`, use `strncpy` and `strncat`.

As with Perl and PHP when programming in C and C++ it is important to check incoming data before passing it to a shell command.

Even though C and C++ scripts are compiled they can still cause the same level of damage if you do not perform the same data integrity checks as you would with a Perl or PHP script.

In fact, a C/C++ script can often cause more damage because there is no controlled space, also called a programming sandbox, where experimental code can be tried out to see if there are any potential problems.

Wrappers

A wrapper is program that runs on your server and helps lessen the security risks associated with CGI scripts. There are several ways this can be done.

The most common method of security control is to allow CGI scripts to be run under the user ID of the site owner—the owner of the directories within which the site resides.

How does allowing scripts to be executed with the same ID as the site owner increase security? In a non-wrapper environment the scripts are executed as the Apache user. This means that the Apache user has to be a member of the same group as the site owner. It also means that anyone on the server has the ability to execute a script, or write to a database in any other site directory on the server.

The two most common wrappers used with Apache are CGIWrap and suEXEC.

CGIWrap

CGIWrap is a very popular wrapper. In addition to the advantages of wrappers already discussed, CGIWrap also performs security checks on the script.

CGIWrap is not installed natively with either Apache or operating systems, so you will need to download and install it. The source code is available from the Unix Tools Web site (`http://www.unixtools.org`). As of this writing the latest version is 3.7.1.

The following instructions are for installation on RedHat 7.1. Please check the CGIWrap installation file for variations of this process for different operating systems.

Start by uncompressing the file:

```
[root@test /root]# tar xvfz cgiwrap-3.7.1.tar.gz
```

Change into the newly created directory:

```
 [root@test /root]# cd cgiwrap-3.7.1/
```

At this point you can either begin the installation process with the program defaults, or you can compile with specific program tags enabled.

You can view the options available by typing:

```
[root@test cgiwrap-3.7.1]# ./configure —help
```

At a minimum you will need to specify the Apache user, and the directory in which you would like to install CGIWrap. An example of a CGIWrap configuration might look something like this:

```
[root@test cgiwrap-3.7.1]# ./configure —with-httpd-user=nobody \
> —with-install-dir=/home/httpd/cgi-bin/ \
> —with-local-contact-email=allan@example.com
```

Finally, you will need to compile and install the program:

```
[root@test cgiwrap-3.7.1]# make && make install
```

You have now successfully installed CGIWrap; the next step is to setup Apache to use CGIWrap. The most common method for doing this is to use the URL Rewriting Engine.

URL Rewriting Engine

The URL Rewriting Engine, or mod_rewrite, is a standard Apache module that allows you to rewrite URL requests on the fly.

Apache processes HTTP requests in phases. The Apache API allows modules to write hooks into these different phases.

Mod_rewrite intercepts an HTTP request in two of these phases. The first place is after the request for a URL has been made, which is the URL to filename translation. The second is when the specific directory configurations are processed.

So between the time Apache determines which server, or virtual server, to send the traffic to and the request is returned to the browser, is when mod_rewrite is activated.

A detailed discussion of mod_rewrite is outside the realm of this chapter, for more information, please visit the URL Rewriting Engine Web site (http://httpd.apache.org/docs/mod/mod_rewrite.html).

Mod_rewrite and CGIWrap

So, how do mod_rewrite and CGIWrap work together? It is actually pretty simple. Let's start by creating a virtual host:

```
<VirtualHost 192.168.0.40>
DocumentRoot /home/httpd/foo/public_html
ServerName test.example.com
</VirtualHost>
```

Add the ScriptAlias directive:

```
ScriptAlias /cgi-bin/ /home/httpd/foo/public_html/cgi-bin/
```

Turn on URL Rewriting for this host:

```
RewriteEngine On
```

Finally, we need to redirect traffic for /cgi-bin to the CGIWrap directory we created earlier:

20

```
RewriteRule ^/~(.*)/cgi-bin/(.*) /home/httpd/cgi-bin/$1/$2 [PT]
```

Put everything together and it should look something like this:

```
<VirtualHost 192.168.0.40>
DocumentRoot /home/httpd/foo/public_html
ServerName test.example.com
ScriptAlias /cgi-bin/ /var/www/cgi-bin/
RewriteEngine On
RewriteRule ^/~(.*)/cgi-bin/(.*) /home/httpd/cgi-bin/$1/$2 [PT]
</VirtualHost>
```

Of course, make sure that you have enabled the mod_rewrite module so it is loaded, and make sure you have enabled ExecCGI for the directory.

Of course you will want to test to see if your new configuration is working. The simplest way to do this is to make a simple Perl script and link to it:

```
#!/usr/bin/perl -Tw
print "Content-type: text/html\n\n";
print "Hello, world!\n";
```

When you click the link to the script you should see a message in the Status Window telling you that you are being redirected (it will probably go by pretty quickly, so don't blink). If you do, congratulations, you have managed to successfully install CGIWrap.

How does this help secure your dynamic content? The cgi-bin has been removed from the root Web directory to another directory to which the site user does not have access. This allows you, as the server administrator, to maintain better control over the scripts that are being used on the server. You can either review code that is submitted by users, or restrict access to only those scripts you have preinstalled.

It also allows you to severely limit the allowed directives within the user's home directory.

suEXEC

Apache includes it's own security wrapper, called suEXEC. As with CGIWrap, suEXEC allows a server administrator to configure sites so that CGI scripts run as the owner of the site, as opposed to the owner of the httpd process.

SuEXEC can also provide performance gains over CGIWrap. Because suEXEC is compiled into the Apache module, it responds faster and resides in memory. It does not have to be called every time a script is executed.

The way suEXEC works is relatively simple. When a request for a CGI or Server-Side Includes file that does not have the same user ID as the Apache Web server is made Apache passes the information to the suEXEC wrapper, which performs a series of checks on the script. If the script passes the checks it is executed. If it does not, an error is created and logged, and a 500 status code is returned.

There are 20 suEXEC checks that a script has to pass before Apache will execute it. You can read more about the specific checks at the Apache suEXEC Web site (`http://httpd.apache.org/docs/suexec.html`).

Before you can configure suEXEC you have to make sure it is installed and running. When you compiled your Apache installation you should have done so using the `−enable-suexec` flag when you installed Apache.

If suEXEC has been successfully compiled into your Apache installation you should see a line appear in your `httpd_error` log when Apache starts, that looks like this:

```
[Fri Nov  2 08:35:40 2001] [notice] suEXEC mechanism enabled
➥(wrapper: /usr/sbin/suexec)
```

The most common way to use suEXEC is with the User and Group directives. When you create a virtual host you can assign a user to that virtual host. That user will now be able to execute scripts with his or her username.

Let's use the same virtual host we set up in the last section to demonstrate this. Change the virtual host configuration to look something like this:

```
<VirtualHost 192.168.0.40>
DocumentRoot /home/httpd/foo/public_html
ServerName test.example.com
ScriptAlias /cgi-bin/ /home/httpd/foo/public_html/cgi-bin/
User allan
Group allan
</VirtualHost>
```

User and group have to be defined in order for suEXEC to work. If only one or the other is defined suEXEC will fail the process and an error will be generated.

A couple of other things you need to worry about with suEXEC. The owner of the Web server process needs to be able to su to the user and group of the script owner. If the Apache user cannot then the script will fail.

Using the hello script created in the last section, set permissions to the user group you defined in the virtual host configuration, and try to execute the script.

To see what an error looks like, change the owner of the script so it does not match what is defined in the virtual host configuration.

You might have to adjust some settings to get suEXEC to work initially; it tends to be more complicated than CGIWrap to configure. However, the additional security it provides, is worth the initial configuration problems.

Checking Code in Existing Scripts

It is not uncommon to install third party CGI scripts on your server. In fact there are hundreds of sites that provide CGI scripts at either a low cost or completely free. Of course, after reading this chapter you are undoubtedly worried about the security measures in those scripts.

The more worried you are the better. Although it is not necessary to never use free scripts, it is important to thoroughly examine anything you install on your server for potential security breaches.

Of course it does help to know what to look for. Reading this chapter has, hopefully, given you some idea of the more common security holes. No matter what language the script is written in, there are several commonalities you can look for to see if it is secure, or, if it is not, if you can fix it to make it more secure.

The biggest security hole to watch out for is scripts that read or write to the system. It's probably been mentioned a dozen times in this chapter, but it bears repeating. Never write unchecked data to your server, and don't allow a script to read from any file on the server.

Look for calls to system programs. Scripts that use Sendmail are the best examples of this. There is nothing inherently wrong with calling system programs, but always make sure the data being passed to those programs is checked.

Hard code system paths into the script. Some programmers prefer to use the PATH CGI environment variable as a shortcut, but that can create security problems.

Someone looking to hack into your site can alter the PATH environment variable to point to the program he wants to execute, as opposed to your program.

If you watch for these three problems and correct them if you do see them, you can save yourself a lot of headaches in the future.

Special Issues with Windows CGI

The security issues discussed so far in this chapter: monitor input, minimize information shared about the server, and avoid system calls all apply to Windows scripting as well. However, there are some special considerations when programming CGI scripts on the Windows platform.

One thing to watch for is that Windows likes to create executable files. This is especially true with FrontPage Extensions. If these executables are created in a directory that has executable permissions, such as a `cgi-bin` directory, then everyone has access to it. One way to avoid this is problem to set permissions for CGI folders to allow scripts to be run, but not allow files to be executed.

Another common security error for parsed scripts is to put the interpreter in the Web server path. When installing Perl or PHP, the executable file should go into a path that the scripts can reach, but that is outside of the Web server root path so an intruder cannot access it.

You can use suEXEC with a Microsoft Windows installation of Apache. The configuration works in the same manner, taking into account the different directory structure. CGIWrap is not currently available for Microsoft Windows installations. Finally, as with other operating systems, be careful with your directory permissions and script permissions.

Summary

CGI scripts and other forms of dynamic content are an integral part of most Web sites.

Although the functionality that dynamic content provides is important to enhance the user experience, it comes with some security risk. The more interaction you create with your users the greater security risk you create for your server.

There are four rules that you can follow to help increase your server's level of security, while still providing the interaction with your site that users want:

- Always validate input. Whether it is from a form, database queries, or any other way of getting data, never accept it blindly.
- Whenever possible use libraries that have been time-tested for security. In addition to shortening your programming cycle the authors of the code have, hopefully, repeatedly tested the code for security. Of course, no matter how secure a library is, it is still important to review it to ensure there are no potential security holes that might have been overlooked.
- It is especially important to validate anything that is going to be sent to a system program. Never pass data to another program without first checking it.
- Do not trust the PATH CGI Variable Environment. Always use hard-coded paths.

If you follow these steps, the security of your server will be greatly enhanced.

20

SECURITY IN
DYNAMIC
CONTENT

Authentication, Authorization, and Access Control

IN THIS CHAPTER

"Mr. Cruncher himself always spoke of the year of our Lord as Anna Dominoes: apparently under the impression that the Christian era dated from the invention of a popular game, by a lady who had bestowed her name upon it."

A Tale of Two Cities—Charles Dickens

Apache has three distinct ways of dealing with the question of whether a particular request for a resource will result in that resource actually being returned. These criteria are called *authorization*, *authentication*, and *access control*.

Authentication is any process by which you verify that someone is who he claims to be. This usually involves a username and a password, but can include any other method of demonstrating identity, such as a smart card, retina scan, voice recognition, or fingerprints. Authentication is equivalent to showing your driver's license at the ticket counter at the airport.

Authorization is finding out if the person, when identified, is permitted to have the resource. This is usually determined by finding out if that person is a part of a particular group, if that person has paid admission, or has a particular level of security clearance. Authorization is equivalent to checking the guest list at an exclusive party, or checking for your ticket when you go to the opera.

Finally, access control is a much more general way of controlling access to a Web resource. Access can be granted or denied based on a wide variety of criteria, such as the network address of the client, the time of day, the phase of the moon, or which browser the visitor is using. Access control is analogous to locking the gate at closing time, or only letting people onto the ride who are more than 48 inches tall—it's controlling entrance by some arbitrary condition which may or may not have anything to do with the attributes of the particular visitor.

Because these three techniques are so closely related in most real applications, it is difficult to talk about them separate from one another. In particular, authentication and authorization are, in most actual implementations, inextricable.

If you have information on your Web site that is sensitive, or, is intended for only a small group of people, the techniques in this chapter will help you make sure that the only people to see those pages are the people that you want to see them.

Basic Authentication

As the name implies, basic authentication is the simplest method of authentication, and for a long time was the most common. However, other methods of authentication have recently passed basic in common usage, because of usability issues that will be discussed shortly.

How Basic Authentication Works

When a particular resource has been protected using basic authentication, Apache sends a `401 Authentication Required` header with the response to the request to notify the client that user credentials must be supplied in order for the resource to be returned as requested.

Upon receiving a `401` response header, the client's browser, if it supports basic authentication, will ask the user to supply a username and password to be sent to the server. If you are using a graphical browser, such as Netscape or Internet Explorer, you will see is a box that gives you a place to type your username and password to be sent back to the server. If the username is in the approved list, and if the password supplied is correct, the resource will be returned to the client.

Because the HTTP protocol is stateless, each request will be treated in the same way, even though they are from the same client. That is, every resource requested from the server will have to supply authentication credentials over again to receive the resource.

Fortunately, the browser takes care of the details here, so that you only have to type your user-name and password one time per browser session. However, you might have to type it again the next time you open up your browser and visit the same Web site.

Along with the `401` response certain other information will be passed back to the client. In particular, it sends a name that is associated with the protected area of the Web site. This is called the *realm*, or just the authentication name. The client browser caches the username and password that you supplied and stores it along with the authentication realm so if other resources are requested from the same realm, the same username and password can be returned to authenticate that request without requiring the user to type them in again. This cacheing is usually just for the current browser session, but some browsers allow you to store them permanently so you never have to type your password again.

The authentication name, or realm, will appear in the pop-up box to identify what the user-name and password are being requested for.

Configuration: Protecting Content with Basic Authentication

Two or three configuration steps must be completed to protect a resource using basic authentication, depending on what you are trying to do.

1. Create a password file
2. Set the configuration to use this password file
3. Optionally, create a group file

Create a Password File

To determine whether a particular username/password combination is valid it will need to be compared to some authoritative listing of usernames and passwords. This is the password file, which you will need to create on the server side and populate with valid users and their passwords.

Because this file contains sensitive information it should be stored outside of the document directory. Although, as you will see in a moment, the passwords are encrypted in the file, therefore, if a cracker were to gain access to the file it would be an aid in their attempt to figure out the passwords. And, because people tend to be sloppy with their passwords, for example, using the same password for Web site authentication as for their bank account, this could potentially be a very serious breach of security, even if the content on your Web site is not particularly sensitive.

> **WARNING**
>
> Encourage your users to use a different password for your Web site than the use for other more essential things. For example, many people tend to use two passwords—one for all their extremely important things, such as the login to their desktop computer and their bank account, and another for less sensitive things, the compromise of which would be less serious.

To create the password file use the `htpasswd` utility that came with Apache. This will be located in the `bin` directory of wherever you installed Apache. For example, it will probably be located at `/usr/local/apache/bin/htpasswd` if you installed Apache from source.

To create the file, type:

```
htpasswd -c /usr/local/apache/passwd/password username
```

`htpasswd` will ask you for the password, and then ask you to type it again to confirm it:

```
# htpasswd -c /usr/local/apache/passwd/passwords rbowen
New password: mypassword
Re-type new password: mypassword
Adding password for user rbowen
```

Note that in the example shown, a password file is being created containing a user called `rbowen`, and this password file is being placed in the location `/usr/local/apache/passwd/passwords`. You will substitute the location and the username, which you want to use to start your password file.

If `htpasswd` is not in your path, you will have to type the full path to the file to get it to run. That is, in the previous example, you would replace `htpasswd` with `/usr/local/apache/bin/htpasswd`.

The `-c` flag is used only when you are creating a new file. After the first time, you will omit the `-c` flag, when you are adding new users to an already-existing password file.

```
htpasswd /usr/local/apache/passwd/passwords sungo
```

The example just shown will add a user named `sungo` to a password file that has already been created earlier. As before, you will be asked for the password at the command line, and then will be asked to confirm the password by typing it again.

> **WARNING**
>
> Be very careful not to use the `-c` flag by mistake when you add new users to an existing password file. Using the `-c` flag will create a new password file, even if you already have an existing file with that name. That is, it will remove the contents of the file that is there and replace it with a new file containing only the one username that you were adding.

The password is stored in encrypted form in the password file, so users on the system will not be able to read the file and immediately determine the passwords of all the users. Nevertheless, you should store the file in as secure a location as possible with whatever minimum permissions on the file so that the Web server itself can read the file. For example, if your server is configured to run as user `nobody` and group `nogroup`, then you should set permissions on the file so that only that user can read the file:

```
chown nobody.nogroup /usr/local/apache/passwd/passwords
chmod 640 /usr/local/apache/passwd/passwords
```

On Windows, a similar precaution should be taken, changing the ownership of the password file to the Web server user, so that other users cannot read the file.

Set the Configuration to Use This Password File

When you have created the password file, you need to tell Apache about it, and tell Apache to use this file to require user credentials for admission. This configuration is done with the directives in Table 21.1:

TABLE 21.1   Configuring Apache to Use the Password File

Directive	Meaning
AuthType	Authentication type being used. In this case, it will be set to Basic.
AuthName	The authentication realm or name.
AuthUserFile	The location of the password file.
AuthGroupFile	The location of the group file, if any.
Require	The requirement(s) which must be satisfied to grant admission.

These directives might be placed in an .htaccess file in the particular directory being protected, or, perhaps, in the main server configuration file in a <Directory> section, or other scope container.

The following example defines an authentication realm called "By Invitation Only." The password file located at /usr/local/apache/passwd/passwords will be used to verify the user's identity. Only users named rbowen or sungo will be granted access, and even then only if they provide a password that matches the one stored in the password file.

```
AuthType Basic
AuthName "By Invitation Only"
AuthUserFile /usr/local/apache/passwd/passwords
Require user rbowen sungo
```

The phrase "By Invitation Only" will be displayed in the password pop-up box, where the user will have to type their credentials.

If these directives were put in the main server configuration file, you will need to restart your Apache server for the new configuration to take effect. Directives placed in .htaccess files take effect immediately because .htaccess files are parsed each time files are served.

The next time you load a file from that directory, you will see the familiar username/password dialog box pop up, requiring that you type the username and password before you are permitted to proceed.

In addition to specifically listing the users to whom you want to grant access, you can specify that any valid user should be let in. This is done with the valid-user keyword:

```
Require valid-user
```

Optionally, Create a Group File

Most of the time, you will want more than one, or two, or even a dozen people to have access to a resource. You want to define a group that has access to that resource, and manage that group by adding and removing members without having to edit the server configuration file and restart Apache each time.

This is handled using authentication groups. An authentication group is, as you would expect, a group name associated with a list of members. This list is stored in a group file, which should be stored in the same location as the password file, so that you are able to keep track of these things.

The format of the group file is exceedingly simple. A group name appears first on a line, followed by a colon, and then a list of the members of the group separated by spaces. For example:

```
authors: rich daniel allan
```

When this file has been created, you can `Require` that someone be in a particular group to get the requested resource. This is done with the `AuthGroupFile` directive, as shown in the following example.

```
AuthType Basic
AuthName "Apache Admin Guide Authors"
AuthUserFile /usr/local/apache/passwd/passwords
AuthGroupFile /usr/local/apache/passwd/groups
Require group authors
```

The authentication process is now one step more involved. When a request is received, and the requested username and password are supplied, the group file is checked first to see if the supplied username is even in the required group. If it is, then the password file will be checked to see if the username there and if the supplied password matches the password stored in that file. If any of these steps fail, access will be forbidden.

Frequently Asked Questions About Basic Authentication

The following questions tend to get asked very frequently with regard to basic authentication. It should be understood that basic authentication is very basic, and, therefore, is limited to the set of features that has been presented previously. Most of the more interesting things that people tend to want need to be implemented using some alternate authentication scheme.

How Do I Log Out?

Since browsers first started implementing basic authentication, Web site administrators have wanted to know how to enable the user log out. Because the browser caches the username and password with the authentication realm, as described earlier in this chapter, this is not a function of the server configuration. It is, however, a question of getting the browser to forget the credential information so that the next time the resource is requested the username and password must be supplied again. There are numerous situations in which this is desirable, such as when using a browser in a public location, and when you don't want to leave the browser logged in so the next person can get into your bank account.

Despite this perhaps being the most frequently asked question about basic authentication, thus far none of the major browser manufacturers have seen this as being a desirable feature to put into their products.

Consequently, the answer to this question is, you can't. Sorry.

How Can I Change What the Password Box Looks Like?

The dialog that pops up for the user to enter their username and password is ugly. It contains unwanted text, it looks different in Internet Explorer and Netscape, and contains different text. It also asks for fields that the user might not understand—for example, Netscape asks the user to type their "User ID". Or, you might want to provide additional explanatory text so that the user has a better idea what is going on.

Unfortunately, these things are features of the browser and cannot be controlled from the server side. If you want the login to look different, then you will need to implement your own authentication scheme. There is no way to change what this login box looks like if you are using basic authentication.

How Do I Make It Not Ask Me for My Password the Next Time?

Your browser forgets your username and password because most browsers only store your password information for the current browser session. So, when you visit the same Web site again, you will need to re-enter your username and password.

There is nothing that can be done about this on the server side.

However, the most recent versions of the major browsers contain the capability to remember your password forever, so that you never have to log in again. Although it is debatable whether this is a good idea because it effectively overrides the entire point of having security in the first place, but it is certainly convenient for the user, and simplifies the user experience.

> **NOTE**
>
> Note that there are alternate authentication methods, such as using cookies, which can make logins persistent, and not require you to log in again the next time you visit the site. But this is not something that you can do on the server side when using Basic authentication.

Why Does It Sometimes Ask Me for My Password Twice?

When entering a password-protected Web site for the first time, you will occasionally notice that you are asked for your password twice. This might happen immediately after you entered the password the first time or it might happen when you click the first link after authenticating the first time.

This happens for a very simple, but nonetheless confusing reason, again having to do with the way that the browser caches the login information.

Browsers store login information based on the authentication realm, specified by the `AuthName` directive and by the server name. This way the browser can distinguish between the `Private` authentication realm on one site and on another. So, if you go to a site using one name for the server, and internal links on the server refer to that server by a different name, the browser has no way to know that they are in fact the same server.

For example, if you were to visit the URL `http://example.com/private/`, which required authentication, your browser would remember the supplied username and password associated with the hostname `example.com`. If, by virtue of an internal redirect or fully qualified HTML links in pages, you are then sent to the URL `http://www.example.com/private/`. Even though this is really the exact same URL, the browser does not know this for sure and is forced to request the authentication information again because `example.com` and `www.example.com` are not exactly the same hostname. Your browser has no particular way to know that these are the same Web site.

Security Caveat

Basic authentication should not be considered secure by any particularly rigorous definition of secure.

Although the password is stored on the server in encrypted format, it is passed from the client to the server in plain text across the network. Anyone listening with any variety of packet sniffer will be able to read the username and password in the clear as it goes across.

Also, remember that the username and password are passed with every request, not just when the user first types them in. So the packet sniffer doesn't need to be listening at a particularly strategic time, but just long enough to see any request come across the wire.

And, in addition to that, the content itself is also going across the network in the clear. So, if the Web site contains sensitive information the same packet sniffer would have access to that information as it went past, even if the username and password were not used to gain direct access to the Web site.

Don't use basic authentication for anything that requires real security. It is a detriment for most users because very few people will take the trouble, or have the necessary software and/or equipment to find out passwords. However, if someone had a desire to get in, it would take very little for him to do so.

Digest Authentication

Addressing one of the security caveats of basic authentication, digest authentication provides an alternate method for protecting your Web content. However, it to has a few caveats.

How Digest Authentication Works

Digest authentication is implemented by the module `mod_auth_digest`. There is an older module, `mod_digest`, which implemented an older version of the digest authentication specification, but probably will not work with newer browsers.

Using digest authentication, your password is never sent across the network in the clear, but is always transmitted as an MD5 digest of the user's password. This way, the password cannot be determined by sniffing network traffic.

The full specification of digest authentication can be seen in the Internet standards document RFC 2617, which you can see at `http://www.ietf.org/rfc/rfc2617.txt`. MD5 itself is described in RFC 1321, which you can find at `http://www.ietf.org/rfc/rfc1321.txt-from` TE. Additional information and resources about MD5 can be found at `http://userpages.umbc.edu/ mabzug1/cs/md5/md5.html`.

Configuration: Protecting Content with Digest Authentication

The steps for configuring your server for digest authentication are very similar to those for basic authentication.

1. Create the password file
2. Set the configuration to use this password file
3. Optionally, create a group file

Creating a Password File (Digest Authentication)

As with basic authentication, a simple utility is provided to create and maintain the password file that will be used to determine whether a particular user's name and password are valid. This utility is called `htdigest`, and will be located in the `bin` directory of wherever you installed Apache. If you installed Apache from some variety of package manager, `htdigest` is likely to have been placed somewhere in your path.

To create a new digest password file, type

```
htdigest -c /usr/local/apache/passwd/digest realm username
```

`htdigest` will ask you for the desired password, and then ask you to type it again to confirm it.

Note that the realm for which the authentication will be required is part of the argument list.

Once again, as with basic authentication, you are encouraged to place the generated file somewhere outside of the document directory.

And, as with the htpasswd utility, the -c flag creates a new file, or, if a file of that name already exists, deletes the contents of that file and generates a new file in its place. Omit the -c flag to add new user information to an existing password file.

Set the Configuration to Use This Password File (Digest Authentication)

When you have created a password file, you need to tell Apache about it to start using it as a source of authenticated user information. This configuration is done with the directives detailed in Table 21.2:

TABLE 21.2 Configuration Directives to Use the Password File(Digest)

Directive	Meaning
AuthType	Authentication type being used. In this case, it will be set to Digest.
AuthName	The authentication realm or name.
AuthDigestFile	The location of the password file.
AuthDigestGroupFile	Location of the group file, if any.
Require	The requirement(s) that must be satisfied in order to grant permission.

These directives might be placed in an .htaccess file in the particular directory being protected, or they might go in the main server configuration file, in a <Directory> section, or another scope container.

The following example defines an authentication realm called "Private." The password file located at /usr/local/apache/passwd/digest will be used to verify the user's identity. Only users named drbacchus or dorfl will be granted access if they provide a password that matches the password stored in the password file.

```
AuthType Digest
AuthName "Private"
AuthDigestFile /usr/local/apache/passwd/digest
Require user drbacchus dorfl
```

The phrase "Private" will be displayed in the password pop-up box, where the user will have to type their credentials.

Optionally, Create a Group File (Digest Authentication)

As you have observed, there are not many differences between this configuration process and that required by basic authentication, described in the previous section. This is true also of group functionality. The group file used for digest authentication is exactly the same as that used for basic authentication. That is, lines in the group file consist of the name of the group, a colon, and a list of the members of that group. For example:

```
admins: jim roy ed anne
```

When this file has been created, you can `Require` that someone be in a particular group to get the requested resource. This is done with the `AuthDigestGroupFile` directive, as shown in the following example.

```
AuthType Digest
AuthName "Private"
AuthDigestFile /usr/local/apache/passwd/digest
AuthDigestGroupFile /usr/local/apache/passwd/digest.groups
Require group admins
```

The authentication process is the same as that used by basic authentication. It is first verified that the user is in the required group, and, if this is true, then the password is verified.

Caveats

Before you leap into using digest authentication instead of basic authentication, there are a few things that you should know.

Digest authentication does give you the advantage of not having to send your password across the network in the clear, however, it is not supported by all major browsers in use today. So, you should not use it on a Web site that you cannot control the browsers that people will be using, such as on your intranet site. In particular, Opera 4.0 or later, Microsoft Internet Explorer 5.0 or later, and Amaya support digest authentication, whereas Netscape, Mozilla, and various other browsers do not.

Next, with regard to security considerations, you should understand two things. Although your password is not passed in the clear all your data is, so this is a rather small measure of security. And, although your password is not really sent at all, but a digest form of it, someone very familiar with the workings of HTTP could use that information—just your digested password—and use that to gain access to the content because that digested password is really all the information required to access the Web site.

The moral of this is that if you have content that really needs to be kept secure, use SSL. (See Chapter 22, "SSL," for more details.)

Authentication, Authorization, and Access Control

CHAPTER 21

295

21

AUTHENTICATION,
AUTHORIZATION,
AND ACCESS

Database Authentication Modules

Basic authentication and digest authentication both suffer from the same major flaw. They use text files to store the authentication information. The problem with this is that looking something up in a text file is very slow. It's like trying to find something in a book that has no index. You have to start at the beginning and work through it one page at a time until you find what you are looking for. Now imagine that the next time you need to find the same thing, you don't remember where it was, so you have to start at the beginning again and work through one page at a time until you find it again. And the next time. And the time after that.

Because HTTP is stateless authentication has to be verified every time that content is requested. So, every time a document is accessed which is secured with basic or digest authentication, Apache has to open up those text password files and look through them one line at a time until it finds the user that is trying to log in and verifies their password. In the worst case, if the username supplied is not in there at all, every line in the file will need to be checked. On average, half of the file will need to be read before the user is found. This is very slow.

Although this is not a big problem for small sets of users, when you get into larger numbers of users (where "larger" means a few hundred) this becomes prohibitively slow. In many cases, valid username/password combinations will get rejected because the authentication module just had to spend so much time looking for the username in the file that Apache will just get tired of waiting and return a failed authentication.

In these cases you need an alternative, and that alternative is to use some variety of database. Databases are optimized for looking for a particular piece of information in a very large data set. It builds indexes to rapidly locate a particular record, and they have query languages for swiftly locating records that match particular criteria.

There are numerous modules available for Apache to authenticate using a variety of different databases. In this section, we'll just look at two modules that ship with Apache.

mod_auth_db and mod_auth_dbm

mod_auth_db and mod_auth_dbm are modules that enable you to keep your usernames and passwords in DB or DBM files. There are few practical differences between DB files and DBM files. And, on some operating systems, such as various BSDs and Linux, they are exactly the same. You should pick whichever of the two modules makes the most sense on your particular platform of choice. If you do not have DB support on your platform, you might need to install it. You can download an implementation of DB at http://www.sleepycat.com/.

Berkeley DB Files

DB files, also known as Berkeley database files, are the simplest form of database, and are ideally suited for the sort of data that needs to be stored for HTTP authentication. DB files store key/value pairs. That is, the name of a variable and the value of that variable. Although other databases allow the storage of many fields in a given record, a DB file allows only this pairing of key and value. This is ideal for authentication, which requires only the pair of a username and password.

> **NOTE**
>
> There are actually a number of implementations that get around this limitation. MLDBM is one of them, for example. However, for the purposes of this discussion, we'll just deal with standard Berkeley DB, which is likely to have shipped with whatever operating system you are already running.

Installing `mod_auth_db`

For the purposes of this chapter, we'll talk about installing and configuring `mod_auth_db`. However, everything that is said here can be directly applied to `mod_auth_dbm` by simply replacing "db" with "dbm" and "DB" with "DBM" in the various commands, filenames, and directives.

Because `mod_auth_db` is not compiled in by default, you will need to rebuild Apache to get the functionality, unless you built in everything when we started. See Chapter 2 for more information about rebuilding Apache with a particular module enabled. Note that if you installed Apache with shared object support, you might be able to just build the module and load it in to Apache.

To build Apache from scratch with `mod_auth_db` built in, use the following `./configure` line in your apache source code directory.

```
./configure —enable-module=auth_db
```

Or, if you had a more complex `configure` command line, you can just add the `-enable-module=auth_db` option to that command line, and you'll get `mod_auth_db` built into your server. See also Chapter 26, "Modules Included with Apache," for details about building your Apache server to include a particular module.

Protecting a Directory with `mod_auth_db`

When you have compiled and loaded the `mod_auth_db` module into your Web server, you'll find that there's very little difference between using regular authentication and using mod_auth_db authentication. The procedure is the same as that we went through with basic and digest authentication:

1. Create the user file.
2. Configure Apache to use that file for authentication.
3. Optionally, create a group file.

Create the User File

The user file for authentication is, this time, not a flat text file, but a DB file (or, if you are using mod_auth_dbm, a DBM file). Fortunately, once again, Apache provides us with a simple utility for the purpose of managing this user file. This time, the utility is called dbmmanage, and will be located in the bin subdirectory of wherever you installed Apache.

dbmmanage is somewhat more complicated to use than htpasswd or htdigest, but it is still fairly simple. The syntax you will usually use is as follows:

```
dbmmanage passwords.db adduser montressor
```

As with htpasswd, you will at this point be prompted for a password, and then asked to confirm that password by typing it again. The main difference here is that rather than a text file being created, you are creating a binary file containing the information that you have supplied.

Type dbmmanage with no arguments to get the full list of options available with this utility.

Creating Your User File with Perl

Note that, if you are so inclined, you can manage your user file with Perl, or any other language that has a DB-file module, for interfacing with this type of database. This covers a number of popular programming languages.

The following Perl code, for example, will add a user "rbowen", with password "mypassword", to your password file:

```perl
use DB_File;
tie %database, 'DB_File', "passwords.dat"
    or die "Can't initialize database: $!\n";

$username = 'rbowen';
$password = 'mypassword';
@chars=(0..9,'a'..'z');
$salt = '', map { $chars[int rand @chars] } (0..1);

$crypt = crypt($password, $salt);
$database{$username} = $crypt;

untie %database;
```

As you can imagine, this makes it very simple to write tools to manage the user and password information stored in these files.

Passwords are stored in Unix crypt format, just as they were in the regular password files. The "salt" that is created in the middle is part of the process, generating a random starting point for that encryption. The technique being used is called a "tied hash." The idea is to tie a built-in data structure to the contents of the file, so when the data structure is changed, the file is automatically modified at the same time.

Configuration Apache to Use This Password File

When you have created the password file, you need to tell Apache about it, and tell Apache to use this file to verify user credentials. This configuration will look almost the same as for basic authentication. This configuration can go in an .htaccess file in the directory to be protected, or can go in the main server configuration, in a <Directory> section, or other scope container directive.

The configuration will look something like the following:

```
AuthName "Members Only"
AuthType Basic
AuthDBUserFile /usr/local/apache/passwd/passwords.dat
require user rbowen
```

Now, users accessing the directory will be required to authenticate against the list of valid users who are in /usr/local/apache/passwd/passwords.dat.

Optionally, Create a Group File

As mentioned earlier, DB files store a key/value pair. In the case of group files, the key is the name of the user and the value is a comma-separated list of the groups to which the user belongs.

Although this is the opposite of the way that group files are stored elsewhere, note that we will primarily be looking up records based on the username, so it is more efficient to index the file by username, rather than by the group name.

Groups can be added to your group file using dbmmanage and the add command:

```
dbmmanage add groupfile rbowen one,two,three
```

In the previous example, groupfile is the literal name of the group file, rbowen is the user being added and one, two, and three are names of the three groups to which this user belongs.

When you have your groups in the file, you can require a group in the regular way:

```
AuthName "Members Only"
AuthType Basic
```

```
AuthDBUserFile /usr/local/apache/passwd/passwords.dat
AuthDBGroupFile /usr/local/apache/passwd/groups.dat
require group three
```

Note that if you want to use the same file for both password and group information, you can do so, but this is a little more complicated to manage because you have to encrypt the password yourself before you feed it to the `dbmmanage` utility.

Access Control

Authentication by username and password is only part of the story. Frequently you want to let people in based on something other than who they are. Something such as where they are coming from. Restricting access based on something other than the identity of the user is generally referred to as *access control*.

Allow and Deny

The `Allow` and `Deny` directives enable you to allow and deny access based on the host name or host address of the machine requesting a document. The directive that goes hand-in-hand with these is the `Order` directive, which tells Apache in which order to apply the filters.

The usage of these directives is

```
allow from address
```

where *address* is an IP address (or a partial IP address) or a fully qualified domain name (or a partial domain name).

For example, if you have someone spamming your message board and you want to keep them out, you could do the following:

```
deny from 205.252.46.165
```

Visitors coming from that address will not be able to see the content behind this directive. If, instead, you have a machine name, rather than an IP address, you can use that.

```
deny from dc.numbersusa.com
```

And, if you want to block access from an entire domain, you can specify just part of an address or domain name:

```
deny from 192.101.205
```

```
deny from cyberthugs.com
```

```
deny from ke
```

Using `Order` will enable you to be sure that you are actually restricting things to the group that you want to let in by combining a deny and an `allow` directive:

```
Order Deny,Allow
Deny from all
Allow from dev.rcbowen.com
```

Listing just the `allow` directive would not do what you want because it will let users from that host in, in addition to letting everyone in. What you want is to let in only users from that host.

Satisfy

The `Satisfy` directive can be used to specify that several criteria might be considered when trying to decide if a particular user will be granted admission. `Satisfy` can take as an argument one of two options—all or any. By default, it is assumed that the value is `all`. This means that if several criteria are specified, then all of them must be met in order for someone to get in. However, if set to any then several criteria might be specified, but if the user satisfies any of these then they will be granted entrance.

A very good example of this is using access control to assure that, although a resource is password protected from outside your network, all hosts inside the network will be given free access to the resource. This would be accomplished by using the `Satisfy` directive, as shown here.

```
<Directory /usr/local/apache/htdocs/sekrit>
   AuthType Basic
   AuthName intranet
   AuthUserFile /www/passwd/users
   AuthGroupFile /www/passwd/groups
   Require group customers
   Allow from internal.com
   Satisfy any
</Directory>
```

In this scenario, users will be let in if they either have a password, or, if they are in the internal network.

Summary

The various authentication modules provide a number of ways to restrict access to your host based on the identity of the user. They offer a somewhat standard interface to this functionality, but provide different back-end mechanisms for actually authenticating the user.

And the access control mechanism allows you to restrict access based on criteria unrelated to the identity of the user.

SSL

IN THIS CHAPTER

"The only system that is truly secure is one that is switched off and unplugged, locked in a titanium-lined safe, buried in a concrete bunker, and surrounded by nerve gas and very highly-paid armed guards. Even then, I wouldn't stake my life on it."

Gene Spafford

This chapter presents you with the security technologies involved in conducting secure transactions over the Internet. It explains the installation and configuration of mod_ssl, the SSL protocol module for Apache 2.0. SSL stands for Secure Socket Layers and enables Web browsers and servers to protect their communications. Configuring a secure server is a complex task and requires an understanding of the underlying protocols. The chapter starts with an introduction to several security-related concepts and algorithms. If you are already familiar with this background material you can skim through the initial sections. Later sections explain the steps necessary to get SSL up and running with Apache 2.0. Pointers to useful resources are provided at the end of the chapter.

Cryptography

As the Internet grows and Web technologies evolve an increasing number of business and individuals use this global network to conduct financial transactions and transmit sensitive information. Hence, the parties need to protect these communications from potential attackers.

The threats are easy to understand, but the solutions can be fairly complex. Consider the typical scenario in which an individual wants to buy a book online. Let's call this person Alice (this is a convention started in one of the original academic cryptographic papers, where Alice and Bob are two figured individuals trying to communicate securely).

> **NOTE**
>
> For more information on these papers you can refer to Rivest, R.L., Shamir, A., and Adleman, L.M., "On Digital Signatures and Public Cryptosystems" Technical Report, MIT Laboratory for Coumputer Science, January 1979. These are the fathers of public key cryptography, and invented the RSA algorithm, named after them.

To buy a book, Alice needs to transmit her credit-card number to the book merchant, but she does not want an attacker to be able to intercept this information. With this information *confidentiality* needs to be protected. Alice wants to make sure the attacker cannot successfully modify or replay her order so she does not end up with a different book or several instances of the same book. The *integrity* of the information needs to be preserved. Finally, Alice wants to make sure that she is communicating with the legitimate merchant Web site, and not a rogue Web site set up by an attacker. She needs to *authenticate* the identity of the remote end. Cryptography studies the algorithms and methods used to securely transmit messages to ensure confidentiality, integrity, and authenticity.

Confidentiality

Encryption is a common method of guaranteeing the confidentiality of an electronic message transmitted over an insecure network. The original message (*plaintext*) is converted by the sender into a new, encrypted, message (*ciphertext*) using a certain piece of information (*key*). The receiver can then use his own key to convert the ciphertext to the original message. The ciphertext looks like random data to an attacker. Only someone with the appropriate key can decrypt that message and make sense out of it.

Symmetric Cryptography

If the key used to encrypt and decrypt the message is the same then the process is known as symmetric cryptography. DES, Triple-Des, RC4 and RC2 are algorithms used for symmetric key cryptography. Many of these algorithms can have different key sizes, measured in bits. In general, given an algorithm, the greater the number of bits of the key, the more secure the algorithm is and the slower it will run, because of the increased computational needs of performing the algorithm.

Public Key Cryptography

Key distribution is the main problem with symmetric cryptography. The encryption/decryption key is a shared secret between sender and receiver and needs to be securely transmitted to both parties. Public key cryptography takes a different approach. Instead of both parties sharing the same key, there is a pair of keys, one public, and the other private. The public key can be widely distributed, whereas the owner keeps the private key secret. These two keys are complementary; a message encrypted with one of the keys can only be decrypted by the other.

Anyone wanting to transmit a secure message to you can encrypt the message using your public key; assured that only the owner of the private key, you, can decrypt it. Even if the attacker has access to the public key, he cannot decrypt the communication. In fact, you want the public key to be as widely available as possible. Public key cryptography can also be used to provide message integrity and authentication. RSA is the most popular public key algorithm.

The assertion that "only the owner of the private key can decrypt it" means that with the current knowledge of cryptography and availability of computing power, an attacker will not be able to break the encryption by brute force alone. If the algorithm or its implementation are found to be flawed, then realistic attacks are possible.

Public key cryptography is similar to giving away many identical lockpads and retaining the key that opens them all. Anybody who wants to send you a message privately can do so by putting it in a safe and locking it with one of those lockpads (*public keys*) before sending it to you. Only you have the appropriate key (*private key*) to open that lockpad (*decrypt the message*).

Integrity

A message digest is a method to create a fixed-length representation of an arbitrary message that uniquely identifies it. You can think of it as the fingerprint of the message. A good message digest algorithm should be irreversible and collision-resistant: Irreversible means that the original message cannot be obtained from the digest and collision-resistant that no two different messages should have the same digest.

Message digests alone, however, do not guarantee the integrity of the message, because an attacker could change the text *and* the message digest. Examples of digest algorithms are MD5 and SHA.

Message Authentication Codes

Message Authentication Codes, or MACs, are similar to message digests, but incorporate a shared secret key in the process. The result of the algorithm depends both on the message and the key used. Because the attacker has no access to the key, he cannot modify both the message and the digest. HMAC is an example of a message authentication code algorithm.

To help you understand what a digest is, think about the following primitive digest algorithm—take a text and assign a number to each letter in the text. The number corresponds to the place it occupies in the alphabet (a=1, b=2, and so on). Add all the numbers. The resulting number is a digest of that message. If you modify the message the digest changes. This is just a simple example and the algorithm is not practical. Although you cannot reconstruct the original message from that number, it is feasible to carefully modify the original message while keeping the number constant. The algorithms used in practice are much more sophisticated and secure for all practical purposes.

Authentication

Public key cryptography can be used to digitally "sign" messages. In fact, just by encrypting a message with your secret key the receiver can guarantee it came from you. Other digital signature algorithms involve first calculating a digest of the message and then signing the digest.

Certificates

Thanks to digital signatures, you can tell that the person who created that public and private key pair is the one sending the message. But how can you know that person is the one you think he is? An attacker could impersonate his identity and distribute a different public key, claiming it is the legitimate one. It is necessary to have a mechanism that links an individual or organization with its public key. This is achieved by using digital certificates. Digital certificates are electronic documents that contain a public key and information about its owner (name, address, and so on). To be useful, the certificate needs to be signed by a trusted third party (Certification Authority). There are many different kinds of Certificate Authorities, as described later on the chapter. Some of them are commercial entities, providing certification services to companies conducting business over the Internet. Others are created by companies looking to provide internal certification services.

The Certification Authority guarantees that the information in the certificate is correct and that the key belongs to that individual or organization. Certificates have a period of validity and can expire or be revoked. Finally, certificates can be chained. That means that the certification process can be delegated. For example, a trusted entity can certify companies, which in turn can certify their own employees.

If this whole process is to be effective and trusted, the Certificate Authority must require appropriate proof of identity from individuals and organizations before it issues a certificate.

We have seen how confidentiality can be achieved via encryption, integrity via message authentication codes, and authentication via certificates and digital signatures. These concepts have been incorporated into the SSL protocol to enable secure communications on the Internet. The next section explains in detail the inner workings of SSL.

Introduction to SSL

In this section you will learn how encryption, digital signatures, and certificates all work together to provide Alice with a secure shopping experience.

> **NOTE**
>
> TLS stands for Transport Layer Security. SSL and TLS is a family of protocols originally designed for securing communications based on the HTTP protocol, but they can be used to protect a variety of other protocols. Netscape released SSL version 2 in 1994 and SSL version 3 in 1995. TLS is an IETF standard designed to standardize SSL as an Internet protocol. It is mostly just a modification of SSL version 3 with a small number of added features and minor cleanups. The name TLS is the result of some silly politics between Microsoft and Netscape over the naming of the protocol.

The requirement for SSL connections is indicated by replacing the http scheme in URLs with https (for HTTP over SSL). Examples of such URLs are `https://www.modssl.org`, `https://www.ibm.com`, or `https://www.microsoft.com`. The default port for HTTPS is 443.

The browser will tell you when a secure connection has been established—Netscape and Microsoft browsers will show a small locked padlock in one of the lower corners. The next section explains the details of the SSL protocol.

SSL Overview

When Alice's browser wants to send an encrypted request to a secure server, it first establishes a secure channel based on SSL. It then communicates using HTTP over this connection.

An SSL connection is divided into two phases, the handshake and data transfer phases. The handshake enables Alice to authenticate the remote server and agree on a set of keys to be used for encrypting the information in the data transfer phase.

The handshake process is the following:

1. The browser sends an initial request with information about the protocol version and algorithms supported. The request includes a random number—r1.

2. The server answers with information about the algorithms to be used, a server certificate, and a random number r2.

3. The browser makes sure the certificate is valid. It then generates a secret string r3, which is encrypted, using the server public key found in the certificate.

4. Both browser and server use r1, r2, and r3 to compute the symmetric encryption keys and the MAC keys using what is called a key-exchange algorithm.

5. The browser calculates a MAC of all the handshake messages and sends it to the server.

6. The server does the same and transmits it to the browser.

The last two steps are necessary to prevent an attacker from manipulating the handshake phase itself (for example by intercepting the messages and modifying the set of algorithms server and client agree to use). Certificate contents and verification are explained in more detail in later sections of this chapter.

During the data transfer phase, HTTP messages are divided into individual pieces. A MAC is calculated and encrypted together with the fragment that is then transmitted. The message is received at the other end, decrypted, and the MAC is calculated.

By using the SSL protocol, Alice achieves:

- **Confidentiality**: After the handshake phase, sender and receiver have agreed on a secret key that they can use to encrypt the data being transmitted, such as Alice's credit card.

- **Integrity**: SSL messages are transmitted together with MACs that prevent them from being altered or replayed. So Alice does not end up buying ten copies of the same book.

- **Authentication**: The server provides Alice with a certificate that provides information about the company or individual running the remote site. Alice can validate the certificate checking that the certificate has been issued or signed by a Certificate Authority that she trusts. The certificates of several well-known CAs are included by default in Microsoft and Netscape browsers.

NOTE

If a certificate has expired, does not match the name of the host you are accessing, or otherwise is invalid, the browser will pop up a window asking you if you still want to connect.

A properly configured SSL server helps secure the communication between a browser and a server. But security can still be compromised in a variety of other ways. An attacker can gain remote access to the server machine and modify the application logic that handles the credit-card transactions. Those credit-card numbers themselves could be stored in an SQL database connected to the Internet with a default password. The attacker could have physical access to the client machine and install a modified version of the browser or a key-logging program.

SSL is an important component of a secure-Internet infrastructure but by no means is the only one. An attacker will always choose the weakest link in your security infrastructure to try to break in into your systems.

Installing SSL

SSL support for Apache is provided by mod_ssl, a module included with Apache 2.0. mod_ssl requires the OpenSSL library. OpenSSL is an open source implementation of the SSL/TLS protocols and a variety of other cryptographic algorithms. OpenSSL is based on the SSLeay library developed by Eric A. Young and Tim J. Hudson. You can learn more about mod_ssl and OpenSSL in the Web sites noted in the reference at the end of the chapter.

OpenSSL

This section explains how to download and install the OpenSSL toolkit for both Windows and Unix variants.

Windows

The required OpenSSL libraries are included with the Windows installer of Apache 2.0 and no further installation or download is necessary. openssl.exe is included in the bin/ directory of the Apache distribution. It is a utility for generating certificates, keys, certificate signing requests, and so on.

Unix

If you are running a recent Linux or FreeBSD distribution, OpenSSL might already be installed in your system. Use the package management tools bundled with your distribution to determine if that is the case or install it otherwise

Installing from Source

OpenSSL can be downloaded from http://www.openssl.org. After you have downloaded the software, you need to uncompress it and change into the created directory:

```
# gunzip < openssl*.tar.gz | tar xvf -
# cd openssl*
```

OpenSSL contains a config script to help you build the software. You need to provide the path to which the software will install. The path we use in this chapter is /usr/local/ssl/install, and you probably need to have superuser privileges to install the software there. You can install the software as a regular user, but to do so you will need to change the path. Then you need to build and install the software:

```
# ./config --prefix=/usr/local/ssl/install \
➡--openssldir=/usr/local/ssl/install/openssl
# make
# make install
```

If everything goes well, you have now successfully installed the OpenSSL toolkit. The `openssl` command-line tool will be located in `/usr/local/ssl/install/bin/`.

This tool is used to create and manipulate certificates and keys and its usage is described in a later section on certificates.

mod_ssl

SSL extensions for Apache 1.3 needed to be distributed separately because of export restrictions. These restrictions no longer exist and mod_ssl is bundled and integrated with Apache 2.0. This section describes the steps necessary to build and install this module. mod_ssl depends on the OpenSSL library, so a valid OpenSSL installation is required.

Windows

You can download a binary distribution of Apache 2.0 for the Windows platform from `http://www.apache.org` that includes mod_ssl.

Unix

If you are using the Apache 2.0 server that came installed with your operating system, chances are it already includes mod_ssl. Use the package management tools bundled with your distribution to install mod_ssl if it is not present in the system.

Installing from Source

When you build Apache 2.0 from source you need to pass the following options to enable and build mod_ssl:

```
--enable-ssl -with-ssl=/usr/local/ssl/install/openssl
```

This assumes you installed OpenSSL in the location described in previous sections.

If you compiled mod_ssl statically into Apache you can check if it is present by issuing the following command, which provides a list of compiled in modules:

```
# ./usr/local/apache2/bin/httpd -l
```

The command assumes you installed Apache in the `/usr/local/apache2` directory.

Certificates

We have seen in previous sections the role certificates play in SSL. In this section we explain in detail the information contained in a certificate and how to create and manage certificates and keys using the `openssl` command-line tool.

The main standard for certificates is X.509, adapted for Internet usage. A certificate contains information about:

- The issuer is the name of the signer of the certificate.
- The subject is the person holding the key being certified.
- The subject public key is the public key of the subject.
- Control information such as the dates in which the certificate is valid.
- Signature is the signature that covers the previous data.

You can check a real-life certificate by connecting to a secure server with your browser. You can click the locked padlock icon to open information on the SSL connection. You can open the property pages by clicking on File, Properties, Certificates. Netscape browsers provide a similar interface.

Open the `https://www.ibm.com` URL in your browser and analyze the certificate, following the steps outlined in the above paragraph. You can see how the issuer of the certificate is the Equifax Secure E-business Certification Authority, which in turn has been certified by the Thawte CA. The page downloaded seamlessly because Thawte is a trusted CA that has its own certificates bundled with Internet Explorer and Netscape Navigator.

To check which are the certificates bundled with your Internet Explorer browser, go to the top menu and select Tools, Internet Options, Content, Certificates, Trusted Root Certification Authorities.

You can see that both issuer and subject are provided as distinguished names (DN), a structured way of providing a unique identifier for every element on the network. In the case of the IBM certificate, the DN is C=US, S=New York, L=Armonk, O=IBM, CN=www.ibm.com.

C stands for Country, S for State, L for Locality, O for organization and CN for Common Name. In the case of a Web site certificate the common name identifies the fully qualified domain name of the Web site (FQDN). This is the server name part of the URL, in this case `www.ibm.com`. If this does not match what you typed in the top bar, the browser will issue an error.

You now need to learn to use the `openssl` command-line tool to create and manage keys and certificates. It assumes OpenSSL was installed in the path described in the OpenSSL installation section. The examples refer to the Unix version. All the steps work the same for Windows you just need to use `openssl.exe` instead.

Creating a Key Pair

We need to have a public/private key pair before we can create a certificate request. We assume the FQDN for the certificate you want to create is www.yourdomain.com. (You will need to substitute this name for the FQDN of the machine you have installed Apache on). You can create the keys by issuing the following command:

```
# ./usr/local/ssl/install/bin/openssl genrsa -des3 -rand file1:file2:file3 \
  ➥-out www.yourdomain.com.key 1024
```

- genrsa indicates to OpenSSL that we want to generate a key pair.
- des3 indicates that the private key should be encrypted and protected by a pass phrase.
- The rand switch is used to provide OpenSSL with random data to assure that the generated keys are unique and unpredictable. Select several large, relatively random files for this purpose (such as compressed log files, kernel image, and so on). This switch is not necessary on Windows, because the random data is automatically generated by some other means.
- The out switch indicates where to store the results.
- 1024 indicates the number of bits of the generated key.

The result of this command looks like

```
625152  semi-random bytes loaded
Generating RSA private key, 1024 bit long modulus
.....++++++
.......................++++++
e is 65537 (0x10001)
Enter PEM pass phrase:
Verifying password - Enter PEM pass phrase:
```

As you can see, you will be asked to provide a pass phrase. Choose a secure one. The pass phrase is necessary to protect the private key and you will be asked for it whenever you want to start the server. You can choose not to protect the key. This is convenient because you will not need to enter the pass phrase during reboots, but it is highly insecure and a compromise of the server means a compromise of the key as well. In any case, you can choose to unprotect the key either by leaving the -des3 switch out in the generation phase or by issuing the following command:

```
# ./usr/local/ssl/install/bin/openssl rsa -in www.yourdomain.com.key \
      ➥-out www.yourdomain.com.key.unsecure
```

It is a good idea to backup the www.yourdomain.com.key file. You can learn about the contents of the key file by issuing the following command:

```
# ./usr/local/ssl/bin/openssl rsa -noout -text -in www.yourdomain.com.key
```

Creating a Certificate Signing Request

To get a certificate issued by a CA you need to submit what is called a Certificate Signing Request. To create the request, issue the following command:

```
# ./usr/local/ssl/install/bin/openssl req -new -key www.yourdomain.com.key
 -out www.yourdomain.com.csr
```

You will be prompted for the certificate information:

```
Using configuration from /usr/local/ssl/install/openssl/openssl.cnf
Enter PEM pass phrase:
You are about to be asked to enter information that will be incorporated
into your certificate request.
What you are about to enter is what is called a Distinguished Name or a DN.
There are quite a few fields but you can leave some blank
For some fields there will be a default value,
If you enter '.', the field will be left blank.
-----
Country Name (2 letter code) [AU]:US
State or Province Name (full name) [Some-State]:CA
Locality Name (eg, city) []: San Francisco
Organization Name (eg, company) [Internet Widgits Pty Ltd]:.
Organizational Unit Name (eg, section) []:.
Common Name (eg, YOUR name) []:www.yourdomain.com
Email Address []:administrator@yourdomain.com
Please enter the following 'extra' attributes
to be sent with your certificate request
A challenge password []:
An optional company name []:
```

The certificate is now stored in www.yourdomain.com.csr. You can learn about the contents of the certificate via the following command:

```
# ./usr/local/ssl/install/bin/openssl req -noout -text \
    ➥-in www.yourdomain.com.csr
```

You can submit the certificate signing request file to a CA for processing. Verisign and Thawte are two of those CAs. You can learn more about their particular submission procedures at their Web sites:

Verisign: http://digitalid.verisign.com/server/apacheNotice.htm

Thawte: http://www.thawte.com/certs/server/request.html

Creating a Self-Signed Certificate

You can also create a self-signed certificate. That is, you are going to be the issuer and the subject of the certificate. Although this is not very useful for a commercial Web site, it will allow you to test your installation of mod_ssl or to have a secure Web server while you wait for the official certificate from the CA.

```
# ./usr/local/ssl/install/bin/openssl x509 -req -days 30  \
-in www.yourdomain.com.csr -signkey www.yourdomain.com.key \
-out www.yourdomain.com.cert
```

You need to copy your certificate www.yourdomain.com.cert (either the one returned by the CA or your self signed one) to /usr/local/ssl/install/openssl/certs/ and your key to /usr/local/ssl/install/openssl/private/.

You need to protect your key file by issuing the following command:

```
# chmod 400 www.yourdomain.key
```

SSL Configuration

In the previous sections we have introduced the (not so basic) concepts behind SSL and you have learned how to generate keys and certificates. Now, finally, you can configure Apache to support SSL. mod_ssl needs either to be compiled statically or, if you have compiled as a loadable module, the appropriate LoadModule directive needs to be present in the file.

Add the following configuration snippet to your Apache configuration file:

```
Listen 80
Listen 443

<VirtualHost _default_:443>
ServerName www.yourdomain.com
SSLEngine on
SSLCertificateFile \
/usr/local/ssl/install/openssl/certs/www.yourdomain.com.cert
SSLCertificateKeyFile \
/usr/local/ssl/install/openssl/certs/www.yourdomain.com.key
</VirtualHost>
```

With the previous configuration, we setup a new virtual host that will listen in port 443 (the default port for HTTPS) and we enable SSL on that virtual host.

You will need to tell the server the location of the certificate and the file containing the associated key. We do so using SSLCertificateFile and SSLCertificateKeyfile directives.

Now you can stop the server if it was running, and start it again. If your key is protected by a pass phrase you will be prompted for it. After this, Apache will start and you should be able to connect securely to it via the `https://www.yourdomain.com/` URL.

If you are unable to restart your server, check the Apache error log for clues to what might have gone wrong. For example, if you cannot bind to the port make sure that Apache is not running somewhere else. You need to have administrator privileges to bind to port 443, otherwise change the port to 8443 and access the URL via `https://www.yourdomain.com:443`.

mod_ssl provides a comprehensive technical reference documentation. We are not going to reproduce that information here, but rather explain what is possible and which configuration directives you need to use. You can then refer to the online documentation at `http://www.modssl.org` for the specific syntax or options.

Algorithms

You can control which ciphers and protocols are used via the `SSLCipherSuite` and `SSLProtocol` commands. For example, you can configure the server to use only strong encryption with the following configuration:

```
SSLProtocol all
SSLCipherSuite HIGH:MEDIUM
```

Client Certificates

Similar to how clients can verify the identity of servers using server certificates, servers can verify the identity of clients by requiring a client certificate and making sure it is valid.

`SSLCACertificateFile` and `SSLCACertificatePath` are two Apache directives used to specify trusted CAs. We can then use `SSLVerifyClient` to restrict access to clients certified by these CAs.

Performance

SSL is a protocol that requires intensive calculations. mod_ssl and OpenSSL allow several ways to speed up the protocol by caching some of the information about the connection (this can be configured using the `SSLcache`, `SSLCachetimeout` directives), and by providing support for specialized cryptographic hardware to perform CPU intensive computations.

Logging

mod_ssl hooks up into Apache's logging system and provides support for logging any SSL-related aspect of the request, ranging from the protocol used to the information contained in specific elements of a client certificate. This information can also be passed to CGI scripts via environment variables. `SSLLog` and `SSLLogLevel` allow you to specify where to store SSL-specific errors and which kind of errors to log.

SSL Options

Many of these options can be applied in a per-directory or per-location basis. The SSL parameters might be renegotiated for those URLs. This can be controlled via the SSLoptions directive.

Name-Based Virtual Hosts

A common problem for people is how to make name-based virtual hosts work with SSL. The answer is that you can't. Name-based virtual hosts depend on the Host header of the HTTP request, but the certificate verification happens when the SSL connection is being established and no HTTP request can be sent. There is a protocol for upgrading an existing HTTP connection to TLS, but it is mostly unsupported by current browsers (RFC 2817).

Further Reading

The book on cryptography:

Applied Cryptography, Second Edition, by Bruce Schneier ISBN 0471117099

An excellent book on the SSL protocol, especially useful if you are programming with SSL libraries:

SSL and TLS: Designing and Building Secure Systems, by Eric Rescorla, ISBN 0201615983

OpenSSL project: http://www.openssl.org

ModSSL project: http://www.openssl.org

OpenBSD, a free Unix-server operating system with focus on security: http://www.openbsd.com

Apache reference, by the author of mod_ssl: http://www.apacheref.com

SSLv2 Specification: http://home.netscape.com/eng/security/SSL_2.html

SSLv3 Specification: http://home.netscape.com/eng/ssl3/draft302.txt

SSL related RFCs. RFCs can be obtained from http://www.rfc-editor.org/

- Internet X.509 PKI: 2459
- Transport Layer Security: 2246
- Upgrading to TLS Within HTTP/1.1: 2817

22

SSL

Summary

This chapter has introduced you to the SSL protocol and to mod_ssl, which allows Apache to support SSL. You have learned basic installation and configuration of mod_ssl and certificate generation and management. You can access the mod_ssl reference documentation for in-depth syntax explanation and additional configuration information.

Web Spiders

IN THIS CHAPTER

I got remote control and a color T.V.
I don't change channels so they must change me.

Close to the Borderline—Billy Joel

When the Web was young—or at least when you were new to the Web—it was interesting to spend hours clicking links and looking at Web pages. Eventually, you got over that, and now you just want the information you want, when you want it, and you no longer want to do the work for yourself. That's where spiders come in.

Spiders are programs that walk the Web for you, following links and grabbing information. They're also known as robots and crawlers. You can find a list of many of the currently available and active spiders online at `http://info.webcrawler.com/mak/projects/robots/active/html/index.html`.

Spiders are very useful, but they can also cause a lot of problems. If you have a Web site on the Internet, you will find that a steady percentage of the visits to your site are from spiders. This is because most of the major search engines use spiders to index the Web, including your Web site, for inclusion in their database.

This chapter discusses what a spider is, how spiders can make your life easier, and how to protect your Web site against spiders that you don't want to let in. You'll also learn how to give spiders the right information about your site when they visit. Finally, you'll learn briefly about writing your own spider.

What Are Spiders?

The Web Robots FAQ defines a robot as "a program that automatically traverses the Web's hypertext structure by retrieving a document and recursively retrieving all documents that are referenced." (You can find the Web Robots FAQ at `http://info.webcrawler.com/mak/projects/robots/faq.html`.) What this means is that a spider starts with some page and downloads all the pages that page has links to. Then, for each of those pages, it downloads all the pages they are linked to, and so on, ad infinitum. This is done automatically by the spider program, which will presumably be collecting this information for some useful purpose.

Spiders might be collecting information for a search engine, collecting e-mail addresses for sending spam, or downloading pages for offline viewing.

Some examples of various common types of robots are

- Scooter is the robot responsible for the AltaVista search engine. Scooter fetches documents from the Web, which are then incorporated into AltaVista's database. You can search that database at `http://www.altavista.com/`. Most major search engines also use some type of spider to index the Web, and you will see many of them in your server logs.

- EmailSiphon, and various other spiders with similar names, rove the Web, retrieving e-mail addresses from Web pages. The people who run EmailSiphon then sell those addresses to various low-lifes who then send unsolicited bulk e-mail (also known as spam) to those addresses. See the later section on excluding spiders from your site to learn how to deny access to these robots and protect your mailbox.

- MOMspider is one that you can download and use on your own site to validate links and generate statistics. You can run it from your server or from your desktop. There are a large number of similar products for Web site developers to use on their own sites.

Spiders: The Good and the Bad

In general, spiders are good things. They can help you out in a number of ways, such as indexing your site, searching for broken links, and validating the HTML on your pages.

A common use for spiders is collecting documents from the Web for you, so that you can look at them at your leisure when you aren't online. This is called offline browsing or caching, among other things, and the products that do this are sometimes called personal agents or personal spiders. One such product, called AvantGo (`http://www.avantgo.com`), will even download Web content to your hand-held computer so that you can look at your favorite Web pages while on an airplane or bus.

Conversely, spiders also can cause a lot of problems on your Web site, because their traffic patterns are not the sort that you typically plan for.

Server Overloading

One potential problem is server overload. Whereas a human user is likely to wait at least a few seconds between downloading one page and the next, the spider can start on the next page immediately after receiving the first page. Also, it can fork multiple processes and download several pages at the same time. If your server isn't equipped to handle that many simultaneous connections, or if you don't have the bandwidth to handle the requests, this might cause visitors to have a long wait for their pages to load, or even cause the server to become overloaded.

Black Holes

Occasionally, poorly written spiders might get trapped in some infinite portion of your Web site, such as a CGI program that generates pages with links back to itself. The spider might spend hours or days chasing its tail, so to speak. This can cause your log files to grow at an alarming rate, skew any statistical information that you might be collecting, and lead to an overloaded server.

23

WEB SPIDERS

Recognizing Spiders in Your Log Files

Before you try to keep spiders out of your site, you might want to get a good idea of what spiders are visiting your site and what they're trying to do. You'll notice log entries from spiders in several ways:

1. The first thing that will stand out will be the user agent (if you are logging the user agent in your log files). It won't look like an ordinary browser (because it's not) and will tend to have a name such as harvester, black widow, Aracnophilia, and the like. You can see a full listing of the various known spiders in the Web Robots FAQ, discussed earlier in this chapter.

   Of course, it's also important to understand what spiders, like any other Web client, are free to provide whatever client description they choose, and so they could just as easily say that they are Netscape, IE, or "Bob's Handy-Dandy Browser". There is no guarantee whatsoever that the USER_AGENT string can be trusted to be true.

2. You might notice that a large number of pages are requested by the same client, often in quick succession.

3. The address from which the client is connecting can tell you quite a lot. Connections from the various search engines are frequently spiders indexing your site. For example, a connection from lobo.yahoo.com is a good indication that your site is being indexed for the Yahoo! Internet directory.

Excluding Spiders from Your Server

You can keep spiders off your site—or at least off certain parts of your site—in several different ways. These methods usually rely on the cooperation of the spider itself. However, you can do a number of things at the server level to deny access.

As mentioned earlier, you will probably want to keep spiders out of your CGI directories. You also will want to keep them out of portions of your site that change with such regularity that indexing would be fruitless. And, of course, there might be parts of your site that you'd just rather not have indexed, for whatever reason.

Robot Exclusion with robots.txt

The Robots Exclusion Protocol, also known as A Standard for Robot Exclusion, is a document drafted in 1994 that outlined a method for telling robots what parts of your site you want them to stay out of. You can find the full text of this document on the WebCrawler Web site at http://info.webcrawler.com/mak/projects/robots/norobots.html.

To implement this exclusion on your Web site, you need to create a text file called
`robots.txt`, and place it in your server's document root directory. When a spider visits your
site, it is supposed to fetch this document before going any further, to find out what rules you
have set.

The file contains one or more `User-agent` lines, each followed by one or more `Disallow` lines
specifying any directories that particular user agent (spider) is not permitted to access. Most
commonly, the user agent specified will be *, which should be obeyed by all robots. In the following sample `robots.txt` file, all user agents are requested to stay out of the directories
`/cgi-bin/` and `/datafiles/`:

```
User-agent: *

Disallow: /cgi-bin/

Disallow: /datafiles/
```

In the following example, a particular user agent, Scooter, is requested to stay out of the directory `/dont-index/`:

```
User-agent: Scooter

Disallow: /dont-index/
```

`robots.txt` files can also contain comments. Anything following a hash character (#), until the
end of that line, is a comment and will be ignored.

Unfortunately, it is very easy to write a spider but considerably more difficult to write one that
is well behaved. Consequently, many people write spiders that blatantly ignore your
`robots.txt` file. Like many parts of Internet standards, it's just a suggestion, and particular
implementations are free to ignore the suggestion.

The ROBOTS Meta Tag

Another method for requesting that spiders not enter your Web site is the ROBOTS meta tag.
This HTML tag can appear in the <HEAD> section of any HTML page. The format of the tag is
as follows:

```
<HTML>

<HEAD>

<META NAME="ROBOTS" CONTENT="arguments">

<TITLE>Title here</TITLE>
```

```
</HEAD>

<BODY>
```

...

Possible arguments to the CONTENT attribute are as follows:

- FOLLOW tells the spider that it's okay to follow any links that appear on this document.
- INDEX tells the spider that it's okay to index this document. That is, the contents of this document can be cached or added to a search engine database.
- NOFOLLOW tells the spider not to follow any links from this page.
- NOINDEX tells the spider not to index this page.

Any of these arguments can be combined, separated by commas, as shown in the following example:

```
<META NAME="ROBOTS" CONTENT="INDEX,NOFOLLOW">
```

Two other directives also specify a grouping of the preceding arguments. ALL is equivalent to INDEX,FOLLOW, and NONE is equivalent to NOINDEX,NOFOLLOW.

As with the robots.txt file, obeying the rules specified in this tag is optional. Most major search engines follow any requests that you make with this meta tag.

Contacting the Operator

If a spider appears to be running wild on your site or visiting parts of your site that you really don't want it to, you should first attempt to contact the operator. You have the client's address in the log files. Try to e-mail an administrator at the offending site to get hold of whoever is running the robot. Tell him what his robot is doing to your server and ask him nicely to stop, or at least to obey your robots.txt file.

Blocking a Spider by Address

If you can't get any response or if the operator refuses to pay any attention to you, you can shut out the spider completely with some well-placed deny directives:

```
<Directory /usr/web/docs>
Order allow,deny
Allow from all
Deny from unfriendly.spiderhost.com
</Directory>
```

If all else fails, have the spider's traffic blocked at your network's router or firewall. This has a disadvantage, however, in that it will also block traffic from any legitimate users coming from that system.

Blocking a Spider by `Deny from Env`

If you want to block a spider by something other than the address, such as the user agent, this can be done most effectively with the `Deny from Env` syntax, in conjunction with the `SetEnvIf` directive.

If, for example, you want to block traffic from a spider with useragent `EmailSiphon`, you might use the following approach.

```
SetEnvIf User-Agent EmailSiphon Spammers
Order Allow,Deny
Allow from all
Deny from env=Spammers
```

The `SetEnfIf` directive sets an environment variable if a particular condition is satisfied. In this case, it will see the environment variable `Spammers` if the `User-Agent` contains the string `EmailSiphon`.

The `Deny from Env` directive will deny access if a particular environment variable is set. In this case, it looks for the existence of the environment variable `Spammers`, which we have set in the case of a particular user agent, and deny access from that user agent.

Place this directive in your main server configuration file, in a `<Directory>` section that encompasses your entire site, and you will be able to keep this spider from looking at your site.

Writing Your Own Spider

Perhaps you want to write your own special-purpose spider to do some work for you. The best advice I can give you is, simply, don't write your own spider. A plethora of spiders are already available online, most of which you can download for free. They do everything from checking links on your site, to getting the latest basketball scores, to validating your HTML syntax, to telling you that your favorite Web site has been updated. It is very unlikely that you have a need so specialized that someone has not already written a spider to do exactly what you need. You can find a spider to suit your needs at

`http://info.webcrawler.com/mak/projects/robots/active/html/index.html`.

It can be difficult to write a spider that correctly implements the Robots Exclusion Protocol (that is, obeys all the suggestions given in the `robots.txt` file and any `ROBOTS` meta tags), so you might as well use one that someone else has already written.

23

WEB SPIDERS

If you really feel that you must write your own spider, the best tool for the job is probably Perl. Perl's main strength is processing large quantities of text and pulling out the information that's of interest to you. Spiders spend most of their time going through Web pages (text files) and pulling out information, as well as links to other Web pages.

Several Perl modules are used specifically for processing HTML pages. These modules are available on CPAN (http://www.cpan.org/). Of particular interest would be the LWP modules, in CPAN's modules/by-module/LWP/ directory, and various HTML::* modules in CPAN's modules/by-module/HTML/ directory.

Listing 23.1 shows a very simple spider, implemented in Perl. This subroutine gets a Web page, does something with that page, and then gets all the pages linked from the first page, recursively. The HTML::LinkExtor module extracts all links from an HTML document. HTML::FormatText formats an HTML page as text, so that you can get to the information without all the HTML markup. And LWP::Simple is a simple way to fetch documents from the network.

LISTING 23.1   A Simple Spider

```perl
use HTML::LinkExtor;
use HTML::FormatText;
use LWP::Simple;

my $p = HTML::LinkExtor->new();
my $Docs = {};

searchpage(0, 'http://www.yoursite.com/', $Docs);

sub searchpage  {
    my ($cur_depth, $url, $Docs) = @_;
    my ($link, @links, $abs);
    print "Looking at $url, at depth $cur_depth\n";
    $Docs->{$url} = 1; # Mark site as visited
    my $content = get($url);
    $p->parse($content);
    $content = HTML::FormatText->new->format(parse_html($content));
    DoSomethingWith($url, $content);
    @links = $p->links;

    for $link (@links)  {
        $abs = url($link->[2], $url)->abs if
            ($link->[0] eq 'a' && $link->[1] eq 'href');
        $abs =~ s/#.*$//;
```

Listing 23.1 continued

```
        $abs =~ s!/$!!;

        # Skip some URLs
        next if $abs=~/^mailto/i; # Email link
        next if $abs=~/(gz|zip|exe|tar|Z)$/; # Binary files
        next if $abs=~/\?\S+?=\S+/; # CGI program

        searchpage($cur_depth+1, $abs, $Docs)
            unless ($Docs->{$abs});
    }
} # End sub searchpage
```

The function call in the middle—DoSomethingWith($url, $content)—is, of course, where you would fill in whatever it is you wanted to do with the content you were collecting from the page.

The section labeled Skip some URLs contains regular expressions that match certain patterns in order to skip files that would be a particularly bad idea to spider. The first regular expression matches mailto links, and skips those so that your spider does not start sending e-mail. The second, regex, skips any files that might be binary files. You might add any number of additional patterns here, such as pdf or doc. The third pattern skips URLs that contain arguments on the end in GET form syntax, indicating that they are CGI links. This is not perfect, but eliminates some links to CGI programs that could trap the spider in an infinite URL space.

23

Web Spiders

> **Caution**
>
> Be careful when using this code, because it can put a heavy load on a server very quickly. It doesn't follow the standard for robot exclusion, as discussed earlier, and it continues to fetch pages forever because the recursion has no exit condition. (A good approach might be to exit from the loop as soon as $cur_depth reaches a certain value.) Test it on your server not mine.

Summary

Spiders are very useful tools for doing tedious work that we don't want to do manually. If carelessly written or used, however, they can wreak havoc on your Web server. This chapter focused on the various uses for spiders, as well as the ways they can be misused. You learned how to block them from your site and even how to write your own spider.

Logging

IN THIS CHAPTER

"Quickly, bring me a beaker of wine, that I may wet my brain and say something clever."

Aristophanies

Apache comes with built-in mechanisms that log activity on your server. In this chapter I'll talk about the standard way that Apache writes log files, and some of the tricks for getting more useful information and statistics out of your server.

If you have done a default installation of Apache two log files will be written when you run your server. These files are called `access_log` (`access.log` on Windows) and `error_log` (`error.log` on Windows). These files can be found (if you did a default installation) in `/usr/local/apache/logs`. On Windows, the logs are in the `logs` subdirectory of wherever you installed Apache. Some package managers put the log files in various other places, and you'll have to poke around to find them, or check in the configuration file for the configured location. Common places include `/var/log/` and `/usr/adm/`.

access_log

`access_log` is, as the name suggests, the log of all accesses to your server. A typical entry in this file would look like

```
216.35.116.91 - - [19/Aug/2000:14:47:37 -0400] "GET / HTTP/1.0" 200 654
```

This Line contains seven pieces of information. Actually, two of them are blank in this example, but there is space for seven pieces of information.

The first piece of information is the address of the remote host. That is, who is looking at your Web site. In the previous example, the host visiting my Web site is 216.35.116.91, which is, incidentally, the IP address of the machine called `si3001.inktomi.com`. (I figured that out by looking up the address in DNS, with the `nslookup` utility.) `inktomi.com` is a company that makes Web searching software. (I looked at their Web site.) Because the same IP address requested the file `robots.txt` just a few seconds earlier, I suspect that this is a Web searching spider that was indexing my Web site. (See Chapter 23, "Web Spiders," for more information about spiders and `robots.txt`.) So, just based on that first piece of information, and a glance back in the log file, I've already found out quite a bit of information about my visitors.

By default, this address is just the IP address of the remote host. You can tell Apache to look up all the hostnames, and put those hostnames in the log instead of the IP address. This is not a very good idea because it greatly slows down the logging process, and, therefore, slows down your entire server. (See Chapter 13, "Performance Tuning," for more tips about performance.) Various other tools will go through your log after the fact and resolve all the IP addresses to hostnames, so there's no real advantage to doing this anyway.

But, if you want to, you can tell Apache to do these lookups with the directive:

`HostNameLookups on`

Setting `HostNameLookups` to `double`, rather than `on`, will cause the logging process to do a reverse lookup on the name that it finds to verify that it points back to the IP address that you started with. The value is set to off by default.

The second slot, is blank, and almost always will be. The "-" is a placeholder for the second piece of information, where you're supposed to get the identity of the visitor in that location. Not just their login name but their e-mail address, or another unique identifier. This information is supposed to be returned by `identd`, or directly by the browser. In the old days, back when Netscape 0.9 was the dominant browser, you would usually have e-mail addresses in this spot. However, it did not take long for unsavory marketing types to think that it would be a good idea to collect those e-mail addresses and send them unsolicited e-mail (also known as spam). So, before very long, this feature was removed from just about every browser on the market. You will almost never find information in this field.

The third piece of information is also blank. The information that would appear there is the username with which the visitor authenticated. This will appear, of course, only when you have required authentication for a particular resource. So for the majority of entries in your log file, and for most sites, this will be blank. See Chapter 21, "Authentication and Authorization," for more details.

Next we have the time when the request was made. This information is enclosed in square brackets, and is in what is called standard-English format. So the request in the previous example was made at 14:47:37 on Saturday, August 19. The `-0400` on the end of the field means that the server is in the time zone four hours before UTC.

The next piece of information is probably the most useful piece in the record. It tells what request was actually made of the server. This is typically in the format `METHOD RESOURCE PROTOCOL`.

In the previous example, the `METHOD` is `GET`. The other most common methods will be `POST` and `HEAD`. There are a number of other valid methods, but those three are what you will see most of the time.

The `RESOURCE` is the actual document, or URL, that was requested from the server. In this example, the client requested `/`, which is the root, or front page, of the server. In most configurations, this corresponds to the file `index.html` in the `DocumentRoot` directory, but could be something else, depending on your server configuration.

The `PROTOCOL` is usually going to be `HTTP`, followed by a version number. The version number will be either `1.0` or `1.1`, with the proportions being roughly even. HTTP is the protocol that

24

LOGGING

makes the Web work. HTTP/1.0 was the earlier version of this protocol, and 1.1 is the more recent version.

The sixth piece of information is a status code. This tells you whether the request was successful, or if it encountered some problem. Most of the time this is 200, which means that the transfer was successful, and everything went well. In general, a status code that starts with 2 was successful. Starting with a 3 means that the request was redirected somewhere else for some reason. Starting with a 4 means that the user did something wrong, and starting with a 5 means that the server did something wrong.

The exact meanings of these status codes are included in the table at the end of this section.

The seventh and final piece of information is the total number of bytes that were transferred to the client. This can tell you if a transfer was interrupted (if the number is different from the size of the file). Adding them up will tell you how much data your server transferred in a day, or week, or whatever.

The following is a complete listing of possible values for the status codes—the sixth piece of information in an access_log entry.

TABLE 24.1   100-Series HTTP Status Codes

100	*Informational*
100	Continue: The client should continue with the request.
101	Switching protocols: The server is willing to comply with the client's request to upgrade protocols.

TABLE 24.2   200-Series HTTP Status Codes

200	*Successful*
200	OK: The request was successfully completed.
201	Resource created: The resource was successfully created.
202	Accepted: The request has been accepted for processing, but the processing has not been completed.
203	Nonauthoritative information: The information is not the definitive set as available from the origin server, but has been gathered from a local or third-party copy.
204	No content: The request was fulfilled, but no content needs to be returned.

TABLE 24.2   continued

200	*Successful*
205	Reset content: The request has been fulfilled, and the client should reset the document view that caused the request to be sent. For example, reset the contents of an HTML form so that the user can enter new information into that form.
206	Partial content: The partial GET request has been completed. This will be in response to a GET request that included a Range header, requesting only a portion of the resource.

TABLE 24.3   300-Series Server Status Codes

300	*Redirection*
300	Multiple choices: The requested resource can be fulfilled with any one of several choices.
301	Moved permanently: The requested resource has been permanently moved to a new location.
302	Found: The resource is temporarily located somewhere else, but the client should continue to use the same URL in the future.
303	See other: Usually the same as a 302. The response to the requested URL can be found at another location and should be retrieved from there.
304	Not modified: The document has not been modified since the specified date.
305	Use proxy: The requested resource must be requested through the specified proxy, which is sent in the Location header.
306	Unused
307	Temporary redirect: The resource has temporarily moved to a new location, and the client should repeat the request using that new location.

TABLE 24.4   400-Series Server Status Codes

400	*Client error*
400	Bad request: The request was not understood by the server.
401	Unauthorized: The request requires user authentication. This response is accompanied by a request for the necessary credentials. See Chapter 21 for more details.

24

LOGGING

TABLE 24.4   continued

400	*Client error*
402	Payment required: Not yet used.
403	Forbidden: The request was understood, but is being refused.
404	Not found: The requested resource could not be located.
405	Method not allowed: The method used is not one of the methods permitted for the requested resource.
406	Not acceptable: The requested resource is only available in representations which the client has indicated are not acceptable. See Chapter 10, "Content Negotiation," for more information on Content Negotiation and `Accept` headers.
407	Proxy authentication required: Similar to 401, but indicates that a proxy server requires authentication.
408	Request timeout: The client did not produce a request in the time that the server was willing to wait.
409	Conflict: The request could not be completed because of a conflict.
410	Gone: The resource is no longer available, and there is no known forwarding address.
411	Length required: The server will not accept the request without a `Status-Length` header.
412	Precondition Failed: A precondition specifies in the request header evaluated is false.
413	Request entity too large: The request was larger than the server was willing or able to process.
414	Request URI too long: The request URI is longer than the server is willing to interpret. Note that this is not the same as 413, which refers to the entire request entity, including headers.
415	Unsupported Media Type: The request is in a format not supported by the requested resource for the requested method.
416	Request range not satisfiable: The client request included a `Range` specifier, which does not specify a valid range for the requested resource. For example, it requests a byte-range that extends past the size of the requested file.
417	Expectation failed: The expectation expressed in the `Expect` request header could not be met by the server.

TABLE 24.5 500-Series Server Status Codes

500	*Server Error*
500	Internal server error: The server encountered an unexpected condition that prevented it from fulfilling the request.
501	Not implemented: The server does not support the functionality required to fulfill the request.
502	Bad gateway: While acting as a gateway or proxy, the server received an invalid request.
503	Service unavailable: The server is currently unavailable.
504	Gateway timeout: When acting as a gateway or proxy, the server did not receive a timely response from the upstream server.
505	HTTP version not supported: The server does not support the HTTP protocol that was specified in the request.

Location and Format of the `access_log` File

Where the `access_log` is located is actually a configuration option. If you look in your configuration file, `httpd.conf`, you should see a line that looks like the following:

```
CustomLog /usr/local/apache/logs/access\_log common
```

NOTE

If you're running an older version of Apache, this line might look a little different. It might be the `TransferLog` directive instead of the `CustomLog` directive. If that is the case, I really recommend that you upgrade if at all possible.

The `CustomLog` directive specifies where a particular log file should be stored, and what format that log should be in. The log format described previously is the `common` log format, which has been in use as the standard since the beginning of Web servers. That's why it still contains the ident information field, even though almost no clients actually pass that information to the server.

The path specified there is the location of the log file.

24

LOGGING

LogFormat

The LogFormat directive defines the actual format of the log file. Long ago, log files came in one format, called the common format, and you were pretty much stuck with it. Then came custom log file format, and it turned out to be such a good idea that even the common format was reimplemented as a custom log file format.

LogFormat sets up a format and gives it a nickname by which you can refer to it. CustomLog sets up an actual log file, and indicates the format (by nickname, usually) that the file will use.

For example, in your default httpd.conf file, you'll find the following line:

```
LogFormat "%h %l %u %t \"%r\" %>s %b" common
```

This directive creates a log format called common, which is in the format specified in quotes. Each one of those letters means a particular piece of information, which is put into the log file in the order indicated.

The available variables, and their meanings, are listed in the documentation, and are reproduced in table 24.6:

TABLE 24.6 LogFormat Variables

Variable	Meaning
%...a:	Remote IP-address
%...A:	Local IP-address
%...B:	Bytes sent, excluding HTTP headers
%...b:	Bytes sent, excluding HTTP headers. In CLF format that is, a "-" rather than a 0 when no bytes are sent
%...{FOOBAR}e:	The contents of the environment variable FOOBAR
%...f:	Filename
%...h:	Remote host
%...H	The request protocol

TABLE 24.6   continued

Variable	Meaning
%...{Foobar}i:	The contents of Foobar: header line(s) in the request sent to the server
%...l:	Remote logname (from identd, if supplied)
%...m	The request method
%...{Foobar}n:	The contents of note Foobar from another module
%...{Foobar}o:	The contents of Foobar: header line(s) in the reply
%...p:	The canonical Port of the server serving the request
%...P:	The process ID of the child that serviced the request
%...q	The query string (prepended with a ? if a query string exists, otherwise an empty string)
%...r:	First line of request
%...s:	Status. For requests that got internally redirected, this is the status of the original request—%...>s for the last
%...t:	Time, in common log format time format (standard-English format)
%...{format}t:	The time, in the form given by format, which should be in strftime(3) format (Potentially localized)
%...T:	The time taken to serve the request, in seconds
%...u:	Remote user (from auth; might be bogus if return status (%s) is 401)
%...U:	The URL path requested
%...v:	The canonical ServerName of the server serving the request
%...V:	The server name according to the UseCanonicalName setting

24

In each case, the "..." indicates an (optional) condition. If the condition is met, then the specified variable is displayed. If the condition is omitted, then the variable will be replaced with a "-" if it is not defined. I'll give some examples of this in a shortly.

The LogFormat line shown in the previous example, from the default httpd.conf file, creates a log format called common, which contains the remote host, remote logname, remote user, the time of the transaction, the first line of the request, the status of the request, and the number of bytes sent. This is the common log format explained in the previous section.

Sometimes you'll only want a particular piece of information logged if it is defined. These are what the "..." referred to previously provide for. If, between the % and the variable, you put one or more HTTP status codes, the variable will only be logged in the event that the request returns one of those status codes. So, if you're trying to keep a log of all the broken links on your site, you might have the following:

```
LogFormat %404{Referer}i BrokenLinks
```

Conversely, if you want to log requests that *don't* match a particular code, put a ! in there:

```
LogFormat %!200U SomethingWrong
```

CustomLog

After you have set up one or more `LogFormats`, you just have to apply them to a particular log file. This is done with the `CustomLog` directive. You can set up as many log files as you like. Each one needs to specify a log file location and which `LogFormat` you want to use:

```
CustomLog /var/log/httpd/bogus_log SomethingWrong
CustomLog /usr/local/apache/logs/broken BrokenLinks
CustomLog /usr/local/apache/logs/access_log common
```

The only disadvantage to doing this is that if you get some "off the shelf" log analysis application, it will assume that you are using `common` or `combined` log format because those are the ones that are most widely in use. However, many log analysis packages are able to do a good job of guessing what format you are using, if you have something other than the expected format.

Error Logs

The format of the entries in the error log is rather different from the entries in the access log that we saw previously.

But the two logs are similar because they both provide a lot of useful information, which you can use in analyzing how your server is being used, and what is going wrong.

Location of the Error Log

Your error log file should be in the same location as your access log file. It will be called `error_log`, or, on Windows machines, `error.log`.

The location of your error log can be configured with the `ErrorLog` directive:

```
ErrorLog logs/error.log
```

The location, unless it has a leading slash, is assumed to be relative to the `ServerRoot` directory.

In a default Apache installation the log file is located in /usr/local/apache/logs. As with the access log, if you installed with one of the various package managers out there, you might find it just about anywhere.

What's in It?

The error log, as the name suggests, contains a record of everything that went wrong while your server was running. It also contains general diagnostic messages, such as a notification of when your server was restarted, or shut down.

You can set your log level higher or lower to control the amount, and type, of messages that appear in your log file. This is configured with the LogLevel directive. The default setting of this directive is error, which tells you about error conditions. The complete list of possible settings is contained in Table 24.7.

TABLE 24.7   LogLevel Values

Level	Description	Example
emerg	Emergencies—system is unusable.	"Child cannot open lock file. Exiting"
alert	Action must be taken immediately.	"getpwuid: couldn't determine user-name from uid"
crit	Critical Conditions.	"socket: Failed to get a socket, exiting child"
error	Error conditions.	"Premature end of script headers"
warn	Warning conditions.	"child process 1234 did not exit, sending another SIGHUP"
notice	Normal but significant condition.	"httpd: caught SIGBUS, attempting to dump core in ..."
info	Informational.	"Server seems busy, (you may need to increase StartServers, or Min/MaxSpareServers)..."
debug	Debug-level messages.	"Opening config file ..."

24

LOGGING

In most cases, the things that you see in your log file will be in two categories: document errors and CGI errors. You will also occasionally see configuration errors, server start, and server stop messages.

Document Errors

Document errors are things that are in the 400 series of server response codes. The most common of these is 404—Document Not Found. 404's are followed in frequency, on most servers, by authentication errors.

A 404 error occurs whenever someone requests a resource—a URL—that is not on your server. Either they have mistyped something, there was a typo in a link somewhere, or you moved or deleted a document that used to be on your server.

> **NOTE**
>
> Jakob Nielsen, who is a highly respected usability expert, says that you should never move or delete any resource from your Web site without providing a redirect of some variety. If you're not already familiar with Nielsen's writings, you should take a look sometime at http://www.useit.com/.

When a client is unable to locate a document on your server, you'll see an entry like this in your logs:

```
[Fri Aug 18 22:36:26 2000] [error] [client 192.168.1.6] File does not exist:
/usr/local/apache/bugletdocs/Img/south-korea.gif
```

Note that, as in the case of the access_log file, this record is broken down into several fields.

First, we have the date/time stamp. The first thing that you might notice is that the format is not the same as the format in the access_log. The format that we called the standard-English format. This is merely an accident of history.

> **NOTE**
>
> The logging mechanisms for access and error logs were implemented by different people, who just happened to use different date formats. By the time they were cooperating a little more closely, there already existed log parsing applications that were counting on the particular date formats that had been used, and it was deemed to be too late to change.

Next, we have the level of the message. This will be one of the levels specified in the documentation for LogLevel (see previous). error is right between warn and crit. This simply indicates how serious the problem is. A 404 error means that you irritated someone, but it's not actually a critical condition affecting the health of your server.

The next field indicates the address of the client machine that made the request. In this case, it is a machine on my local network.

The last part of the log entry is the actual error message. In the case of a 404, it gives you the full path of the file that the server tried to serve. This is particularly useful when you're getting a 404 on a file that you just *know* is there. Frequently you have a configuration wrong, or the file is on a different virtual host than you thought, or some other strangeness.

Note that document errors, because they are a direct result of a client request, will be accompanied by an entry in `access_log` as well.

Authentication errors will look very much the same:

```
[Tue Apr 11 22:13:21 2000] [error] [client 192.168.1.3] user rbowen
authentication failure for "/cgi-bin/hirecareers/company.cgi": password
mismatch
```

CGI Errors

Perhaps the most useful purpose of the error is troubleshooting misbehaved CGI programs (or other content generation programs, such as `mod_perl`). Anything that a CGI program emits to STDERR (Standard Error) gets appended directly to the error log for your perusal. This means that (well-written) CGI programs, when they have problems, will tell you, via the log file, exactly what that problem is.

The downside to this is that you end up with stuff in the error log that is not in any well-defined format, and so it makes it very hard to have any automatic error-log parsing to get useful information out.

What follows is an example of an entry in an error log from problematic Perl CGI code:

```
Wed Jun 14 16:16:37 2000] [error] [client 192.168.1.3] Premature
end of script headers: /usr/local/apache/cgi-bin/TestProg/announcement.cgi
Global symbol "$rv" requires explicit package name at
/usr/local/apache/cgi-bin/TestProg/announcement.cgi line 81.
Global symbol "%details" requires explicit package name at
/usr/local/apache/cgi-bin/TestProg/announcement.cgi line 84.
Global symbol "$Config" requires explicit package name at
/usr/local/apache/cgi-bin/TestProg/announcement.cgi line 133.
Execution of /usr/local/apache/cgi-bin/TestProg/announcement.cgi
aborted due to compilation errors.
```

Although this entry actually does follow the same format as the previous 404 error, in that it has a date, error level, and a client address, the error message itself is several lines long, which tends to confuse some log-parsing software.

Even if you don't know Perl, you should be able to look at the previous error messages and glean some useful information about what went wrong. At the very least, you can tell on what lines the program had problems. Perl is very good about telling you where you made a mistake. Your mileage may vary based on what language you are using.

Without logs, it would be very difficult to troubleshoot most CGI programs because running it from the command line is a rather different environment than running it from a Web server.

Watching the Error Log

When actively developing a CGI program, or a content-generation application using some other technology, such as mod_perl, it's a good idea to actively watch the error log, so that when error conditions happen, you have immediate feedback.

This is done using the utility called tail. tail is a standard part of any Unix operating system, and tail clones are available for other operating systems.

At the command prompt, type the following:

```
tail -f /usr/local/apache/logs/error_log
```

This will show the last few lines of your log file, and, as lines are added to the file, it will show you those as they happen. The f stands for "follow" because it follows the log as it grows.

If you want to use tail (and other Unix utilities) on Windows, you may want to try AINTX, which is a collection of AIX utilities for NT. You can find these at http://maxx.mc.net/jlh/nttools/html/nttools.htm.

It's extremely good practice to keep several terminal windows open, with your error log tailing in one window, and your access log tailing in the other, while you work on your site. This will tell you what is going on as it happens, so you know about problems before the customer has a chance to call you about them.

Log File Analysis

Although there is an enormous amount of information in the log files it's not much good in its raw form.

Your marketing department, or the customer you are running the Web site for, will typically want to know how many people visited the site, what they looked at, how long they stayed, and where they found out about your site. All that information is (or might be) in your log files.

They will also want to know the names, addresses, and shoe sizes of those people, and, hopefully, their credit-card numbers. That information is not there and you need to know how to explain to your employer that not only is it not there, but the only way to get it is to explicitly ask your visitors for it and be willing to be told "no."

What Your Log Files Can Tell You

A lot of information is available to put in your log files, including the following:

1. **Address of the remote machine**: This is almost the same as "who is visiting my Web site," but not quite. More specifically, it tells you where that visitor is from. This will be something like `buglet.rcbowen.com` or `proxy01.aol.com`.

2. **Time of visit:** When did this person come to my Web site? This can tell you something about your visitors. If most of your visits come between the hours of 9 a.m. and 4 p.m., then you're probably getting visits from people at work. If it's mostly 7 p.m. through midnight, people are looking at your site from home.

   Single records, of course, give you very little useful information, but across several thousand hits, you can start to gather useful statistics.

3. **Resource requested**: What parts of your site are most popular? Those are the parts that you should expand. Which parts of the site are completely neglected? Perhaps those parts of the site are just really hard to get to. Or, perhaps they are genuinely uninteresting, in which case you should spice them up a little. Of course, some parts of your site, such as your legal statements, are boring and there's nothing you can do about it, but they need to stay on the site for the two or three people that want to see them.

4. **What's broken?** And, of course, your logs tell you when things are not working as they should be. Do you have broken links? Do other sites have links to your site that are not correct? Are some of your CGI programs malfunctioning? Is a robot overwhelming your site with thousands of requests per second?

What Your Log Files Don't Tell You

HTTP is a stateless, anonymous protocol. This is by design, and is not, at least in my opinion, a shortcoming of the protocol. If you want to know more about your visitors, you have to be polite, and actually ask them. And be prepared to not get reliable answers. This is amazingly frustrating for marketing types. They want to know the average income, number of kids, and hair color of their target demographic. And they don't like to be told that that information is not available in the log files. However, it is quite beyond your control to get this information out of the log files. Explain to them that HTTP is anonymous.

24

LOGGING

Even what the log files do tell you is occasionally suspect. For example, you can expect to have numerous entries in your log files indicating that a machine called something like `cache-mtc-am05.proxy.aol.com` has visited your Web site. This tells you that this is a machine that is on the AOL network. But because of the way that AOL works, this might be one person visiting your site many times, or it might be many people visiting my site one time each. All requests coming from the AOL network are proxied. A proxy server is one that one or more people sit behind. They type an address into their browser. It makes that request to the proxy server. The proxy server gets the page (generating the log file entry on my Web site). It then passes that page back to the requesting machine. This means that I never see the request from the originating machine, but only the request from the proxy.

Another implication of this is that if, 10 minutes later, someone else sitting behind that same proxy requests the same page a log file entry is not generated at all. They type the address, and that request goes to the proxy server. The proxy sees the request and thinks "I already have that document in memory. There's no point asking the Web site for it again." So instead of asking my Web site for the page, it gives the copy that it already has to the client. So, not only is the address field suspect, but the number of requests is also suspect.

Most proxies will not cache dynamic content, such as the results of a CGI program, as that can change from one client to the next.

It might sound like the data that you receive is so suspect that it's useless. This is in fact not the case. It should just be taken with a grain of salt. The number of hits that your site receives is almost certainly not really the number of visitors that came to your site. But it's a good indication. And it still gives you some useful information. Just don't rely on it for exact numbers.

Getting Useful Statistics From Your Logs

So, to the real meat of all this. How do you actually generate statistics from your Web server logs?

There are two main approaches that you can take here. You can either do it yourself, or you can get one of the existing applications that is available to do it for you.

Unless you have custom log files that don't look anything like the Common log format, you should probably get one of the available apps out there. There are some excellent commercial products, and some really good free ones, so you just need to decide what features you are looking for.

The following are some of the available programs on the market. This should not be considered a comprehensive list, and you should do your own research before choosing one for your site because they all have somewhat different feature sets and different reports.

The programs that I have chosen here either all have versions that will run on Unix and NT operating systems, or are in Perl, and will consequently run anywhere.

- **Analog:** The Analog Web site (`http://www.statslab.cam.ac.uk/sret1/analog/`) claims that about 29% of all Web sites that use any log analysis tool at all use Analog. They claim that this makes it the most popular log analysis tool in the world.

  The example report, which you can see on the Analog Web site, seemed very thorough and contained all the stats that I might want. In addition to the pages and pages of detailed statistics, there was a very useful executive summary, which will probably be the only part that your boss will really care about.

  Analog is free software.

- **WebTrends:** WebTrends provides astoundingly detailed reports on your log files, giving you all sorts of information that you did not know you could get out of these files. And there are a lot of pretty graphs generated in the report.

  It is, however, rather on the expensive side. You can look up the actual price on their Web site `http://www.webtrends.com/default.htm`.

  It is also very slow, in comparison to other programs listed here.

- **WWWStat:** WWWStat has been around for a very long time. It's fast, full-featured, and it's free. What more could you want? You can get it at `http://www.ics.uci.edu/pub/websoft/wwwstat/` and there is a companion package (linked from that same page) that generates pretty graphs.

  It is very easy to automate WWWStat so that it generates your log statistics every night at midnight, and then generates monthly reports at the end of each month.

- **Wusage:** Wusage has also been around a very long time. It is a great program, full-featured, inexpensive, and generates useful graphical reports.

  You can get Wusage at `http://www.boutell.com/wusage/`.

Parsing the Log Files Yourself

If you want to do your own log parsing and reporting, the best tool for the task is Perl. In fact, Perl's name (Practical Extraction and Report Language) is a tribute to its capability to extract useful information from logs and generate reports. (In reality, the name "Perl" came before the expansion of it, but I suppose that does not detract from my point.)

The `Apache::ParseLog` module, available from your favorite CPAN mirror, makes parsing log files simple, and, therefore, takes all the work out of generating useful reports from those logs.

For detailed information about how to use this module, install it and read the documentation. After you have installed the module, you can get at the documentation by typing `perldoc Apache::ParseLog`.

Trolling through the source code for WWWStat is another good way to learn about Perl log file parsing.

Because the log file format is so simple, writing code to chop it up into its component parts and do statistical analysis of it is rather simple.

Logging to a Process

You don't have to log to a file; you can log to a process. This is particularly useful if you want your logs to go to a database, or to some process that will give some type of real-time statistics on your Web site traffic.

Using the `<CustomLog>` directive, you can, instead of specifying a file to which the log should be written, specify |, followed by the name of a program that is to receive the logging information.

For example:

```
CustomLog |/usr/bin/apachelog common
```

Where `/usr/bin/apachelog` is some program that knows what to do with Apache log file entries. This might be as simple as a Perl program that processes the log entries in some fashion, or it might be something that writes entries to a database.

The main thing to be cautious about if you're going to do this is security. Log files are opened with the permission of the user that starts the server. This is usually root, and it applies as well to logging to a process. Make sure that the process to which you are logging is secure. If you log to an unsecure process (one that some non-root user can tinker with) you run the risk of having that process being replaced by another that does unsavory things. If, for example, `/usr/bin/apachelog.pl` is world-writable, any user could edit it to shut down your server, mail someone the password file, or delete important files. This would be done with root permissions.

Secondly, you should be careful about buffering. If, for example, you log to a process written in Perl, you might find that, although your Web site appears to be active, nothing is being logged by your Perl program. However, when you shut down the server, it suddenly logs everything. This is because it is buffering the output, and does not write anything out until the process terminates. Make sure you turn off output buffering if you want to get any sort of real-time reporting.

If you want to log to a process of some kind, you might be well advised to look for a module that already implements the functionality that you are looking for. Check out `http://modules.apache.org/` for a list of some of the modules available to do all sorts of cool things with Apache.

Note that logging to a process always uses more system resources than just logging to a text file. Unless you have an exceptionally good reason to log to a process, you will usually find that post-processing your log files is a better solution. It's a good idea to copy your log files off onto another machine for processing, so that there is no performance impact on your machine while the logs are being crunched.

Rotating Your Log Files

Log files get big. If you're not careful, you can end up filling up the drive (or partition) on which your log files are sitting, which can bring your server to a grinding halt.

The way around this is to move your log files to some other place before they get too big. This can be accomplished a number of different ways. Some Unix variants come with a `logrotate` script that handles this for you. RedHat, for example, comes preconfigured to rotate your logs for you every few days, based on either their size or their age.

Logfile::Rotate

If you want to do this yourself, you can use a Perl module (freely available from CPAN) called `Logfile::Rotate`. The following code, run periodically (perhaps once a week?) by cron, will rotate out your log file, keeping five previous log files at any given time. Each backup log file will be gzipped to conserve space.

```perl
#!/usr/bin/perl
use Logfile::Rotate;
foreach $log (qw(error_log access_log)) {
    $logfile = new Logfile::Rotate(
        File => "/usr/local/apache/logs/$log",
        Count => 5,
        Gzip => '/bin/gzip',
        Post => sub {
            `/usr/local/apache/bin/apachectl restart`;
        }
    }
);
```

The Perl module takes care of all the details. You'll end up with files called things such as `access_log.1.gz`, `access_log.2.gz`, and so on. Each file will get bumped up one number each time and the file that used to be `access_log.5.gz` will be deleted each time. The `Count` parameter specifies how many log files are kept.

This keeps you from running out of space on your log drive, and keeps as much of an archive as you like.

logrotate

Additionally, Apache ships with a utility called `logrotate`, which enables you to rotate log files on a regular basis. You can use the `logrotate` utility by adding it to your Apache configuration file as a process to which you will log. The syntax will look like this:

```
CustomLog "|/usr/local/apache/bin/rotatelogs /var/log/archive/apachelog
➥86400" common
```

The parameter 86400 here is the number of seconds after which the log will be moved and a new log started.

The path `/var/log/archive/apachelog` specifies where the old log files will be put for archival purposes. More specifically, the log file will be backed up to a file named by taking this argument, and appending a timestamp.

86400 seconds, by the way, is 24 hours.

Logging for Multiple Virtual Hosts

When you have more than one virtual host on the same machine, you should have separate log files for each host. This will eliminate the problems related to trying to pull log files apart into accesses from the various hosts after the fact.

In each of your `VirtualHost` sections, simply specify a log file for that host. You can then handle each log file separately when it comes time to run reports.

There are some concerns with available file handles. That is, if you are running hundreds of virtual hosts, and have a log file per host, you may encounter a situation where you run out of available file handles. This can cause system instability and can even cause your system to halt. This is primarily a concern on servers that are hosting a very large number of virtual hosts. In that condition, you will need to consult the documentation for your particular operating system regarding the available number of file handles.

Summary

In this chapter, we've talked about various aspects of logging with Apache. You should now be equipped to log whatever information you're interested in, and get all sorts of useful statistics out of those log files.

Modules

PART
V

IN THIS PART

Introduction to Apache Modules

IN THIS CHAPTER

"While I'm still confused and uncertain, it's on a much higher plane, d'you see, and at least I know I'm bewildered about the really fundamental and important facts of the universe."

Treatle nodded. "I hadn't looked at it like that," he said, "But you're absolutely right. He's really pushed back the boundaries of ignorance."

Discworld scientists at work—Terry Pratchett, Equal Rites

As you have already seen throughout this book, most of the interesting functionality in Apache is implemented in modules rather than in the Apache core.

Apache, like many large software projects, operates on a modular model, where a very minimal set of crucial features are put into a core, or kernel, and everything else is implemented as a module, or plug-in, to that core. In this way, you can build Apache to have the smallest possible feature set, and, therefore, reduce the total size.

The Apache core implements an API (Application Programmer Interface), which modules can make calls into to access the basic functions the core provides, such as outputting HTTP headers, writing to the log files, and sending content to the client.

An Apache module extends the functionality of Apache and provides either directives or handlers (or filters in 2.0), which give the Web server administrator a way to affect the behavior of Apache in some way.

When a module is loaded it registers a list of the configuration directives and handlers that it provides with the core. When parsing the server configuration file at server startup, the value of each directive will be passed to the particular module that is responsible for it.

For example, mod_speling provides the CheckSpelling directive, which is used to set whether the spelling correction behavior is desired or not. When Apache encounters this directive while parsing the configuration file, it looks up who provides the directive and upon finding that mod_speling does, informs mod_speling of the setting.

You can see what modules you have installed, and the directives they provide, in one of two ways.

If you have mod_info installed and configured, you can view its output to get this information. (See Chapter 14, "Handlers and Filters," for details about configuring mod_info.)

Or, from the command line you can run the httpd binary, providing it with the -l flag to see what modules have been built into Apache, or with the -L flag to see what configuration variables are made available by these modules.

The -l flag provides a simple listing of modules. Here is an example output from this command.

```
rbowen@rhiannon:~% /usr/local/apache/bin/httpd -l
Compiled-in modules:
  http_core.c
  mod_env.c
  mod_log_config.c
  mod_mime.c
  mod_negotiation.c
  mod_status.c
  mod_info.c
  mod_include.c
  mod_autoindex.c
  mod_dir.c
  mod_cgi.c
  mod_asis.c
  mod_imap.c
  mod_actions.c
  mod_speling.c
  mod_userdir.c
  mod_alias.c
  mod_rewrite.c
  mod_access.c
  mod_auth.c
  mod_setenvif.c
  mod_perl.c
```

The -L flag returns much more detailed information, listing every available directive, what module provides it, and a one-to-three-line description of what the directive is for. For example, one directive might look like the following:

```
CheckSpelling (mod_speling.c)
        whether or not to fix miscapitalized/misspelled requests
        Allowed in *.conf anywhere and in .htaccess
        when AllowOverride includes Options
```

A section like this appears for every directive defined by every module you have installed. For modules that you have installed as DSOs (dynamic shared objects), you will get this information only for modules that you have loaded under your current configuration.

In Chapter 2, "Acquiring and Installing Your Apache Server," there is more discussion of shared objects and installing modules as shared objects.

25

INTRODUCTION TO
APACHE MODULES

The Apache API

First of all, this is not a book about writing Apache modules. For that, you should read *Writing Apache Modules with Perl and C*, from O'Reilly and Associates (http://www.oreilly.com/catalog/wrapmod/), which is an excellent reference to writing Apache modules.

The Apache Web site contains a complete listing of the Apache API, which is located at http://dev.apache.org/apidoc/. It provides each of the functions, a description of what it does, and an example of how to use it.

The Apache documentation also contains a short tutorial on using the Apache API. The tutorial has examples from real modules and it shows how to interact with the Apache API. It can be found at http://httpd.apache.org/docs/misc/API.html. Part of the Apache distribution is a module, called mod_example, which provides an example of how to write an Apache module and shows you how to go about accessing the Apache API. You should read that before you attempt to write your first Apache module.

Installing Modules

As you saw in Chapter 2, there are two ways to install modules. When you build Apache you can either specify what modules you want installed, or you can build it as a shared object and decide in your configuration file whether or not to load that module. Each method has its advantages and disadvantages, but one method is not clearly better than the other for all Apache installations.

Building the Module into `httpd`

The first of the two methods of installing modules is building them into the `httpd` binary. This is frequently called "statically linked" because the various parts are compiled together into one final binary file, and it is not possible to dynamically swap out various components.

Advantages and Disadvantages

There are a number of things that you should know about installing a module this way, but whether each is an advantage or disadvantage really depends on your perspective and interpretation.

Building your modules into `httpd` requires that you know at compile time what modules you are going to need. The list of modules is passed to the `configure` script, and these modules are then compiled into the binary for the Apache daemon. You are not able to go back and change your mind on what modules you want, except by rebuilding the server.

httpd itself will be much larger, with all the modules built into it, than if you use mod_so to load them at the time your server starts.

Apache will start up slightly faster because it will not have to locate and load the various module files.

How to Install a Module

To add a particular module to Apache at compile time, you need to only add an argument to the list that is passed to the configure script.

For example, if you want to add mod_auth_db to your build of Apache, which is not compiled in by default, you would use a configure command line similar to the following:

```
./configure —prefix=/usr/local/apache —enable-module=auth_db
```

This will work for any module that is included with the Apache distribution.

This command should be run in the directory where you have unpacked your Apache source code, and should be followed by the commands make and make install to complete the installation.

See the next chapter for a listing of all the modules that come with Apache, and whether or not they are compiled in by default.

To build in a module that was not distributed with Apache—a third-party module—you will need to follow the instructions that came with that module. However, the general procedure in such a case is as follows:[1]

```
./configure —prefix=/usr/local/apache \
    —add-module=/path/to/mod_thirdparty.c
```

In the previous example, mod_thirdparty.c is the C language source code file for the module that you are including.

Some modules, such as mod_perl or mod_ssl, have very specific installation instructions that you need to follow, so always read the documentation for the third-party module before trying the previous technique.

Dynamic Shared Objects

The second way to install a module is as a DSO, or Dynamic Shared Object. This involves building Apache and its modules separately, and then loading the ones you want when you start the Apache server.

---

[1]*The backslash character at the end of the line is a continuation character, telling the shell that the command continues on the next line. Most shells understand this notation. You can also just type the entire command on one line. It is broken into shorter lines to make its format fit the book.*

25

INTRODUCTION TO APACHE MODULES

Advantages and Disadvantages

As with statically linking the modules, whether you consider a particular thing an advantage or a disadvantage, with respect to DSOs, is purely your opinion.

Building modules as shared objects allows you to decide to change what modules you have loaded on a moment's notice, just by changing the configuration file. If you want to add a new module, you only have to build that module, rather than rebuilding Apache. You then add a `LoadModule` directive to your main server configuration file, and restart the server.

Apache will start up slightly slower on restart, because it has to locate and load each of the `.so` files. However, this is seldom actually a noticeable slowdown, and does not translate into any slower performance after the startup is completed.

The main `httpd` binary will be substantially smaller than it would be if all the modules were built into it. But the combined size of the `httpd` binary and the various `.so` files will be roughly the same as the httpd binary with all the same modules built in.

Installing Modules As Shared Objects

To install a module as a shared object, rather than statically linked, you need merely to add the `-enable-shared` argument when you run `configure`.

For example, to install `mod_rewrite` as a DSO, you would use the following command:

```
./configure —prefix=/usr/local/apache \
    —enable-module=rewrite \
    —enable-shared=rewrite
```

You are not required to choose one method or the other—that is, you can install some modules statically, and other dynamically.

As before, the previous command needs to be followed by the commands `make` and `make install` to complete the process.

If you want to build all the modules that came with Apache as shared objects use the following convenience syntax:

```
./configure —prefix=/usr/local/apache \
    —enable-module=most \
    —enable-shared=max
```

This will build most, but not all, of the modules that are distributed with Apache. The ones left out are those considered experimental, and those, such as `mod_auth_db`, which require external libraries that might not be present.

The `-enable-shared=max` syntax can be used without the other parts of this command, if you want to ensure that all modules are installed as DSOs.

```
./configure —prefix=/usr/local/apache —enable-shared=max
```

This will build Apache with the standard list of enabled modules, and build them all as DSOs. Again, see the next chapter for a full list of the modules distributed with Apache, and the ones compiled by default.

The DSO functionality is implemented by `mod_so`, which *must* be built in to load the other modules. You can't build `mod_so` as a DSO.

Summary

Modules implement all the interesting functionality in Apache, with the core doing as little as possible. In Apache 2.0, the core does even less than it does in 1.3, with more of the functionality being pulled out into modules.

Modules can be installed statically or dynamically, as shared objects, if your operating system supports that functionality.

25

INTRODUCTION TO APACHE MODULES

Modules Included with Apache

IN THIS CHAPTER

"We shall not cease from exploration
And the end of all our exploring
Will be to arrive where we started
And know the place for the first time."

T.S. Eliot

As we saw in the previous chapter, modules are the heart and soul of why Apache is so great. The Apache core is lightweight and does as little as possible. All the really interesting functionality is implemented in modules.

In this chapter, we talk about the standard modules that ship with Apache. Some of them are not compiled in by default, but can be enabled by a flag at compile time. We'll talk about what each module does, and how to get it installed on your server.

Note that this chapter does not contain comprehensive documentation of these modules. That documentation is available online, in the official Apache module documentation, at `http://httpd.apache.org/docs/mod/index.html`. More importantly, the official documentation is improved upon on an almost daily basis, therefore printing it here will guarantee that it is almost immediately out of date.

The source code for each of these modules is located in the `src/modules` subdirectory when you unpack the Apache distribution file. In particular, these standard modules are in the `standard` directory. There is also an `experimental` directory containing modules that are not yet considered to be production quality.

> **NOTE**
>
> You should also note that, as of this writing, Apache 2.0 is in beta, and the list of standard modules is still subject to change. A few of the modules listed here will go away, and some new ones are sure to be added.

The Modules

The following are the modules that are distributed with Apache. You should note that this is the list of modules that are distributed with Apache only if you download Apache from the official Apache Web site. If you get your Apache distribution from somewhere else, that vendor might have added or removed modules from this list. A number of distributions will add mod_perl or mod_ssl to their Apache installation to eliminate the difficulty usually associated with installing those modules.

Modules Included with Apache

359

CHAPTER 26

26

MODULES
INCLUDED WITH
APACHE

mod_access

Name	mod_access
On by default?	Yes
Docs	http://httpd.apache.org/docs/mod/mod_access.html

mod_access provides access control based on client hostname, IP address, or other characteristics of the client request.

mod_actions

Name	mod_actions
On by default?	Yes
Docs	http://httpd.apache.org/docs/mod/mod_actions.html

Provides for executing CGI scripts based on media type or request method.

mod_alias

Name	Mod_alias
On by default?	Yes
Docs	http://httpd.apache.org/docs/mod/mod_alias.html

Mapping different parts of the file system into the document tree and URL redirection.

mod_asis

Name	mod_asis
On by default?	Yes
Docs	http://httpd.apache.org/docs/mod/mod_asis.html

Sending files that contain their own HTTP headers.

mod_auth

Name	mod_auth
On by default?	Yes
Docs	http://httpd.apache.org/docs/mod/mod_auth.html

Basic HTTP authentication, using text files to contain user and group information.

mod_auth_anon

Name	mod_auth_anon
On by default?	No
Docs	http://httpd.apache.org/docs/mod/mod_auth_anon.html

Anonymous user access to authenticated areas.

mod_auth_db

Name	mod_auth_db
On by default?	No
Docs	http://httpd.apache.org/docs/mod/mod_auth_db.html

Basic HTTP authentication, using Berkeley DB files to contain user and group information.

mod_auth_dbm

Name	mod_auth_dbm
On by default?	No
Docs	http://httpd.apache.org/docs/mod/mod_auth_dbm.html

Basic HTTP authentication, using DBM files to contain user and group information.

mod_auth_digest

Name	mod_auth_digest
On by default?	No
Docs	http://httpd.apache.org/docs/mod/mod_auth_digest.html

MD5 digest authentication.

mod_autoindex

Name	mod_autoindex
On by default?	Yes
Docs	http://httpd.apache.org/docs/mod/mod_autoindex.html

Automatic directory listings.

mod_cern_meta

Name	mod_cern_meta
On by default?	No
Docs	http://httpd.apache.org/docs/mod/mod_cern_meta.html

Support for HTTP header metafiles.

mod_cgi

Name	mod_cgi
On by default?	Yes
Docs	http://httpd.apache.org/docs/mod/mod_cgi.html

Support for execution of CGI programs.

mod_digest

Name	mod_digest
On by default?	No
Docs	http://httpd.apache.org/docs/mod/mod_digest.html

Provides MD5 authentication, but has been replaced by mod_auth_digest.

mod_dir

Name	mod_dir
On by default?	Yes
Docs	http://httpd.apache.org/docs/mod/mod_dir.html

Provides for mapping URLs with a trailing slash to an index file, typically called index.html.

mod_env

Name	mod_env
On by default?	Yes
Docs	http://httpd.apache.org/docs/mod/mod_env.html

Handles the passing of environment variables to CGI programs.

mod_example

Name	mod_example
On by default?	No
Docs	http://httpd.apache.org/docs/mod/mod_example.html

An example module, demonstrating the Apache API, and the technique of writing Apache modules.

mod_expires

Name	mod_expires
On by default?	No
Docs	http://httpd.apache.org/docs/mod/mod_expires.html

Gives the capability to apply Expires: headers to resources.

mod_headers

Name	mod_headers
On by default?	No
Docs	http://httpd.apache.org/docs/mod/mod_headers.html

Add arbitrary HTTP headers to resources.

mod_imap

Name	mod_imap
On by default?	Yes
Docs	http://httpd.apache.org/docs/mod/mod_imap.html

Handles server-side image map files.

mod_include

Name	mod_include
On by default?	Yes
Docs	http://httpd.apache.org/docs/mod/mod_include.html

Server-parsed documents (Server-side includes).

mod_info

Name	mod_info
On by default?	No
Docs	http://httpd.apache.org/docs/mod/mod_info.html

Provides the `server-info` handler for providing information about server configuration. See Chapter 14, "Handlers and Filters," for more details.

mod_log_agent

Name	mod_log_agent
On by default?	No
Docs	http://httpd.apache.org/docs/mod/mod_log_agent.html

Logging of user agent (browser). This module is superseded by the `LogFormat` directive in `mod_log_config`.

mod_log_config

Name	mod_log_config
On by default?	Yes
Docs	http://httpd.apache.org/docs/mod/mod_log_config.html

Allows you to build custom log files. See Chapter 24, "Logging," for detailed discussion of the various logging directives and techniques.

mod_log_referer

Name	mod_log_referer
On by default?	No
Docs	http://httpd.apache.org/docs/mod/mod_log_referer.html

Provides logging of document references. That is, logs the places that have links to your content. This module is superseded by the LogFormat directive in `mod_log_config`.

mod_mime

Name	mod_mime
On by default?	Yes
Docs	http://httpd.apache.org/docs/mod/mod_mime.html

Determining document types by file extensions. See Chapter 8 for more discussion of MIME types and the related directives.

mod_mime_magic

Name	mod_mime_magic
On by default?	No
Docs	http://httpd.apache.org/docs/mod/mod_mime_magic.html

Determining document types using "magic numbers"—that is, by looking at the contents of the file, and, based on the frequency of occurrence of certain patterns or characters, determining what the file type probably is.

mod_mmap_static

Name	mod_mmap_static
On by default?	No
Docs	http://httpd.apache.org/docs/mod/mod_mmap_static.html

Mapping files into memory to improve performance of serving static document. This module is marked as experimental.

mod_negotiation

Name	mod_negotiation
On by default?	Yes
Docs	http://httpd.apache.org/docs/mod/mod_negotiation.html

Content negotiation (see Chapter 10).

mod_proxy

Name	mod_proxy
On by default?	No
Docs	http://httpd.apache.org/docs/mod/mod_proxy.html

A caching proxy server.

mod_rewrite

Name	mod_rewrite
On by default?	No
Docs	http://httpd.apache.org/docs/mod/mod_rewrite.html and http://apache/httpd-docs-1.3/htdocs/manual/misc/rewriteguide.html

Provides the capability to rewrite incoming URL requests to do all the things that you wish mod_alias did.

mod_setenvif

Name	mod_setenvif
On by default?	Yes
Docs	http://httpd.apache.org/docs/mod/mod_setenvif.html

Set environment variables based on client information.

mod_so

Name	mod_so
On by default?	No
Docs	http://httpd.apache.org/docs/mod/mod_so.html

Dynamically load modules as shared objects at runtime.

mod_speling

Name	mod_speling
On by default?	No
Docs	http://httpd.apache.org/docs/mod/mod_speling.html

Automatically correct minor typos in URLs, such as character transposing, wrong capitalization, or other small errors.[1]

mod_status

Name	mod_status
On by default?	Yes
Docs	http://httpd.apache.org/docs/mod/mod_status.html

Display server status in a convenient HTML report.

mod_unique_id

Name	mod_unique_id
On by default?	No
Docs	http://httpd.apache.org/docs/mod/mod_unique_id.html

Generate unique identifiers for each incoming request for tracking purposes.

---

[1]*Yes, the name is* mod_speling, *not* mod_spelling. *Someone thinks they're funny.*

mod_usertrack

Name	mod_usertrack
On by default?	No
Docs	http://httpd.apache.org/docs/mod/mod_usertrack.html

User tracking using cookies. Make sure you know what you are doing before enabling this. It sends a lot of cookies.

mod_vhost_alias

Name	mod_vhost_alias
On by default?	No
Docs	http://httpd.apache.org/docs/mod/mod_vhost_alias.html

Dynamically configure a large number of virtual hosts without changing your server configuration file.

Installing or Omitting a Standard Module

To install one of the standard modules that is not enabled by default, you need to add an additional parameter during the configuration phase of installation. For example, to add mod_usertrack to your set of modules, you would use the following command:

```
./configure —enable-module=usertrack
```

Note that this argument is in addition to any others that you might already have in effect. This module is added to the list of modules that is already enabled by default. The modules that are already enabled by default need not be mentioned in your configuration options.

Similarly, if you want to disable one of the modules that is enabled by default, you do so with the -disable-module parameter. For example, if for some reason you wanted to remove mod_auth from the list of enabled modules, you would use the following command:

```
./configure —disable-module=auth
```

Apache 2.0

The list of standard modules will change some with Apache 2.0. Most importantly, perhaps, SSL will be distributed with Apache by default (it is a separate distribution with Apache 1.3), and will be enabled by default.

Modules Included with Apache

CHAPTER 26

367

26

MODULES
INCLUDED WITH
APACHE

The syntax for enabling and disabling modules is somewhat different as well, with a directive for each module. For example, to enable mod_auth_db, which is not enabled by default, you would use the -enable-auth-db parameter, as shown in this example:

```
./configure —enable-auth-db
```

And, similarly, to disable mod_negotiation, you would use the -disable-negotiation parameter:

```
./configure —disable-negotiation
```

For a complete list of these possible parameters, you will use the same syntax as with Apache 1.3:

```
./configure —help
```

As of this writing, Apache 2.0 is in beta and the list of standard modules is still subject to change.

Summary

In summary, here is a list of all the modules that are included with the Apache distribution, and an indication of whether they are enabled by default. This list is possibly subject to change from one release of Apache to the next (although, in practice, it seldom does). You can get the authoritative list for the version that you are using by going to the Apache source code directory and typing ./configure -help.

access=yes	actions=yes	alias=yes
asis=yes	auth=yes	auth_anon=no
auth_db=no	auth_dbm=no	auth_digest=no
autoindex=yes	cern_meta=no	cgi=yes
digest=no	dir=yes	env=yes
example=no	expires=no	headers=no
imap=yes	include=yes	info=no
log_agent=no	log_config=yes	log_referer=no
mime=yes	mime_magic=no	mmap_static=no
negotiation=yes	proxy=no	rewrite=no
setenvif=yes	so=no	speling=no
status=yes	unique_id=no	userdir=yes
usertrack=no	vhost_alias=no	

Special-Purpose Apache Modules

IN THIS CHAPTER

"My girl came to the study and said Help me;
I told her I had a time problem which meant:
I would die for you but I don't have ten minutes."

Time Problem—Brenda Hillman

As you have seen in the last two chapters Apache is built around modules.[1] Apache is distributed with a substantial list of modules that perform the tasks necessary for a normal Web site.

But you don't have a normal Web site. Who does? You have that strange customer with those unusual demands. You need to authenticate users against your Windows NT domain. You need to embed Perl code in your pages. You need to generate a gallery of thumbnail graphics so that you can serve up files from your digital camera. And Apache does not do any of these things, right?

Well, yes, and no. Remember, technically, Apache does not do much of anything, and everything interesting that it does do, it does by virtue of a module.

The modules that are distributed with Apache represent things that Apache did not do, which someone thought that it should do. So, in the spirit of open software development, those people went off to scratch their personal itch and wrote functionality to do those things that they wanted done, and then contributed their work back to the ASF.

After a while, there were just too many modules to include with the Apache distribution. The decision of whether or not to include a particular module had to be made, based largely on the demand for that module, as well as on the complexity of the module.

`mod_perl`, `mod_php`, and `mod_ssl`, for example, are large enough and complex enough that despite the fact that they are in high demand, they are distributed separately, and maintained by a different set of programmers.[2]

Finally, you need to understand that modules that are not part of the official Apache distribution are not formally tested by the Apache Software Foundation. There may be interoperability problems with other modules or module combinations, or with particular versions of Apache.

---

[1] *Or, modules are built around Apache, depending on your perspective.*

[2] *Note that* `mod_ssl`, *perhaps under a different name; will be distributed with Apache 2.0.*

Finding Apache Modules

There are, however, an enormous number of available Apache modules that are not included in the distribution. These modules are available primarily from two locations. The main location for Apache modules that are written in C is `http://modules.apache.org`, whereas `http://www.cpan.org/modules/by-module/Apache` is the primary place for Apache/mod_perl modules written in Perl.

modules.apache.org

`modules.apache.org`—the Apache Module Registry—is where Apache modules can be found, if they are not included in the Apache distribution. Many Apache module developers around the world are developing modules for some special purpose, which might be extremely specific to their particular situation. Some of these modules, however, turn out to be of interest to more people than just the developer, but not to enough people to warrant including it in the distribution. The Apache Module Registry provides a place for these people to advertise these modules, allow people to download or buy them, and participate in the continuing development of these modules.

The Module Registry is maintained by Covalent Technologies, Inc., and contains just a few dozen modules at the time of this writing.

If you write an Apache module that you think would be of general interest please consider registering your module and source code at the Module Registry, so that others can benefit from it, and improve on it.

CPAN

CPAN, the Comprehensive Perl Archive Network, is a global network of mirror sites that contain close to a gigabyte of Perl modules, scripts, documentation, and the Perl source code.

A portion of the CPAN mirror, located in the `/modules/by-module/Apache` directory, contains Apache `mod_perl` modules, as well as other Apache-related Perl modules. These modules can be dropped onto your `mod_perl`-enabled Apache server and put into production immediately, doing a variety of things from cookie-based authentication to streaming MP3 audio to e-mailing system administrators when their unpatched IIS server attempts to infect you with the Code Red worm.

CPAN can be found at `http://www.cpan.org/`. A CPAN mirror closer to you can be found on the mirror list at `http://www.cpan.org/SITES.html`.

Search for Them

And, if all else fails, check a search engine.

A search for "apache modules" on www.google.com turned up 335,000 Web sites with Apache modules on them. Of course, many of these are CPAN mirrors, but if you are searching for something specific, you can narrow this down a great deal.

Announce Mailing List

There is a mailing list for the purpose of announcing new Apache modules. If you are interested in extending your Apache server, then you might want to subscribe to this list to be kept abreast of new modules that are being developed.

To subscribe to the list, send an empty e-mail message to the address apache-modules-announce-subscribe@covalent.net.

To unsubscribe from the list, send an empty e-mail message to the address apache-modules-announce-unsubscribe@covalent.net.

Examples of Modules

The following are two examples of modules that are available, and do things that will hopefully be useful to many readers. However, the idea here is to show you how to find, install, and configure a module that is not included in the Apache distribution.

User Authentication with LDAP

You've gone to all the trouble to put your entire organization on an LDAP server, and would like to have Apache use this information for authentication, rather than having to maintain a different password file on your Apache server. Having a single point of authentication is a very good thing, as users only have to remember one set of credentials, and, therefore, are less likely to have a list of passwords on a PostIt note on their monitor. Using the username and password that they are already using for other things means that there is no new behavior to learn, and, therefore, fewer tech support calls for you.

Searching for "ldap" on modules.apache.org actually returns nine results. Apparently this is a fairly popular thing to do. We'll try the first one, which advertises itself as just "LDAP auth module for Apache," which is just what we are looking for.

Looking at a few of the other options the search pulled up, we run into a number of red flags that steer us away from several of them. Some of them have not been modified in more than a year. Another gives us the module source code, but no documentation. Still another is just a broken link. It appears that we have chosen the right one.

The link takes us to software by Muhammad A Muquit, called `mod_auth_ldap`. At first glance it appears that we have picked a good one because there is a great deal of documentation immediately available, so one this should be easy to set up.

The URL for `mod_auth_ldap` is

`http://www.muquit.com/muquit/software/mod_auth_ldap/mod_auth_ldap.html`

The extensive documentation walks you through compiling Apache with the new module and configuring Apache to use the module. It is available for both Unix and Windows, and is available as a precompiled DLL for Windows. It also appears to be frequently maintained and updated.

Photo Album

You have a snazzy new digital camera and want to put all your photos on your Web site, but you don't want to have to go to all the trouble of creating HTML to list all the files, make thumbnail images, and lay it all out in nice tables.

Fortunately, this is one of the things available as an Apache `mod_perl` module on CPAN. One of the better ways to locate modules on CPAN is with the CPAN search engine, at `http://search.cpan.org/`, which enables you to search for modules by looking for particular words in the documentation.

After trying a few different words, searching for "album" opens `Apache::Album`, which sounds promising.

`Apache::Album` is well-documented and does exactly what we are looking for. It generates thumbnails of all the images in a particular directory, and links these to the original image, as well as a few intermediate sizes of the image.

It is a `mod_perl` module, so this means that you must have `mod_perl` installed to use it. It is configured by a variety of `PerlSetVar` directives in your Apache configuration file, which allow you to control the size of the thumbnails, the attributes of the HTML page (such as background color or what the footer says), and whether there are three various-sized images generated.

The module also allows for upload of images so that you can manage the album from your Web browser.

See your nearest CPAN mirror to download this module.

Summary

Although the Apache documentation includes the modules that most people will agree are useful, special needs give rise to dozens of special-purpose modules that are floating around.

`http://modules.apache.org/` and `http://search.cpan.org/` are two places where you might find just the module you are looking for.

Appendixes

IN THIS PART

The Apache Software License

The following is the Apache Software License, under which the Apache server is released.

The Apache Software License, Version 1.1

Copyright © 2000-2001 The Apache Software Foundation. All rights reserved.

Redistribution and use in source and binary forms, with or without modification, are permitted provided that the following conditions are met:

1. Redistributions of source code must retain the above copyright notice, this list of conditions and the following disclaimer.

2. Redistributions in binary form must reproduce the above copyright notice, this list of conditions and the following disclaimer in the documentation and/or other materials provided with the distribution.

3. The end-user documentation included with the redistribution, if any, must include the following acknowledgment:

   "This product includes software developed by the Apache Software Foundation (`http://www.apache.org/`)."

   Alternately, this acknowledgment may appear in the software itself, if and wherever such third-party acknowledgments normally appear.

4. The names "Apache" and "Apache Software Foundation" must not be used to endorse or promote products derived from this software without prior written permission. For written permission, please contact apache@apache.org.

5. Products derived from this software may not be called "Apache," nor may "Apache" appear in their name, without prior written permission of the Apache Software Foundation.

THIS SOFTWARE IS PROVIDED "AS IS" AND ANY EXPRESSED OR IMPLIED WARRANTIES, INCLUDING, BUT NOT LIMITED TO, THE IMPLIED WARRANTIES OF MERCHANTABILITY AND FITNESS FOR A PARTICULAR PURPOSE ARE DISCLAIMED. IN NO EVENT SHALL THE APACHE SOFTWARE FOUNDATION OR ITS CONTRIBUTORS BE LIABLE FOR ANY DIRECT, INDIRECT, INCIDENTAL, SPECIAL, EXEMPLARY, OR CONSEQUENTIAL DAMAGES (INCLUDING, BUT NOT LIMITED TO, PROCUREMENT OF SUBSTITUTE GOODS OR SERVICES; LOSS OF USE, DATA, OR PROFITS; OR BUSINESS INTERRUPTION) HOWEVER CAUSED AND ON ANY THEORY OF LIABILITY, WHETHER IN CONTRACT, STRICT LIABILITY, OR TORT (INCLUDING NEGLIGENCE OR OTHERWISE) ARISING IN ANY WAY OUT OF THE USE OF THIS SOFTWARE, EVEN IF ADVISED OF THE POSSIBILITY OF SUCH DAMAGE.

This software consists of voluntary contributions made by many individuals on behalf of the Apache Software Foundation. For more information on the Apache Software Foundation, please see `http://www.apache.org/`.

Portions of this software are based upon public domain software originally written at the National Center for Supercomputing Applications, University of Illinois, Urbana-Champaign.

A

THE APACHE
SOFTWARE
LICENSE

Configure Command-Line
Options

This appendix contains a complete listing of the command-line options available to the configure script. This listing can also be seen by typing `./configure -help` in the unpacked Apache source code tree.

Usage: configure [options] [host]

Options: [defaults in brackets after descriptions]

Configuration:

—cache-file=FILE	cache test results in FILE
—help	print this message
—no-create	do not create output files
—quiet, —silent	do not print 'checking...' messages
—version	print the version of autoconf that created configure

Directory and file names:

—prefix=PREFIX	install architecture-independent files in PREFIX
	[/usr/local/apache2]
—exec-prefix=EPREFIX	install architecture-dependent files in EPREFIX
	[same as prefix]
—bindir=DIR	user executables in DIR [EPREFIX/bin]
—sbindir=DIR	system admin executables in DIR [EPREFIX/sbin]
—libexecdir=DIR	program executables in DIR [EPREFIX/libexec]
—datadir=DIR	read-only architecture-independent data in DIR
	[PREFIX/share]
—sysconfdir=DIR	read-only single-machine data in DIR [PREFIX/etc]
—sharedstatedir=DIR	modifiable architecture-independent data in DIR
	[PREFIX/com]
—localstatedir=DIR	modifiable single-machine data in DIR [PREFIX/var]
—libdir=DIR	object code libraries in DIR [EPREFIX/lib]

—includedir=DIR	C header files in DIR [PREFIX/include]
—oldincludedir=DIR	C header files for non-gcc in DIR [/usr/include]
—infodir=DIR	info documentation in DIR [PREFIX/info]
—mandir=DIR	man documentation in DIR [PREFIX/man]
—srcdir=DIR	find the sources in DIR [configure dir or ..]
—program-prefix=PREFIX	prepend PREFIX to installed program names
—program-suffix=SUFFIX	append SUFFIX to installed program names
—program-transform-name=PROGRAM	run sed PROGRAM on installed program names

Host type:

—build=BUILD	configure for building on BUILD [BUILD=HOST]
—host=HOST	configure for HOST [guessed]
—target=TARGET	configure for TARGET [TARGET=HOST]

Features and packages:

—disable-FEATURE	do not include FEATURE (same as —enable-FEATURE=no)
—enable-FEATURE[=ARG]	include FEATURE [ARG=yes]
—with-PACKAGE[=ARG]	use PACKAGE [ARG=yes]
—without-PACKAGE	do not use PACKAGE (same as —with-PACKAGE=no)
—x-includes=DIR	X include files are in DIR
—x-libraries=DIR	X library files are in DIR

—enable and —with options recognized:

—with-optim=FLAG	obsolete (use OPTIM environment variable)
—with-port=PORT	Port on which to listen (default is 80)
—enable-debug	Turn on debugging and compile time warnings
—enable-maintainer-mode	Turn on debugging and compile time warnings
—enable-layout=LAYOUT	
—enable-modules=MODULE-LIST	
—enable-mods-shared=MODULE-LIST	
—disable-access	host-based access control

B

—disable-auth	user-based access control
—enable-auth-anon	anonymous user access
—enable-auth-dbm	DBM-based access databases
—enable-auth-db	DB-based access databases
—enable-auth-digest	RFC2617 Digest authentication
—enable-file-cache	File cache
—enable-dav-fs	DAV provider for the filesystem
—enable-dav	WebDAV protocol handling
—enable-echo	ECHO server
—enable-charset-lite	character set translation
—enable-cache	dynamic file caching
—enable-disk-cache	disk caching module
—enable-ext-filter	external filter module
—enable-case-filter	example uppercase conversion filter
—enable-generic-hook-export	example hook exporter
—enable-generic-hook-import	example hook importer
—enable-optional-fn-import	example optional function importer
—enable-optional-fn-export	example optional function exporter
—disable-include	Server-Side Includes
—disable-http	HTTP protocol handling
—disable-mime	mapping of file-extension to MIME
—disable-log-config	logging configuration
—enable-vhost-alias	mass hosting module
—disable-negotiation	content negoatiation
—disable-dir	directory request handling
—disable-imap	internal imagemaps
—disable-actions	Action triggering on requests
—enable-speling	correct common URL misspellings
—disable-userdir	mapping of user requests
—disable-alias	translation of requests
—enable-rewrite	regex URL translation
—disable-so	DSO capability
—enable-so	DSO capability
—disable-env	clearing/setting of ENV vars
—enable-mime-magic	automagically determining MIME type

—enable-cern-meta	CERN-type meta files
—enable-expires	Expires header control
—enable-headers	HTTP header control
—enable-usertrack	user-session tracking
—enable-unique-id	per-request unique ids
—disable-setenvif	basing ENV vars on headers
—enable-tls	TLS/SSL support
—with-ssl	use a specific SSL library installation
—with-mpm=MPM	Choose the process model for Apache to use.
MPM={beos,threaded,prefork, spmt_os2,perchild}	
—disable-status	process/thread monitoring
—disable-autoindex	directory listing
—disable-asis	as-is filetypes
—enable-info	server information
—enable-suexec	set uid and gid for spawned processes
—disable-cgid	CGI scripts
—enable-cgi	CGI scripts
—disable-cgi	CGI scripts
—enable-cgid	CGI scripts
—enable-shared[=PKGS]	build shared libraries [default=no]
—enable-static[=PKGS]	build static libraries [default=yes]
—enable-fast-install[=PKGS]	optimize for fast installation [default=yes]
—with-gnu-ld	assume the C compiler uses GNU ld [default=no]
—disable-libtool-lock	avoid locking (might break parallel builds)
—with-program-name	alternate executable name
—with-suexec-caller	User allowed to call SuExec
—with-suexec-userdir	User subdirectory
—with-suexec-docroot	SuExec root directory
—with-suexec-uidmin	Minimal allowed UID
—with-suexec-gidmin	Minimal allowed GID
—with-suexec-logfile	Set the logfile
—with-suexec-safepath	Set the safepath
—with-suexec-umask	umask for suexec'd process

B

CONFIGURE
COMMAND-LINE
OPTIONS

Regular Expressions

A regular expression is a pattern that describes a set of strings. Regular expressions are constructed analogously to arithmetic expressions by using various operators to combine smaller expressions.

The fundamental building blocks are the regular expressions that match a single character. Most characters, including all letters and digits, are regular expressions that match themselves. Any metacharacter with special meaning can be quoted by preceding it with a backslash.

A list of characters enclosed by [and] matches any single character in that list; if the first character of the list is the caret then it matches any character not in the list. For example, the regular expression [0123456789] matches any single digit. A range of characters can be specified by giving the first and last characters, separated by a hyphen. Finally, certain named classes of characters are predefined. Their names are self explanatory, and they are [:alnum:], [:alpha:], [:cntrl:], [:digit:], [:graph:], [:lower:], [:print:], [:punct:], [:space:], [:upper:], and [:xdigit:].

For example, [[:alnum:]] means [0-9A-Za-z], except the latter form depends upon the POSIX locale and the ASCII character encoding, whereas the former is independent of locale and character set. (Note that the brackets in these class names are part of the symbolic names and must be included in addition to the brackets delimiting the bracket list.) Most metacharacters lose their special meaning inside lists. To include a literal] place it first in the list. Similarly, to include a literal ^ place it anywhere but first. Finally, to include a literal - place it last.

The period . matches any single character. The symbol \w is a synonym for [[:alnum:]] and \W is a synonym for [^[:alnum]].

The caret ^ and the dollar sign $ are metacharacters that respectively match the empty string at the beginning and end of a line. The symbols \< and \> respectively match the empty string at the beginning and end of a word. The symbol \b matches the empty string at the edge of a word, and \B matches the empty string provided it's not at the edge of a word.

A regular expression may be followed by one of several repetition operators:

TABLE A.1   Repetition Operators

Operator	Meaning
?	The preceding item is optional and matched at most once.
*	The preceding item will be matched zero or more times.
+	The preceding item will be matched one or more times.
{n}	The preceding item is matched exactly n times.
{n,}	The preceding item is matched n or more times.
{n,m}	The preceding item is matched at least n times, but not more than m times.

Two regular expressions can be concatenated; the resulting regular expression matches any string formed by concatenating two substrings that respectively match the concatenated subexpressions.

Two regular expressions can be joined by the infix operator | ; the resulting regular expression matches any string matching either subexpression.

Repetition takes precedence over concatenation, which in turn takes precedence over alternation. A whole subexpression can be enclosed in parentheses to override these precedence rules.

The backreference \n, where n is a single digit, matches the substring previously matched by the nth parenthesized subexpression of the regular expression.

In basic regular expressions the metacharacters ?, +, {, |, (, and) lose their special meaning; instead use the backslashed versions \?, \+, \{, \|, \(, and \).

mod_perl Example Code

The following are a few code examples that were omitted from Chapter 17, "mod_perl," in the interests of brevity.

mod_perl Form Handler Code

In Chapter 17, code was presented that would parse the contents of a HTML form, or the contents of URL "command-line" arguments in ?key=value&key=value syntax.

The portion of this code that does the actual form parsing is the single line that follows:

```
my %form = $r->method eq 'POST' ? $r->content : $r->args;
```

This line uses the Perl ? : syntax, which functions exactly like an if/else clause. This syntax allows for a simple if/else clause to be expressed in one line, as shown in the example. If written out fully, the statement would look like the following block:

```
my %form; # Declare the form variable
if ($r->method eq 'POST') { # was the data posted?
    %form = $r->content;    # Get the form contents
} else {
    %form = $r->args;       # Otherwise, read arguments from the URL
}
```

It is very important to note that the example code *does not* work for forms that contain multiple-select lists, and so should not be used for any production code. The following subroutine solves this problem, and you will probably want to use this instead.

A detailed explanation of the code is not provided in this appendix.

The following function returns the contents of the form as a hash reference. The keys of the hash are the names of the form fields, whereas the values are the values of those fields. The only exception to this is a multiple-select list, where more than one element of the list was selected. In this case, the value that is put into the hash is actually a reference to a list of the selected value. An example of this is provided following the example function.

```
sub form {
    my $r = Apache->request();
    my @form = $r->method eq 'POST' ? $r->content : $r->args;
    my %form;
    foreach my $i (0..@form) {
        my $key = $form[$i];
        my $value = $form[++$i];
        next unless $value;

        if ($form{$key}) {
            my $temp  = $form{$key};
            if(ref $temp) {
```

```
                push @{$form{$key}},$value;
            } else {
                $form{$key} = [ $temp, $value ];
            }
        } else {
            $form{$key} = $value;
        }
    }
    return \%form;
}
```

In your handler code, you will access this method as follows:

```
my $form = form();
my $color = $form->{favorite_color};
```

If accessing a value that was returned from a multiple select list, you will need to test the value to determine if more than one element was selected, as shown in this example:

```
if ( ref $form->{favorite_food} ) {
    @food = @{ $form->{favorite_food} }; # Dereference the array
} else {
    $food = $form->{favorite_food}; # There's just one value
}
```

Please note that the examples provided here are just that[md]examples, not fully functioning programs, and, therefore, are not intended to be blindly copied into your code.

Numerous modules on CPAN can help you do this stuff and should be used in preference to examples printed in this, or any other, book. CPAN can be found at http://www.cpan.org/, as well as at hundreds of mirrors worldwide.

Apache History

IN THIS APPENDIX

According to Netcraft (`http://www.netcraft.com/`), the Apache Web server is used more than all other Web servers combined. Of the approximately 33 million Web sites on the World Wide Web, about 19 million of them (57%) are running Apache. If you also count server software that is based on the Apache code, this figure is closer to 62%. In the following few pages, you'll see how this project came to be, and why it has become so popular.

Before the Beginning

If you're really interested in hunting down the origins of the World Wide Web, you may want to find a copy of the paper titled "As We May Think," by Vannevar Bush. This paper was written in 1945 (no, that's not a typo) and talked about ways to organize information. His ideas look a lot like hypertext.

> **NOTE**
>
> You can find "As We May Think" at `http://www.theatlantic.com/unbound/flashbks/computer/bushf.htm`

In the Beginning

The WWW is still a very young phenomenon. Tim Berners-Lee invented the WWW in late 1990, while he was working at CERN—the European Laboratory for Particle Physics. He developed it so physicists working at various universities all over the world could have instantaneous access to information, to enable their collaboration on a variety of projects.

Tim defined URLs, HTTP, and HTML, and together with Robert Cailliau, wrote the first Web server, along with the first Web client software, which was later dubbed a browser.

Just a few years ago, it would have been necessary to explain what these concepts meant to all but the most technically aware audience. Now, there are few people (at least in developed nations) who are unaware of the WWW.

Shortly after Tim's initial work, a group at the National Center for Supercomputing Activities (NCSA) at the University of Illinois at Urbana-Champaign (UIUC) developed the NCSA HTTPd Web server, and the NCSA Mosaic graphical Web browser. Mosaic was not the first graphical Web browser, although it is almost universally remembered as such. That honor rightfully belongs to Viola, written by Pei Wei, and available before Mosaic. But Mosaic quickly stole the spotlight, and most of the users, becoming the most widely used WWW browser some time in 1992.

NCSA HTTPd was the server most used on the WWW for the first several years of its existence. However, in 1994, Rob McCool, who had developed NCSA HTTPd, left NSCA, and the project fizzled. Because the source code of the server was publicly available many of the folks using it had developed their own bug fixes, and additional features that they needed for their own sites. These patches were shared via Usenet, but there was no centralized mechanism for collecting and distributing these patches.

Who's Responsible?

In February of 1995, Brian Behlendorf and Cliff Skolnick put together a mailing list, got some space on a machine, and bandwidth donated by HotWired. This provided a way for a group of developers to collect their code modifications in one place, and produce a combined product. Starting with NCSA httpd 1.3, they started applying these patches. The first release of this product, which got the name Apache, was version 0.6.2, released in April of 1995.

A rumor quickly sprang up that the name was a pun on "patch", because the server was built on patches to NCSA HTTPd, and hence it was "a patchy" server. The name is actually derived from the governmental structure of the Apache people, who govern by a meritocracy, meaning that those who contribute most to society get to be the leaders. This is how the Apache software projects work also.

The eight original core members of the Apache Group were Brian Behlendorf, Roy T. Fielding, Rob Hartill, David Robinson, Cliff Skolnick, Randy Terbush, Robert S. Thau, and Andrew Wilson.

Shortly after the initial release, Robert Thau designed a completely new architecture, and starting with version 0.8.8, in August of 1995, Apache was switched to this new code base.

Netcraft shows Apache passing NCSA as the leading HTTP server sometime in early 1996.

What's Happened Recently

Suddenly, publications like The Wall Street Journal and Forbes are using the term "Open Source" in front page articles. This seems a little strange to those of us who have been familiar with the concept for a few decades and are used to it being ignored, or actively snubbed, by people in the commercial software industry.

In May of 1997, Eric Raymond gave his talk, entitled "The Cathedral and the Bazaar," at the Linux Kongress. This started a chain of events, not least of which was Netscape's decision to release the source code for their WWW browser. The software world was no longer able to ignore the "free software" movement, a branch of which renamed itself "Open Source" to shed some of the negative associations surrounding the free software movement.

In June of 1998, the Apache Group announced that they were entering in an agreement with IBM for the continuing development of the Apache server, so that IBM could include that code in their WebSphere product. This was one of the first examples of a major software company endorsing an existing Open Source project, and was one of the lynch pins in making the Open Source movement appear viable to the rest of the software world.

E

APACHE HISTORY

A consequence of the Apache-IBM agreement was the development of a Microsoft Windows version of the server. The Apache Group warns that Apache on Windows should not be considered as reliable as Apache on Unix and Unix-line platforms (for example, Linux), but improvements are still being made, and Apache 2.0 for Windows is a substantial improvement, in all measurable ways, over the 1.3 server on Windows.

In June of 1999, the Apache Software Foundation was incorporated as a not-for-profit corporation, in order to provide the necessary legal and financial protection for the members, and enable the group to receive financial donations.

Why It Works So Well

Apache is just a fantastic product. It does everything you want it to do and none of the stuff that you don't want it to do. It's fast, reliable, and inexpensive. What more could you want from a piece of software?

Apache is able to be all of these things because it is Open Source. That means that everyone that uses the product has access to the source code. If they have an idea that would be useful, they can write the code for that feature and submit it back to the Apache Group for possible inclusion in the product.

What this means is that features that make it into Apache are features that real people are actually using on real Web sites, not features that someone suggested in a marketing meeting, after conducting a focus group.

It also means that when bugs are found, many people have access to the code, can determine what is breaking, and suggest fixes for the problem. Contrast this to closed-source software products, where something crashes, you get a cryptic error message, and you are at the mercy of a schedule set by an engineering manager. Hence, bug fixes usually follow closely on the heels of bug discoveries.

> **NOTE**
>
> You can read the official history of Apache on the Apache web site at
> `http://www.apache.org/ABOUT_APACHE.html`.

Summary

Apache was developed by actual users who needed to fix problems with, and add features to, the Web server software that was available in the early days of the WWW. As such, it is a server that does things that real Web sites need. Apache, and Apache derivatives, are used on about 60% of the Web sites on the Internet—more than all other Web servers combined.

Where to Get More Information

If you'd like more information on the Apache server there are just a few places that are highly recommended. I've split these into the following categories:

- Web
- Usenet
- Mailing list
- Print

Web Resources

On the web, the following resources should be considered if you want the right answer, and want it fast.

ApacheAdmin.com

ApacheAdmin.com serves as a companion Web site for this book. It contains errors that were discovered after the book went to press and updates information that has changed since the book was written. It also contains various other information related to Apache and the contents of this book.

The Apache Server Web Site

The official Apache Server Web site (`http://httpd.apache.org/`) is a part of the Web site of the Apache Software Foundation (`http://www.apache.org/`). It is *the* most authoritative source of information on the Apache Server. When changes are made to the Apache documentation they are almost immediately reflected on the Apache Web site. There are a number of mirrors of the Apache Web site. In fact, you can set up your own mirror of the Apache Web site if you want. For information on becoming an Apache mirror site check `http://www.apache.org/info/how-to-mirror.html`.

Apache Week

In addition to producing a weekly mailing list, Apache Week (`http://www.apacheweek.com/`) contains an enormous wealth of articles on a variety of topics relating to Apache, dating back a number of years.

Apache Week is a very important historical archive, and is also the best place to get an idea of the history of the Apache project. Looking back through back issues will tell you about all the major events in the life of the Apache server, all the way back to the earliest releases.

Historical documentation is extremely hard to come by in most computer projects because people are much more interested in the latest and greatest version, rather than considering where we have come from. Web sites like Apache Week and `http://history.perl.org/` are resources that we should support and encourage.

Apache Server Web Ring

Ken Coar's Apache Software Web ring (`http://Apache-Server.Com/WebRing/`) is a collection of sites that contain useful information about the Apache Web Server and related technologies.

Usenet

Usenet, also known as Internet Newsgroups as well as a variety of other names, is a distributed discussion forum. There are just a few Usenet groups that pertain to the Apache server and related subjects.

comp.infosystems.www.servers.*

There are four groups that fall into this category, and which one you read depends on your interest. The four groups are

- `comp.infosystems.www.servers.misc`—Contains general discussion of Web server issues. Much of the discussion is about Apache, simply because most of the Web servers in the world are running Apache.

- `comp.infosystems.www.servers.unix`—Discussion specific to Web servers running on Unix. This group is almost exclusively devoted to Apache because almost all Unix Web servers are running Apache.

- `comp.infosystems.www.servers.windows`—Most of the discussion here is related to IIS because that's what most Windows Web servers are running. There is, however, some discussion here of Apache.

- `comp.infosystems.www.servers.mac`—A rather quiet group because very few Web sites run on Macintosh.

comp.infosystems.www.authoring.cgi

There are a few groups in the `authoring` tree of this branch of Usenet. The CGI one is the one most related to Apache and a lot of Apache-specific discussion goes on there—how to get CGI working on Apache and how to get a particular CGI problem working.

Mailing Lists

There are a few mailing lists that provide quality Apache help via e-mail. Here are three I recommend.

hwg-servers

The hwg-servers mailing list, operated by the HTML Writers Guild (http://www.hwg.org/), is devoted to running a Web server and related issues. You can find out more about hwg-servers at http://www.hwg.org/lists/hwg-servers/index.html.

You can subscribe to hwg-servers by sending e-mail to hwg-servers-request@hwg.org with a message of "subscribe."

hwg-languages

The hwg-languages mailing list is more geared to CGI programming, although there is a lot of non-CGI programming discussion.

You can subscribe to hwg-languages by sending e-mail to hwg-languages-request@hwg.org with a message of "subscribe."

Apache Week Mailing Lists

As mentioned above, Apache Week is a great source of Apache news and articles.

You can choose to receive Apache Week either as a plain text e-mail message, suitable for all mail readers, or in HTML format, for readers that can display HTML.

To join either of the mailing lists, send a message to the address majordomo@apacheweek.com. To receive Apache Week in text format, send the following command in the body of the message: "subscribe apacheweek."

To receive Apache Week in HTML format, send the following command in the body of the message: "subscribe apacheweek-html."

You can unsubscribe to the lists by following the same instructions, but replacing the word "subscribe" with "unsubscribe" in the message body.

Print

There are a lot of Apache books on the market, so I'll try to be selective in what I recommend without being biased.

- *Apache Server Unleashed,* **Sams Publishing, 2000, 0672318083**—Although somewhat dated, *Apache Server Unleashed* is a good solid book for beginners, and a useful reference guide for the experienced Apache administrator.

- *Apache Server for Dummies,* **Hungry Minds, 1998, 0764502913**—Despite the uninspiring name, this book, by Ken Coar, is an excellent beginner's guide to Apache that does not assume you're a dummy, and does not strive to keep you one, as do many books in this unfortunately named series.

- *Apache Server—The Definitive Guide*, **O'Reilly & Associates, 1999, 1565925289**— Although a little dated, this book from O'Reilly is a great guide to Apache, written by Ben Laurie and Peter Laurie.

- *Apache Pocket Reference*, **O'Reilly & Associates, 2000, 1565927060**—This little book, by Andrew Ford, covers all the basics and is a great thing to carry around once you are already familiar with the basics.

Summary

There are a plethora of resources available to help you learn about the Apache server. With this list, you should never be left wanting more information.

INDEX

SYMBOLS

A

Other Related Titles

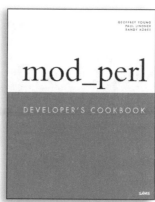

mod_perl Developer's Cookbook
Geoffrey Young
0-672-32240-4
$39.99 US/$59.95 CAN

Maximum Security, Third Edition
Anonymous
0-672-31871-7
$49.99 US/$74.95 CAN

Zope Web Application Construction Kit
Martina Brockmann, Mark Pratt, Katrin Kirchner, Sebastian Luhnsdorf
0-672-32133-5
$49.99 US/$74.95 CAN

PHP Developer's Cookbook, Second Edition
Sterling Hughes
0-672-32325-7
$39.99 US/$59.95 CAN

PHP Developer's Dictionary
Allen Wyke, Michael J. Walker, Robert M. Cox
0-672-32029-0
$39.99 US/$59.95 CAN

Perl Developer's Dictionary
Clinton Pierce
0-672-32067-3
$39.99 US/$59.95 CAN

JavaScript Developer's Dictionary
Alexander Vincent
0-672-32201-3
$39.99 US/$59.95 CAN

Python Developer's Handbook
Andre Lessa
0-672-31994-2
$44.95 US/$67.95 CAN

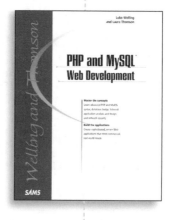

PHP and MySQL Web Development
Luke Welling, Laura Thomson
0-672-31784-2
$49.99 US/$74.95 CAN

Maximum Linux Security, Second Edition
Anonymous
0-672-32134-3
$49.99 US/$74.95 CAN

SAMS

www.samspublishing.com

All prices are subject to change.